7 Tail Feather

Attribution

Guide

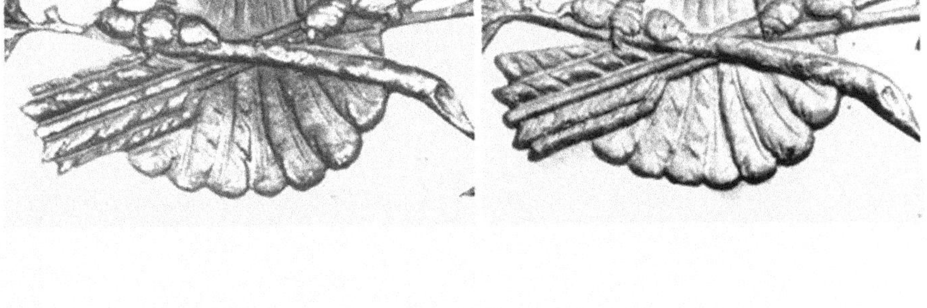

By

Leroy Van Allen

Edited by

Michael S. Fey, Ph.D.

1878 P 7 Tail Feather Morgan Dollar Attribution Guide

Engraved Feather

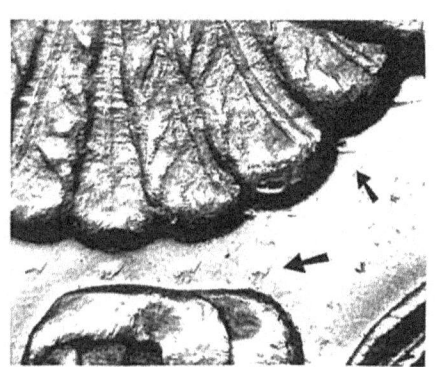

Denticle Impressions

Tripled R

by

Leroy Van Allen

Revised November 2010

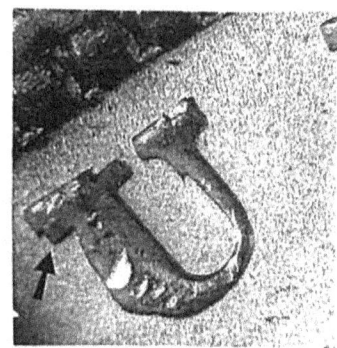

Shifted U

Tripled Star

Doubled R

Published by

Rare Coin Investments (RCI)
P.O. Box C
Ironia, NJ 07845

Copyright © 2021 by Michael S. Fey, Ph.D.

Authors: Leroy C. Van Allen

Library of Congress Catalog Number: 2023904390

ISBN-13 number: 979-8-990-2970-3-6

Printed in the United States

TABLE OF CONTENTS

LIST OF FIGURES

LIST OF CHARTS Page

ACKNOWLEDGMENTS

There are many collectors and dealers the author would like to thank for reporting and sharing the new and revised 1878 P 7 Tail Feather (7TF) Morgan dollar varieties. Their sharing of knowledge and coins for examination and photographing has made possible the preparation and continued updating of this 1878 P 7TF Guide.

The major design changes in the Morgan dollar obverse and reverse designs, including those for the 1878 P 7TF, were first discussed and illustrated in detail in a lengthy article by Neil Shafer in the *Whitman Numismatic Journal,* November 1964 issue, entitled, *Morgan Silver Dollars of 1878–1921.* It concentrated on the 1878 P designs and varieties and was instrumental in the awakening of collectors to the many design types and die varieties for this first year of issue.

A special thanks also goes to David DeRuiter who first discovered and reported the engraved wing feather on the 1878 S between the eagle's right wing and leg in November 1979. It wasn't until August 2002 that Michael Fey discovered and reported a similar type of touch-up engraving between the wing and leg on an 1878 P 7TF reverse die. Since then, seven more dies with engraved wing feathers have been discovered in 2007 for the 1878 P 7TF.

Much appreciation is given to Michael Fey, Bill Fivaz and Jeff Oxman who reported many new and revised 1878 P 7TF die varieties and to Mark Kimpton who reported most of the new clashed die letters of the 1878 P 7TF varieties. Two interesting new B^1 type long nock die combinations were recently reported by Kenneth Robb for VAM 85 and Larry Briggs for VAM 86.

The following are the discoverers of each of the 1878 P 7TF die varieties, plus those that reported significant revisions to the known varieties. Those die combinations denoted by XXX-1,-2, etc., are not included here since they are identified only by minor die scratches and polishing lines and not a sub-variety with listable gouges, die breaks or clashed die letters.

Leroy Van Allen
November 2010

1878 P 7TF DISCOVERERS HALL OF FAME
Comments & corrections welcomed

VAM #	Discoverer	Date Reported
7 TF rev	George Rice	June 1898
Obv types	Neil Shafer	Nov 64
70	Leroy Van Allen	Dec 65
79	Clarence Brown	Jun 66
80	Leroy Van Allen	Dec 65
80A	Logan McKechnie	Oct 05
81	Leroy Van Allen	Dec 65
82	" " "	Dec 65
83	" " "	Dec 65
84	" " "	Dec 65
84A	" " "	May 03
84Arevise	" " "	Sep 04
85	Kenneth Robb	Oct 10
86	Larry Briggs	Nov 10
100	Leroy Van Allen	Dec 65
110	" " "	Dec 65
110revise	Bill Fivaz	Aug 06
111 obv	Neil Shafer	Nov 64
111	Leroy Van Allen	Dec 65
112	" " "	Dec 65
112A	Calvin Goddard	Feb 10
113	Leroy Van Allen	Dec 65
114	" " "	Dec 65
114revise	Jeff Oxman	Aug 06
114A	Mark Kimpton	Jan 04
114Arevise	Jeff Oxman	Aug 06
115	Leroy Van Allen	Dec 65
116	" " "	Dec 65
116A	John Roberts	Aug 07
116B	John Baumgart	Sep 07
116Brevise	Clayton Cristiansen	Sep 09
116C	Jeff Oxman	Sep 99
116Crevise	Clayton Christiansen	Sep 09
117	Leroy Van Allen	Dec 65
117revise	" " "	June 07
118	" " "	Dec 65
119	" " "	Dec 65
119revise	Russell James	Jul 10
120	Guy Messing	Dec 73
121	" "	May 74
122	Guy Messing	July 76
123	Ron Derosier	Dec 97
123revise	Laurence Galbraith	Aug 07
130	Leroy Van Allen	Dec 65
130A	John Baumgart	June 04
130B	Logan McKechnie	Feb 07
130Brevise	John Roberts	Feb 07
130C1	Leroy Van Allen	Dec 65
130C1revise	Brian Raines	May 09
130C2	Michael Ash	May 08
130C3	John Coxe	Nov 08
131	Leroy Van Allen	Dec 65
131A	(in 1965 VA book)	
131Arevise	Rick Davis	Feb 07
131B	(in 1971 VAM book)	
131C1	(in 1965 VA book)	
131C2	Mark Kimpton	Apr 03
131C3	John Roberts	Jan 07
132	Bill Fivaz	Apr 73
132revise	Brian Raines	May 09
133	Leroy Van Allen	Dec 65
133revise	" " "	Apr 07
134	Edward Malinowski	Sep 04
134revise	Brian Raines	Feb 06
134revise	Clayton Christiansen	Sep 09
140 rev	Charles Wallace	Apr 59
140	Leroy Van Allen	Dec 65
140revise	John Roberts	Feb 10
140A	" "	Feb 10
141	Leroy Van Allen	Dec 65
141revise	" " "	Apr 07
141A	Clayton Christiansen	Oct 06
142	Leroy Van Allen	Dec 65
142A	Logan McKechnie	Mar 06
143	Leroy Van Allen	Dec 65
143revise	" " "	Apr 07
144	" " "	Dec 65
144A	Mark Kimpton	May 04
145	Leroy Van Allen	Dec 65
146	" " "	Dec 65

146revise Leroy Van Allen	Apr 07	
160 " " "	Dec 65	
161 " " "	Dec 65	
162 " " "	Dec 65	
163 " " "	Dec 65	
163 rev Melvin Carmichael	Aug 51	
164 Leroy Van Allen	Dec 65	
164revise John Roberts	June 07	
165 Leroy Van Allen	Dec 65	
165revise " " "	June 07	
166 " " "	Dec 65	
167 " " "	Dec 65	
168 " " "	Dec 65	
168revise John Roberts	June 07	
169 Leroy Van Allen	Dec 65	
170 " " "	Dec 65	
170A Michael Ash	May 09	
171 Leroy Van Allen	Dec 65	
185 " " "	Dec 65	
185A Michael Fey	Oct 02	
185B " "	Oct 02	
186 Leroy Van Allen	Dec 65	
186A Clayton Christiansen	Mar 06	
186B " "	Mar 06	
187 Bill Fivaz	Feb 73	
188 Pete Bishal	Dec 74	
189 Michael Fey	Aug 02	
190 Leroy Van Allen	Dec 65	
190A Jeff Oxman	June 05	
195 Leroy Van Allen	Dec 65	
195A " " "	Dec 65	
196 Richard Deters	Sep 73	
196A Leroy Van Allen	Sep 03	
197 ???		
197revise Bill Van Note	July 04	
198 Steve Sabella	Jun 79	
199 Martin Field	Nov 80	
199-1 Jacob Weisel	May 97	
199-2 Jeff Oxman	Sep 99	
200 Leroy Van Allen	Dec 65	
200revise " " "	Dec 99	
200revise " " "	Sep 06	
201 Leroy Van Allen	Dec 65	
201revise " " "	Sep 06	
202 " " "	Dec 65	
202revise " " "	Sep 06	
202A Jeff Oxman	June 05	
203 Leroy Van Allen	Dec 65	
203revise " " "	Dec 99	
203revise " " "	Sep 06	
203A Mark Kimpton	June 03	
203Arevise " "	Jan 04	
203Arevise Leroy Van Allen	Sep 04	
210 " " "	Dec 65	
210revise " " "	Feb 00	
210revise " " "	Sep 06	
210A " " "	Dec 65	
210Arevise " " "	Dec 99	
210Arevise " " "	Sep 06	
210B1 " " "	Feb 00	
210B1revise " " "	Sep 06	
210B2 Mark Kimpton	May 03	
210B2revise Michael Ash	Sep 06	
215 Bob Cohen	Sep 73	
220 rev Neil Shafer	Nov 64	
220 Leroy Van Allen	Dec 65	
220revise " " "	Dec 99	
221 " " "	Dec 65	
221revise Jeff Oxman	Nov 99	
221A Brian Raines	Oct 07	
222 Leroy Van Allen	Dec 65	
222revise Leroy Van Allen	Dec 99	
222A Michael Fey	Oct 99	
222B Brent Fogelberg	Mar 01	
222C Michael Fey	Oct 02	
222D Mark Witkower	Nov 08	
223 Leroy Van Allen	Dec 65	
223revise " " "	Dec 99	
223revise " " "	Nov 02	
224 " " "	Dec 99	
224 168reeds William Wolfsen	Mar 65	
224revise Leroy Van Allen	Nov 02	
225 " " "	Dec 99	
225revise " " "	Nov 02	
225A Michael Fahey	Oct 04	
226 Jym Braun	Mar 00	
226revise Leroy Van Allen	Nov 02	
226revise Norman Salter	May 09	
226A " "	May 09	
227 Tim Hargis	Aug 01	
228 " "	Aug 01	
228revise Leroy Van Allen	Nov 02	
228A Jeff Oxman	Oct 02	
228B Leroy Van Allen	Nov 02	
229 Larry Briggs	Oct 02	
229.1 John Baumgart	Oct 04	
230 Leroy Van Allen	Dec 65	
231 Jeff Oxman	Nov 99	
231revise Leroy Van Allen	Nov 02	
232 " " "	Feb 00	
232revise Russell James	Jul 10	

1878 P 7 TAIL FEATHER MORGAN DOLLAR
ATTRIBUTION GUIDE

INTRODUCTION

This is the fifth revision of the 2002 *1878 P 7 Tail Feather Morgan Dollar Attribution Guide* that covers both of the reverse '78 (B) and reverse '79 (C) types. The previous revisions of December 2003, March 2005, April 2009 and this revision primarily added some new varieties and updated the descriptions and photographs of some existing die varieties. The May/June 2007 revision was much more extensive with many added sections, charts and photographs.

This Guide is for collectors to attribute unknown 1878 P 7 Tail Feather (7TF) coins and for pointing out interesting die varieties, their relative scarcity and background information on some of the unique features of this series. The 1878 P 7TF die varieties are rather complicated with three different obverse design types used plus two sub-types, 33 dual hub dies and two different reverse design types used plus five sub-types. Many of the die varieties have spectacular features, but many are also very similar and require close scrutiny with a good hand magnifier in order to identify them.

The literature of the 1878 P 7TF die varieties includes the book, *Comprehensive Catalog and Encyclopedia of Morgan & Peace Dollars* by Leroy C. Van Allen & A. George Mallis, DLRC Press, third edition, 1992, and WorldWide Ventures reprint in 1998 (Known as the VAM book.) plus the yearly VAM Varieties Supplements by Leroy Van Allen. There are also nine **Top 100** 1878 P 7TF die varieties included in the 1996 booklet, *The Top 100 Morgan Dollar Varieties: The VAM Keys,* by Michael Fey and Jeff Oxman, six **Hot 50** 1878 P 7TF varieties included in the 2000 book, *SSDC Official Guide to the Hot 50 Morgan Dollar Varieties* by Jeff Oxman and nine in the 2009 book, *Official Guide to The Morgan Dollar Hit List 40,* by Jeff Oxman.

An **excellent** Guide for the 1878 P reverse '79 (C) varieties is the *Official Guide To The 1878 Reverse of '79 Varieties,* by Mark Witkower with Jeff Oxman, VAMSTAR, 65 pgs, 2008. It covers all of the reverse of '79 C type 1878 P die varieties with attribution logic trees, detailed close–up photographs of each variety with discussion of rarity and value guides. **Highly recommended** for collectors of 1878 P die varieties.

This Guide includes sections of highlights of some interesting and unique features of 1878 P 7TF varieties, information on the unique dual hub, II/I, obverse dies, special touch-up engraving on the reverse wing similar to that of the 1878 S dies, features of the design types and sub-types, Top 30 collectible 1878 P 7TF die varieties, high interest die varieties, primary scarce varieties, and a summary chart that briefly describes the main features, availability and desirability of each die variety. Detailed attribution procedures are given including suggested step-by-step attribution guidelines, a die combinations summary chart, grouped photographs for the dual hub II/I varieties, obverse and reverse dies to VAM number charts, detailed descriptive listings and close-up photographs of the varieties.

The May/June 2007 Guide revision added new die varieties of VAMs 80A T breaks, 130B die gouges wing, 131C clashed n and die break O in OF, 141A die gouge wing, 142A die chips reverse, 186A spike eyelid, 186B over polished wing and 190A and 202A clashed n. Revisions were VAMs 110 gouge eagle's right leg, 133 polished left wing, 134 doubled die reverse and 117, 141/146, 143, 165 & 168/169 engraved bars and lines at eagle's right wing–body.

April 2009 revisions added new varieties VAMs 116A, B & C die gouges, 130C die breaks obverse, 221A denticle impressions and 222D over polished lower hair. Revisions included VAM 123 with new engraved wing feather, 144 additions plus new die combinations for VAMs 100, 131, 221, 227 and 228. VAM 144B was eliminated as dot to right of date is a planchet flaw or gas bubble.

Current Guide revisions add new varieties VAMs 85 & 86 B[1] reverses, 140A die scratches, 112A clashed G, 170A die chips obverse & 226A clashed n. Revisions include 116B & C die sequences, 117 thread-like impression, 130C1 new obverse die, 132 added die chip cheek and die markers, 134 die polishing sequences, 140 Die 2 and 226 added die marker.

The author can be contacted about any possible new and revised 1878 P 7TF die varieties at: Leroy Van Allen, P.O. Box 196, Sidney, OH 45465 or by e-mail at vams@woh.rr.com.

BACKGROUND

It is estimated that there were around 9 million 1878 P 7TF coins struck with about 5 million of the second reverse, **B**, type with **parallel** top arrow feather and **flat** eagle's breast and about 4 million of the third reverse, **C**, type with **slanted** top arrow feather and **rounded** eagle's breast. The remainder of the 10.5 million 1878 P coins were about 700,000 8TF design and about 800,000 7/8TF dual hubs. This is a small number of coins struck for one year at a mint by modern standards.

The dies used in the first year of the Morgan dollar production were undergoing development and refinement. The number of coins struck per die was **very low** during much of the first year of production with some only striking an average of 30,000 coins while others struck just over 100,000 coins. As a result, there are many die varieties because of the relatively large number of dies used to strike the 1878 P coins. The obverse and reverse hubs tended to have small **breaks** which showed up on a number of dies produced. This enables the sorting of die varieties into several sub-types which makes it easier to narrow down the possible die varieties when attributing coins.

Because the Morgan dollar design was undergoing refinement during the first few months of die production in 1878, there are several basic design types and sub-types for both the obverse and reverse 1878 P 7TF dies. These were used in various die marriage combinations. Also, many of the earlier **I obverse** dies were **re-hubbed** with the later **II obverse** hub which produced 40 **unique** dies with extensive die doubling on many of them. 33 of these II/I dual hub obverse dies were used with the 7 tail feather reverse dies. The second II obverse and B reverse design types had flaws in them which were largely corrected in the III obverse and C reverse design types that began to be used in mid-1878. The II obverse dies didn't strike coins up properly on the Liberty head cheek, and the B reverse dies had weak or missing feathers between the eagle's right wing and leg from the die basining and polishing. Five 1878 P 7TF B reverse dies were touched up in this wing-leg area and five in the wing-body area to engrave back missing feathers. The 1878 S had 41 B reverses with this touch-up engraving that was performed at the San Francisco Mint, a highly **unorthodox** procedure for a branch mint!

There were 65 die varieties and three sub-varieties die combinations listed for the 1878 P 7TF Morgan dollars in the so-called VAM book, *Comprehensive Catalog and Encyclopedia of Morgan and Peace Dollars*, 4th ed. 1998 by Leroy C. Van Allen and A. George Mallis. These were assigned the VAM number blocks of VAMs 70- 230. Because of space limitations, the VAM book necessarily had brief variety descriptions and small photographs with some appearing very much the same. Since the 1998 edition of the VAM book was published, about 15 new varieties and 39 sub-varieties of 1878 P 7TF have been added for a total of 9 B^1, 50 B^2 and 20 C regular varieties and two B^1, 27 B^2 and 13 C sub-varieties. Also, many of the 7TF descriptions have been revised and expanded and new close-up photographs taken. Some multiple die combinations have lately been identified for a few primary die variety listings based on minor die scratches and polishing lines that didn't warrant sub-variety listings. There is increased interest in identifying each 1878 die, even for common die type combinations.

The 1878 P currently has 135 die varieties of 41 8TF, 15 7/8TF, 59 B 7TF and 20 C 7TF, not including any sub-varieties. By comparison, the 1878 S has 105 B 7TF die varieties currently listed with a comparable mintage of 9.8 million coins. Many of the 1878 S die varieties are the result of the 41 engraved wing feather reverses and their die combinations. This contributed to the 1878 S high number of die varieties even though only the II obverse and B reverse designs were used. The 1878 CC has only 13 B 7TF die varieties currently listed because of it's much lower mintage of 2.2 million and there were no dual hub or engraved feather varieties.

The 1878 P 7TF die varieties can lead to a fascinating study of them because of the many **design types**, various **sub-types** and the many **dual hub** obverse II/I dies. There are quite a few spectacular **doubled** obverse dies, **Top 100** and **Hot 50** die varieties, some interesting **engraved** wing feather die varieties, **broken hub** parts that showed up on many working dies, some "*trial*" obverse and reverse dies, **clashed die** letters that include a die that has a partial letter 'E' on reverse and two reverse dies with **denticle impressions** from the obverse die.

1878 P VAM 100 I¹ OBVERSE

1878 P VAM 130 II OBVERSE

1878 P VAM 231 III^2 OBVERSE

1878 P VAM 113 B² REVERSE

1878 P VAM 231 C³ REVERSE

SOME 1878 P 7TF HIGHLIGHTS

Top 100, Hot 50 and Hit List 40

The 1878 P 7 Tail Feather (7TF) varieties are fortunate to have listed nine **Top 100** die varieties in the booklet, *The Top 100 Morgan Dollar Varieties: The VAM Keys,* 1996 by Michael Fey and Jeff Oxman, six **Hot 50** die varieties in the book, *SSDC Official Guide to the Hot 50 Morgan Dollar Varieties*, 2000 by Jeff Oxman and nine **Hit List 40** die varieties in the book, *Official Guide To The Morgan Dollar Hit List 40*, 2009 by Jeff Oxman.

The **Top 100** 1878 P 7TF die varieties are VAMs **70** with Doubled RIB, **100** Type I Obverse, **115** Tripled Blossoms (bolls), **117 & 141** Tripled Star, **171 & 220** Tripled R, **203** Short Leaf and **223** Washed Out L. The **Hot 50** 1878 P 7TF die varieties are VAMs **79** Disconnected Leaf, **145 & 162** Broken N & M, **169** Quadrupled Stars, **170** Doubled Date and **187** Doubled R. The **Hit List 40** 1878 P 7TF die varieties are VAMs 116, A, B, C Double P, 123 Spiked Eye, 166 Tripled Eye, 188 Polished L, 189 Re-Engraved Wing, 22A Face Chip, 224 Low Reed Count, 227-1 and 228B Slashed O. These Top 100, Hot 50 and Hit List 40 die varieties are discussed and illustrated in the Highlights topics.

Dual Hub Obverse

For the 1878 P 7TF, the major die variety feature is the **dual hub, II/I, obverse dies**. There are currently known 40 II/I obverse dies with 33 used with the 1878 P 7TF second type B design reverse. The other seven II/I dies occur with the type A design and B/A, 7/8 Tail Feather dual hub reverse dies. These dual hub obverse dies had the first type I design dies impressed with the second type II design working hub that created the dual hub II/I obverse working dies. Also, six dual hub II/I obverse dies were used with the first reverse type A design with 8 tail feathers and another four II/I obverse dies were used with the dual hub reverse B/A, 7/8 tail feather dies. One II/I 6 obverse die used with 8 tail feather reverse dies and two II/I 7 & 8 dies used with 7/8 TF dies were also used with the 7TF reverse.

Early in 1878, the Philadelphia Mint was under pressure to strike the 2 million Morgan dollars per month required by the Bland-Allison Act. The first obverse type I design dies only struck an average of 30,000 coins per die– less than half the average for the first type A design reverse dies. Because the first obverse type I design and reverse type A design were found to be defective, the San Francisco and Carson City branch mints did not receive any Morgan design dollar dies to aid in the striking of the required monthly quota of coins. To save the time of over a week to prepare new dies, the I obverse design dies were impressed with the improved lower relief obverse type II design hub.

Apparently none of the obverse type I design working dies were lapped and polished down before being impressed with the type II design obverse hub. There were only small differences in the details between the two designs such as the width of ear fill and lobes, width of LIBERTY letters and orientation of some stars. Nonetheless, there are spectacular die doubling of some of II/I obverse dies.

A strongly tripled R in PLURIBUS is shown in Figures 1 and 2 of VAMs 171 and 220. It also has strongly doubled back of the Liberty head and cotton bolls and leaves, Phrygian cap upper fold and bottom edge, all hair below the cap and right inside of the ear. It is the strongest doubled or shifted II/I obverse die.

Another tripled obverse is VAMs 115 and 198 with tripled right edge of cotton bolls and leaves as shown in Figure 3. VAMs 117 and 141 obverse has an **amazing** strongly tripled single second right star as shown in Figure 4 with a doubled eye, tripled eyelid and doubled tops of cotton leaves.

An interesting large shift of the first U in PLURIBUS of VAM 163 is shown in Figure 5. The M in UNUM also has a large shift. VAM 169 has strongly quadrupled left stars as shown in Figure 6 along with doubled right stars and 18–8 in the date. A strongly doubled date of VAM 170 is shown in Figure 7, and it also has doubled left and right stars. All of the II/I obverse dies show some degree of die doubling and design shift, but the above are some of the strongest.

Touched–up Engraved Wing Feather

The mints experienced difficulties in basining and polishing of type B design reverse dies

Figure 1 VAM 171 Tripled R

Figure 2 VAM 171 Doubled Cotton Bolls, Cap

Figure 3 VAM 115 Tripled Cotton Bolls

Figure 4 VAM 117 Tripled Second Rt. Star

Figure 5 VAM 163 Shifted U

Figure 7 VAM 170 Doubled Date

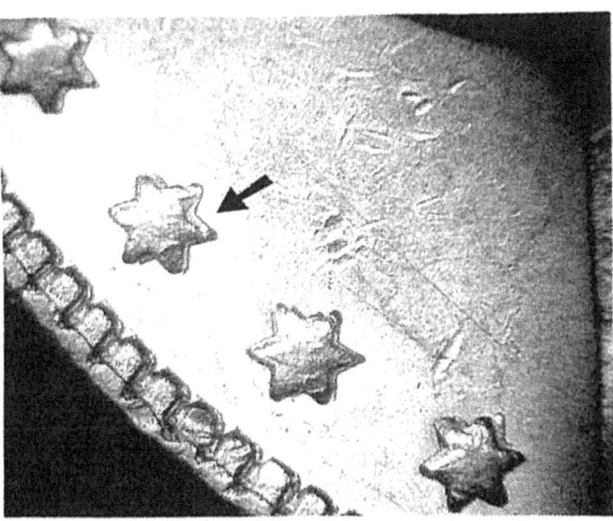

Figure 6 VAM 169 Quadrupled Left Stars

which was necessary in order for the design to strike up evenly across the coin. Basining of the die face was performed by placing the die face against a rotating disk with the desired radius of curvature. Polishing grit and compound mixed with water or oil on the basining disc gave a slight curvature and polish to the die face. This also removed some shallow design features on the type B reverse in the wing next to the eagle's right leg and body and sometimes in the middle of the wings. Figure 8 shows a normal unpolished wing–leg area of VAM 80. Figure 9 shows a typical over polished wing-leg area of VAM 114 and a very over polished wing–leg area is shown in Figure 10 of VAM 116.

The San Francisco Mint engraved a wing feather back into this wing–leg area on 41 working dies. The Carson City Mint did not touch up any type B design reverse dies. In 1878 the Philadelphia Mint **touched up seven B design reverse dies**, in the wing–leg area of VAMs 117, 123, 141, 143/145, 146, 168/169 and 189. Engraved bars and lines were added in the wing-body area for five VAMs 117, 143/145, 165, 168/169 and 189. Small feathers were added at the lower part of the eagle's left and right wings for 16 type A design 8TF working dies.

Figure 11 shows the touched up wing–leg area of VAM 189, a Hit List 40 variety. Some diagonal feather lines were engraved in the missing feather area next to the eagle's right leg with a broad line extending up to the middle of the wing–body area. It was reported by Michael Fey in August 2002 and is the first known and strongest touched up wing–leg area for a 1878 P B design reverse die. VAM 123 a Hit List 40 variety and has vertical bars with fine lines engraved in the wing–leg area as shown in Figure 12. VAM 141 is a Top 100 variety and has three vertical bars with fine lines that was engraved in the wing-leg area as shown in Figure 13. VAM 146 has a feather with a single vertical bar with lines engraved on the wing-leg area as shown in Figure 14. VAM 143/145 has thin vertical fine lines engraved in the wing–leg area as shown in Figure 15. There are two additional weaker engraved wing-leg varieties of VAMs 117 and 168/169 with a single vertical bar.

Doubled Dies

In addition to the dual hub II/I obverse doubled dies, there are some fairly **strongly doubled dies** of the I, II and III obverse types and one for the sub-type B^2 reverse. The $I^2 12$ obverse of VAM 70 has a strongly doubled motto as shown in Figure 16 plus doubled right stars and 878. VAM 187 II 5 obverse has a large shift in the R in PLURIBUS as shown in Figure 17 plus other doubled letters in PLURIBUS UNUM. Figure 18 shows the doubled feathers in the top of the eagle's left wing of VAM 190 $B^2 b$ reverse, which also has doubled God We to the right. VAM 202 $III^1 1$ obverse has a fairly strongly doubled date at the top inside of both 8 loops and left sides of 1 and 7 shafts, plus doubled left and right stars as shown in Figure 19.

Broken Hub Parts

As the II 2 obverse and sub-type B^2 reverse hubs wore out in the 1878, bits and pieces of design elements broke or chipped off creating **missing or weak parts**. The most obvious one on the obverse is the left point of the fourth right star, which gradually broke away to finally show a missing point. Figures 20, 21 and 22 show a complete fourth right star of II 1 obverse of VAM 133, a partial left point missing of II 2 obverse of VAM 131 and the point completely missing of II 2 obverse of VAM 197. For the reverse, the upper arm of the r in Trust gradually broke away. Figure 23 of VAM 190 shows a complete r of $B^2 a$ reverse die. Figure 24 of VAM 160 shows a partial broken r arm of $B^2 c$ with a triangle on the arm and Figure 25 shows an almost completely broken r arm of VAM 163. A minor break of the reverse hub is a chip out of the upper part of the o in God of $B^2 b$ shown in Figure 26 for VAM 141. Another minor reverse hub break of $B^2 e$ is the bottom of D in DOLLAR as shown in Figure 27 for VAM 195 where it is completely missing. Some varieties only show a partially broken D as for $B^1 e$ of VAM 84 shown in Figure 28. An interesting hub break occurs on the lower left serif of N and lower right serif of M in UNUM for II/I obverses. These serifs gradually chip away for VAMs 110 and 145/162 and are finally missing for VAM 200 as shown in Figure 29.

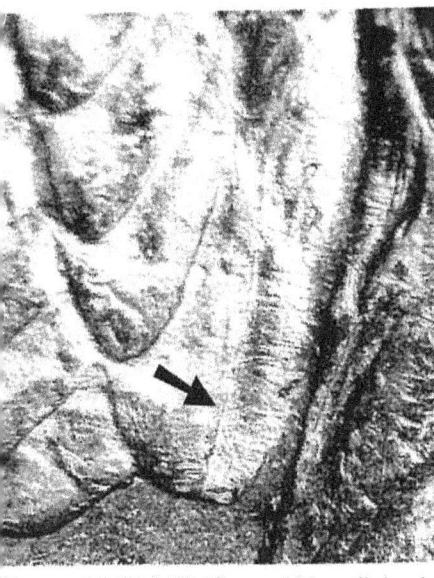  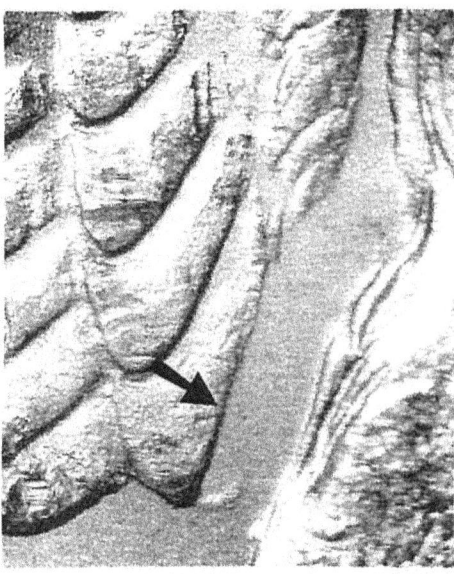

Figure 8 VAM 80 Normal Unpolished Wing-Leg Feather   Figure 9 VAM 114 Typical Over Polished Wing-Leg Feather   Figure 10 VAM 116 Very Over Polished Wing-Leg Feather

Figure 11 VAM 189 Engraved Wing Feathers

Figure 12 VAM 123 Engraved Wing Feather

Figure 13 VAM 141 Engraved Wing Feather

Figure 14 VAM 146 Engraved Wing Feather

Figure 15 VAM 143/145 Engraved Wing Feather

Figure 16 VAM 70 Doubled Motto Letters

Figure 17 VAM 187 Doubled R

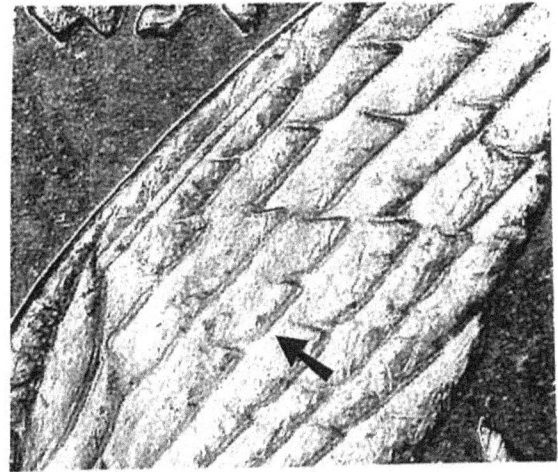

Figure 18 VAM 190 Doubled Wing Feathers

Figure 19 VAM 202 Doubled Date

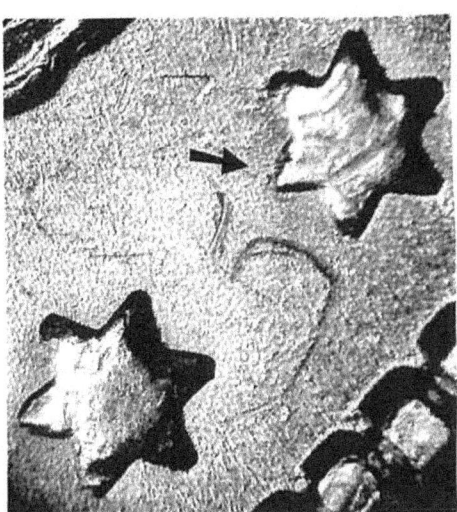

Figure 20 VAM 133 Unbroken 4th Rt. Star

Figure 21 VAM 131 Partial Broken 4th Rt. Star

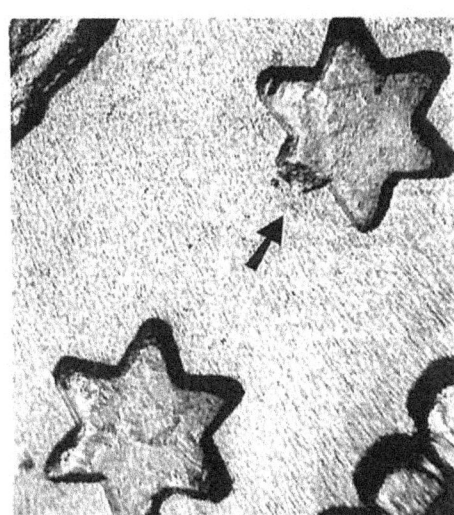

Figure 22 VAM 197 Broken 4th Rt. Star

Figure 23 VAM 190 Unbroken r

Figure 24 VAM 160 Triangle on r Arm

Figure 25 VAM 163 Broken r

Figure 26 VAM 141 Open o in God

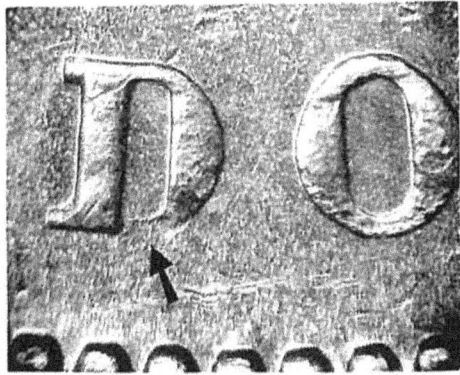

Figure 27 VAM 195 Broken D Bottom

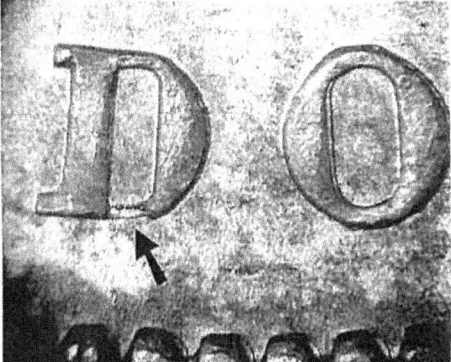

Figure 28 VAM 84 Partially Broken D

-18-

B¹ Reverse With Long Nock or Center Arrow Shaft

There are eight known reverse dies of VAMs 70, 79–86 with the B¹ reverse with **long nock** or **center arrow shaft** for the 1878 P 7TF. VAMs 85 and 86 are additions in October and November 2010 with VAM 80 obverse but new reverse dies. Figure 30 shows the long nock of B¹ reverse of VAM 81 and Figure 31 shows a typical short nock of B² reverse of VAM 111. The long nock die varieties of VAMs 80-84 aren't scarce or command large premium prices. VAM 70 as a Top 100 and VAM 79 as a Hot 50 variety have premium prices as well as the new reported rare VAMs 85 and 86. The B¹ reverse of 1880 CC are also not particularly scarce. The1878 S long nock varieties are scarce to rare and command large premiums in any grade since apparently most were released into circulation.

Initial Obverse Die Type I

There are only two varieties with the 1878 P 7TF reverse that are paired with the **first type I design obverse**. Both are listed as Top 100 varieties. VAM 70 has a I²12 obverse with the long nock B¹a reverse and VAM 100 has a I¹10 obverse with the short nock B²a reverse. Figure 32 shows the thin letters of LIB in LIBERTY of the I obverse of VAM 100, while Figure 33 shows the thick letters of the II/I and II obverse of VAM 133. The difference in the designer's initial, M, is shown in Figure 34 for the incuse initial M of VAM 100 I¹10 and in Figure 35 for the raised initial M of VAM 70 I²12.

Early "Trial" C Reverse Dies

There were **early versions of the type C reverse** with slanted top arrow feather and rounded eagle's breast. The first is the C¹ reverse used on VAMs 200–203 with at least four different reverse dies known. It has the bottom feather of the eagle's right wing next to the leg that is rounded and not connected to the wing as shown in Figure 36 for VAM 202. The C² reverse was used on VAMs 210 and 215 with at least three different reverse dies known. It has the bottom feather of the eagle's right wing next to the leg that is rounded and shallow where it connects to the wing with a thin line between the eagle's leg and left wing feather as shown in Figure 37 for VAM 210. Figure 38 of VAM 224 shows the normal C³ reverse with the bottom feather of the eagle's right wing squared off and raised.

Lowest Edge Reeding Count, 168, For 1878–1904

VAM 224 with a normal II 2 obverse and C³c doubled lower reverse has an edge reeding count of 168 and is fairly scarce. It was reported by William Wolfson in March 1965. That is the **lowest reeding count** for the 1878–1904 Morgan dollars with the next lowest of 176 for some P and O mint coins from 1878 through 1885. Why this low reeding count collar was used with only one pair of dies is not known. The lowest reeding count of 157 was used with a number of 1921 P Infrequent Reeding dies and they aren't very scarce.

Clashed Partial 'E' on Reverse

The 1878 P 7TF occurs with a number of die varieties showing partial clashed letters. Only one variety, VAM 84A, has a **partial clashed 'E'** showing below the eagle's tail feathers as shown in Figure 39. It isn't particularly scarce except for the very high grades.

Die Gouges and Breaks

The 1878 P 7TF is noteworthy for its lack of large die gouges and breaks. It has its share of small ones as the dies wore out, but apparently the workman were careful to not use dies with the obvious large die gouges and breaks. An exception is VAM 143 shown in Figures 40 and 41, which has an unusually **large number of die scratches** in the lower tail feathers and leaves to the left and right of the wreath bow. These were likely caused by coarse grit when the reverse die was polished.

Denticle Impressions

Denticle impressions exist for a number of Morgan dollar reverse dies from 1878 through 1921. They were caused by the edge of the obverse hammer die accidentally falling or coming into contact by other means with the field of the reverse die. This transferred part of the denticle edge design into the fields of the reversed die, which typically shows as raised triangles in a line with spacing between them the same as the denticle spacings. There are two known cases of an 1878 P 7TF reverse die with **denticle impressions** of VAM 221A that has four raised dots in a square to the left of the wheat bow as shown in Figure 42 and was reported by Brian Raines in October 2007. VAM 225A shown in Figure

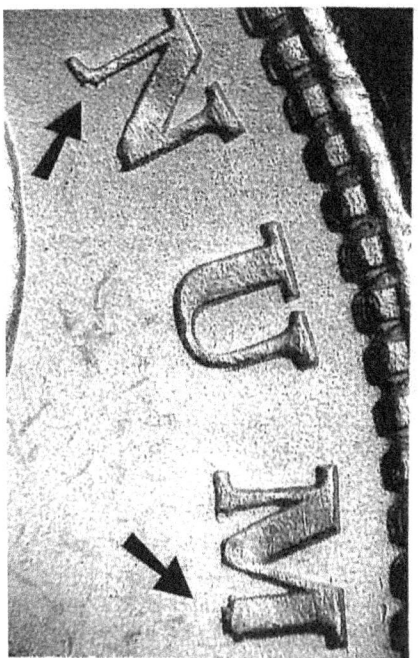

Figure 29 VAM 200 Broken N & M

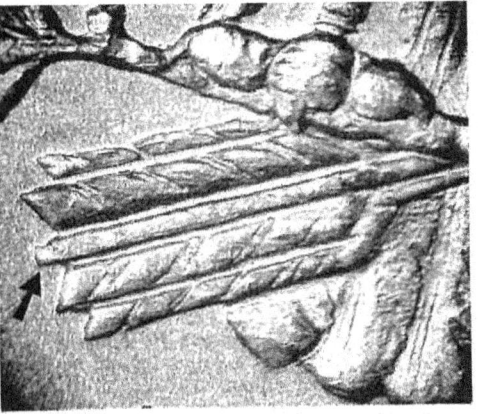

Figure 30 VAM 81 B^1 Long Nock

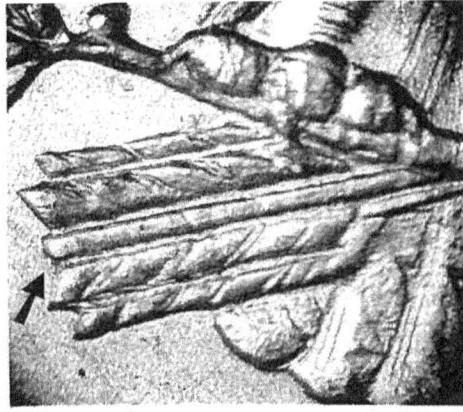

Figure 31 VAM 111 B^2 Short Nock

Figure 32 VAM 100 I Thin LIB Letters

Figure 33 VAM 133 II Thick LIB Letters

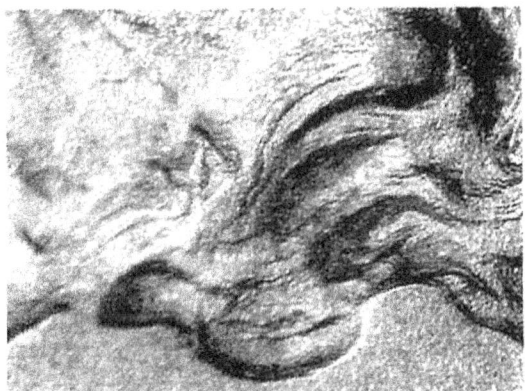

Figure 34 VAM 100 I^1 Incuse Designer's Initial M

Figure 35 VAM 70 I^2 Raised Designer's Initial M

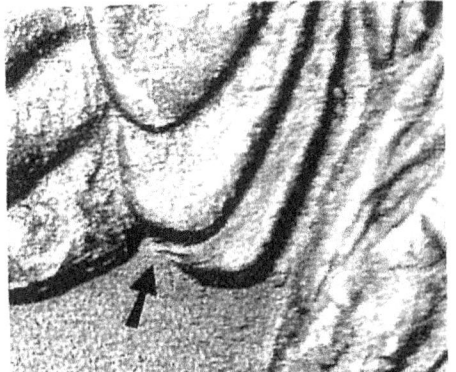

Figure 36 VAM 202 C^{1}Shallow
Feather Next to Leg

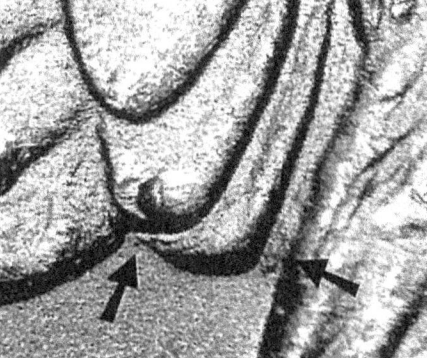

Figure 37 VAM 210 C^2 Line Next to Leg

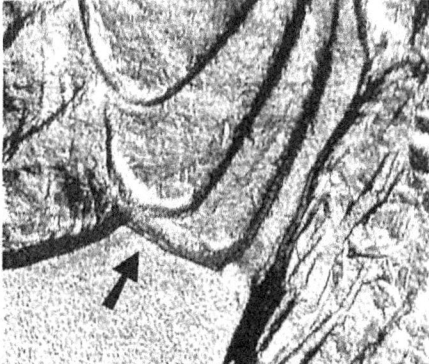

Figure 38 VAM 224 C^3 Raised
Feather Next to Leg

43 and reported by Michael Fahey in October 2004 has four raised dots below the middle tail feathers with spacing between them the same as for the denticles.

Hub Doubling

The C³ reverse type has two cases **hub doubling** which appears the same on a number of dies. The first is the C³b reverse with doubling at the bottom inside of UNITED STATES letters and left edge of some leaves in the left wreath. The key identifier for this C³b hub doubling is the strong doubling at the left inside of the U in UNITED as shown in Figure 44 for VAM 221. This hub doubling also occurs on a few other 1878 P 7TF dies and on some 1879 P, O and S dies.

The second reverse hub doubling is the C³c reverse which also appears the same on a number of dies in the form of doubling of the outside edges of some leaves in the left and right wreaths and tops of the serifs of A next to the star in AMERICA. The doubling on the A serifs sometimes is weak or disappears when the die is excessively polished. Figure 45 shows this A serif doubling for VAM 224. This hub doubling also occurs on a few other 1878 P 7TF dies and some 1879 P, O and 1880 P dies.

1878P 7TF Highlights Summary

In summary, the 1878 P 7TF has some **interesting** and **unique** die varieties:
- There are nine **Top 100** varieties of VAMs 70, 100, 115/117, 141, 171/220, 203 and 223 plus six **Hot 50** varieties of VAMs 79, 145/162, 169, 170 and 187.
- 33 **dual hub II/I** obverse dies were used with 7 TF B reverse with many having significant doubling of motto letters and date digits.
- **Seven** reverse dies of VAMs 117, 123, 141, 143/145, 146, 168/169 and 189 have a **touched–up engraved wing feather** between the eagle's right wing lower part and leg to replace the feather polished away because of a flaw in the B reverse design relief. Five other dies have engraved bars into the wing-body area of VAMs 117, 143/145, 165, 168/169 & 189. This is a small number compared to the 41 engraved wing feathers of 1878 S B² reverse.
- Some significant **doubled dies** exist that weren't the dual hub II/I obverse such as VAMs 70, 187 and 202 obverses and VAM 190 reverse.
- **Broken hub** parts are quite numerous for this first year of use, including broken point of forth right star, broken r in Trust, open o in God, bottom of D in DOLLAR and lower serifs of left U and M in UNUM.
- Eight **long nock B¹** reverse dies are known, but VAMs 80-84 are common compared to scarce1878 S long nock, plus rare VAMs 85 & 86 and VAMs 70 & 79 Top 100 & Hot 50.
- The initial **obverse die type I** exists for only two die pairs, the VAMs 70 and 100.
- Early **"trial" C** reverse design types that are an early sub–type of the C reverse are the C¹ for at least four dies and the C² for at least three different dies.
- The 1878 7TF VAM 224 has the **lowest as reeding count of 168** for the years 1878–1904. Only the 1921 P Infrequent Reeding dies have a lower count of 157.
- VAM 84A has the only **partial clashed 'E'** below the eagles tail feathers for the 1878 P 7TF.
- There are no large die gouges or breaks with 1878 P 7TF, just small ones as the dies wore out. Exceptions are VAM 143, which has **numerous die scratches** in lower tail feathers and in leaves to left and right of wreath bow and VAM 140A with die scratches on lower reverse.
- Two dies of VAM 221A and 225A with **denticle impressions** of four raised dots below the tail feathers exist for the 1878 P 7TF.
- Two cases of **doubled reverse hub** exists. The C³b reverse with strongly doubled left inside of U in UNITED and other doubled letters in UNITED STATES and leaves in left wreath plus the C³c reverse with the doubled serifs on A next to the star in AMERICA and some doubled wreath leaves. These doubled hubs were used to prepare multiple 1878 P 7TF, 1879 P, O and S and one 1880 P dies.

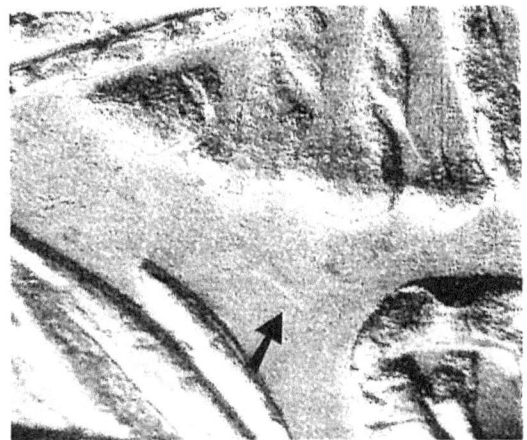

Figure 39 VAM 84A Clashed Partial 'E'

Figure 40 VAM 143 Die Scratches in Tail Feathers

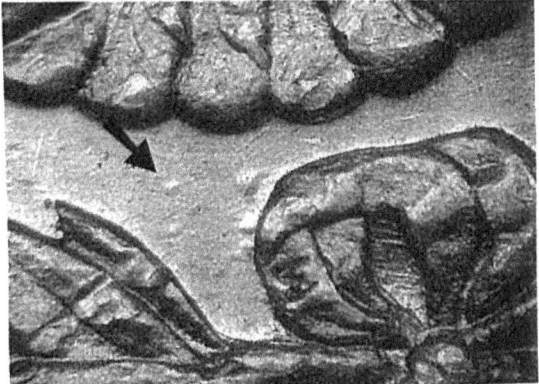

Figure 42 VAM 221A Denticle Impressions

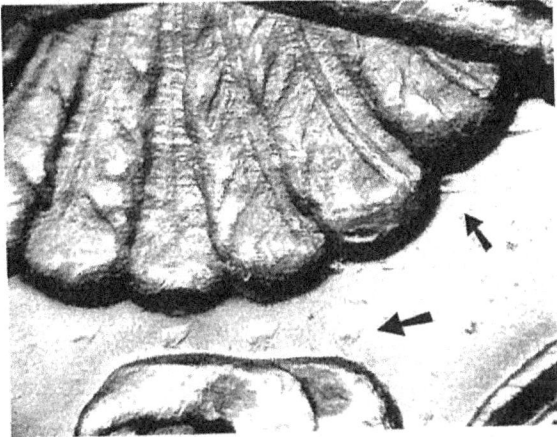

Figure 43 VAM 225A Denticle Impressions

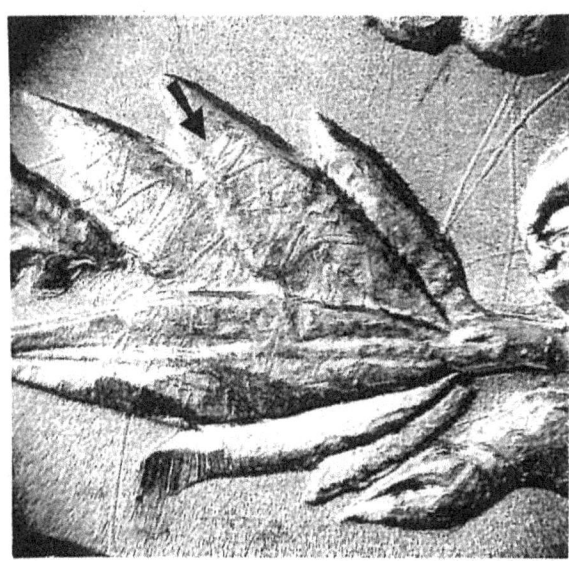

Figure 41 VAM 143 Die Scratches Wreath Leaves

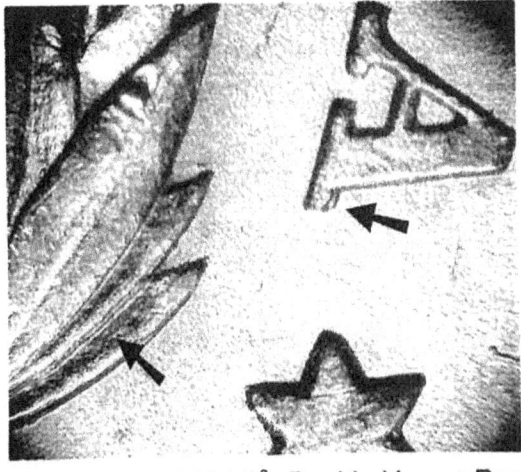

Figure 45 VAM 224 C³c Doubled Lower Reverse, A

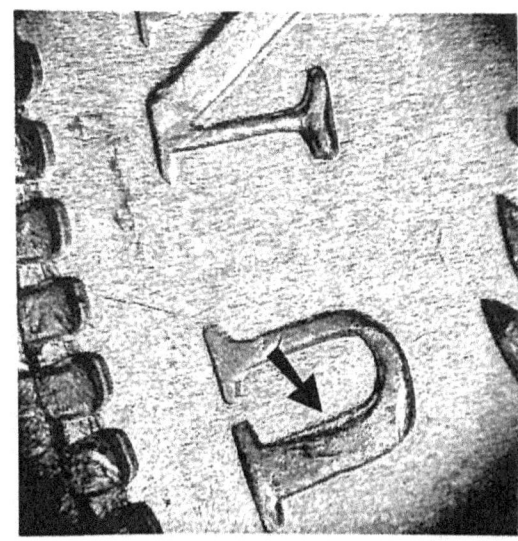

Figure 44 VAM 221 C³b Doubled Left Reverse, U

II/I DUAL HUB OBVERSE

There is one known set of dual hubbing of the obverse working dies, II/I, for the 1878 P Morgan dollar. On the other hand, there are now known multiple sets of dual, tripled or quadrupled hubbing of the 1878 P reverse working dies including A^1/A^0 (designated as A^1 in VAM book), $A^2/A^1/A^0$ (designated as A^2/A^1 in VAM book) and $B^1/A^1/A^0$ and $B^1/A^2/A^1/A^0$ (designated as B/A in VAM book). The multiple hubbing of reverse dies is explored in detail in the booklet, *Morgan Dollar 8 & 7 Over 8 Tail Feather Story*, by Leroy Van Allen, January 2006. The dual hubbing of obverse dies was first reported in the article by Leroy Van Allen, *1878 7/8 Tail Feather Silver Dollar: How and Why*, The Numismatic Scrapbook Magazine, April 1965, pp. 948–953.

The first obverse design type I working dies had a relatively high relief that caused some problems in striking coins as mentioned in engraver George Morgan's letter on April 8, 1878 to Director of the Mint, Dr. Henry R. Linderman:

...I noticed some time ago that when they die had settled a little as they almost invariably do– a place on the cheek which comes opposite of the wing of the eagle– did not come up satisfactorily. In the hub now being used I have cut down this part. I cannot see that it would be of advantage to reduce the relief in any other place.

The hub that Morgan referred to was that of the type II obverse design. In addition, the first type I obverse working dies only struck an average of about 30,000 coins per die, less than half the average of the first type A reverse working dies. These problems of the first design dies were mentioned in a letter from the coiner, O. C. Bosbyshell, to the Superintendent of the Philadelphia Mint, James Pollock, on April 1, 1878:

...the dies however, do not stand as well as could be desired – they crack and sink shortly after entering the presses...

The Philadelphia Mint was under pressure during March and April 1878 to strike the 2 million Morgan dollars each month to meet the provisions of the Bland–Allison Act. Dies had not yet been sent to the San Francisco and Carson City branch mints because of the die imperfections. Some shortcuts were taken to salvage the existing dies by entering the new improved obverse hub of type II design into the older type I design obverse working dies. This also reduced the time to prepare new working dies of from seven to ten days down to a day or two when the obverse dies were re-impressed with the new hub.

Equipment in the Die Room at the Philadelphia Mint in 1901 is shown in Figure 46 that includes lathes and a screw press to hub the dies. This equipment was likely similar or in some cases the same as that used by the Philadelphia Mint in 1878. Figure 47 shows the Metal Room of the Philadelphia mint in 1901 with George Morgan at the bench and hydraulic presses at the left and the screw press at the back. Close-up photos of George Morgan is shown in Figure 48 at age 56 and in Figure 49 at age 65.

Evidence of the dual hubbing of the obverse dies shows up as frequent doubling of the stars, motto letters, date and LIBERTY which aren't the simple misalignment of the hub between the multiple blows required to transfer the design onto a working die. In particular, the letters LIBERTY in the headband are thinner for the type I obverse as shown in Figure 50 for VAM 70 than that for the type II obverse as shown in Figure 51 for VAM 195. The dual hubbing resulted in frequent doubling of the LIBERTY letters in various directions as shown in Figure 52 for VAM 141.

The ear of the type I obverse has an evenly divided rear portion of the ear and a thin pointed inner ear fill as shown in Figure 53 for VAM 70. The type II obverse has an unevenly divided rear portion of the ear and a thick inner ear fill with blunt end as shown in Figure 54 for VAM 195. When the type II design was impressed over the type I design, the wider rear ear portion of the type I design would have remained since it was a wider and deeper cavity in the die face as shown in Figure 55 for VAM 82 II/I obverse.

Figure 46 Die Room, Philadelphia Mint, 1901
George Morgan at back of room, screw press on right
(Report of the Director of the Mint, 1902)

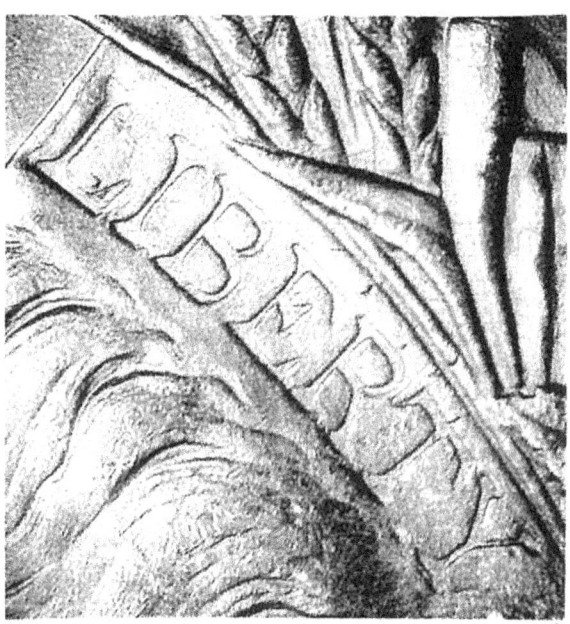

Figure 50 VAM 70 I LIBERTY

Figure 51 VAM 195 II LIBERTY

Figure 52 VAM 141 II/I LIBERTY

Figure 47 Medal Room, Philadelphia Mint, 1901
George Morgan at bench, hydraulic presses at left, screw press at back
(Report of the Director of the Mint, 1902)

Figure 48 George Morgan, Medal Room, Philadelphia Mint, 1901
Morgan wielding hammer with dies and medals, age 56
(Report of the Director of the Mint, 1902)

Figure 49 George T. Morgan, Engraver, 1910, Age 65
(Philadelphia Mint photo)

When the new type II hub was made, the center of the ear was cut out deeper so the inner fill could be made wider. Thus, when the type II hub was impressed into the type I dies, the inner part didn't contact that of the type I dies. Instead, the metal was forced from the area around the ear into the ear's center but not enough to be formed by the type II hub. So the inner ear fill on the type I die was reduced in size somewhat depending how hard the hub was forced into the die and the subsequent die polishing on this high point of the die. As a result, the inner ear fill on the II/I obverse is always very short and pointed and is a key diagnostic for the II/I dies.

There are also isolated cases of strongly doubled and tripled motto letters and stars which don't seem to be due to a regular shift of the hub and die during a blow. Figure 56 of VAM 121 shows a doubled R in PLURIBUS that perhaps is the result of a letter I being punched over the R in the die to strengthen it. Likewise, Figure 57 of VAM 163 shows a strongly shifted U in PLURIBUS while the adjacent R is not, which indicates an individual U punch may have been used. The strongly tripled second right star of VAM 117 is an isolated case again with the adjacent stars being normal as shown in Figure 58. A star punch may have been used to strengthen the star with mixed results.

Most of the type I obverse dies were not lapped and polished before being impressed with the type II obverse hub since the position of the motto letters, date and stars had not changed. In contrast, the B/A dual hub reverse, 7/8 TF, dies were heavily lapped before being re-impressed because of the major differences in the legend letter positions, wreath design and number of tail feather ends.

Currently there are 40 known II/I dual hub obverse dies with 33 used with the 1878 P 7TF second type B design reverse dies. The other seven II/I dual hub obverse dies were used with the type A design and B/A, 7/8 TF dual hub reverse dies. Six dual hub II/I obverse dies were used with the first type A reverse design 8 tail feather dies with one of these obverse dies, II/I 6, also used with the type B 7TF reverse die. Four II/I obverse dies were used with the B/A, 7/8 TF reverse dies and two of these dies, II/I 7 and 8, were also used with the type B 7TF reverse dies.

As a side note, Morgan had some difficulties in preparing the type C reverse design. On May 17, 1878, Morgan reported to Linderman that: *We have made two pairs of dies from the new hubs for the Silver Dollar and tried them in the coining presses...* These were the new type III obverse and type C reverse designs. On June 5, Morgan again reported to Linderman:

Having still about 100 pairs of dies for the silver dollar in stock, we have had no necessity to make dies for this coin during the last two weeks.

With a view of making the work come up easier and more uniform I have made slight alterations in the depth of work and width of border.

The dies were tried in the coining presses but in neither case was the result exactly satisfactory as I wished. I am now engaged in a third attempt which I believe will give us all we want....

These three tries of the dies in the coining presses were likely the interim type C[1] and C[2] reverses with a third attempt being the final type C[3] reverse design.

Figure 53 VAM 70 I Ear

Figure 54 VAM 195 II Ear

Figure 55 VAM 82 II/I Ear

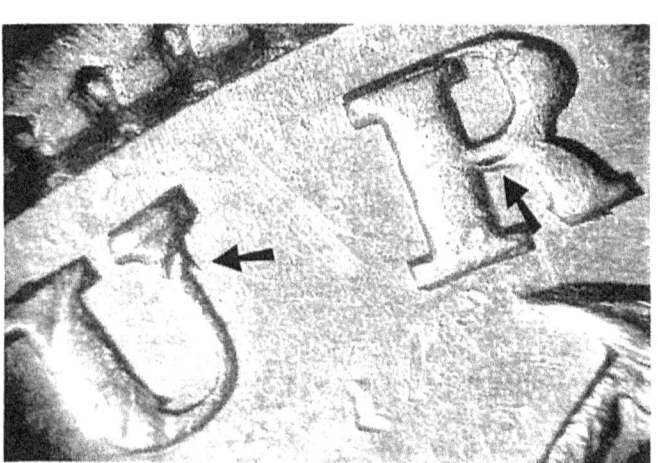

Figure 56 VAM 121 Doubled UR

Figure 57 VAM 163 Shifted U

Figure 58 VAM 117 Tripled Second Rt. Star

ENGRAVED WING FEATHER

There are seven unusual 1878 P seven tail feather reverse die varieties that show engraving bars and lines between the bottom of the eagle's right wing and the leg. This area was frequently over polished with a weak or missing lower wing feather caused by the low die relief and die polishing. In addition, there are five reverse dies that have bars and lines engraved between the eagle's right wing and body, an area that was also frequently over polished.

David DeRuiter sent some 1878 S Morgan dollars for examination in November 1979 and pointed out that the ends of the eagle's bottom right wing feather's next to the leg were different. He stated that many of them had been retouched on the working die. He had also seen similar retouching of the 1879 S with the sub-type B² parallel arrow feather reverse. There are currently known 41 1878 S reverse dies that had been retouched with various hand engraved wing feather's added back onto the die between the eagle's right wing and leg.

It was not until August 2002 that Michael Fey reported that a 1878 P 7TF type B reverse die had also been retouched with added engraved bars in this wing–leg area of VAM 189 (See Figure 59.). This was the first reported and strongest engraved wing feather variety for the 1878 P 7TF type B reverse. Then in April 2007 Leroy Van Allen reported three more engraved wing feather varieties that had small bars and lines added to this same area, VAMs 141, 143/145 and 146 shown in Figures 60, 61 and 62. A thin vertical bar with fine lines at the wing–leg and engraved bars between the eagle's right wing and body was reported by John Roberts in June 2007 for VAM 168/169 as shown in Figures 63 and 64. VAM 117 with engraved bar at wing–leg was then reported in June 2007 by Leroy Van Allen as shown in Figure 65. Similar wing–body engraving on VAMs 117 and 165 and lines on VAM 143/145 shown in Figures 66, 67 and 68 were reported by Leroy Van Allen also in June 2007. The engraved bars at the wing–leg of VAM 123 was later reported in August 2007 by Leroy Van Allen as shown in Figure 69. The engraved bar in the wing–leg area of VAM 189 also extends up between the wing–body as shown in Figure 70 as fifth variety with engraving bars at wing–body. These eight engraved wing feather dies are a small number compared to 41 that the San Francisco Mint had touched up in 1878 plus another five that were used in 1879, but likely left over from being engraved in 1878. The Philadelphia Mint had engraved small feathers at the lower part of the eagle's left and right wings on 16 of type A design eight tail feather working dies to correct weak or missing wing feathers.

Engraver George Morgan indicated problems with the sub-type B² reverse dies in a letter to the Director of the Mint, Dr. Henry R. Linderman on April 17, 1878:

...The reverse dies now fill up quickly, while striking the coin. I am finishing this hub so that I believe this failing will be avoided.

I notice that some places in both dies are apt to get rubbed too low in the polishing...

The polishing that Morgan referred to was the basining of the die face that placed it against a rotating disk that had a desired radius of curvature. Polishing grit and compound mixed with water or oil on the basining disk gave a slight curvature and polish to the die face. This radius of curvature allowed the die design to be struck up evenly across the coin.

A normal wing and leg area that hasn't been over polished is shown in Figure 71 of VAM 80, a fairly rare occurrence for the type B reverse dies. Figure 72 shows a typical over polished wing–leg area for VAM 114, and one that is very over polished in Figure 73 for VAM 116. The majority of the type B reverse dies used at the Philadelphia Mint do not have the wing–leg area touched up while the San Francisco Mint engraved a wing feather back on most of the type B reverse dies used in 1878. The Carson City mint did not engrave any of the type B reverse dies used in 1878 and 1880.

It isn't known who did the touch-up engraving on the wing–leg area of the eight type B reverse dies at the Philadelphia Mint. The engraved area is similar for VAMs 123, 141 and 146 and may have been done by the same engraver or workman. The engraved wing–leg area of VAM 189 is very different with thin diagonal bars and was likely done by a different workman. The specific tools used for the touch-up engraving isn't known. A microscope to view the wing–leg area and abrasive stone, hardened steel chisels and pointed tools were likely used similar to the die touch-up tools used in the 1970s at the Philadelphia Mint as shown in Figures 74 and 75. The subsequent type C reverse design dies basined satisfactory without removing some of the design details and none were touched up.

Figure 59 VAM 189 Engraved Wing Feather

Figure 60 VAM 141 Engraved Wing Feather

Figure 61 VAM 143/145 Engraved Wing Feather

Figure 62 VAM 146 Engraved Wing Feather

Figure 63 VAM 168/169 Engraved Vertical Bar

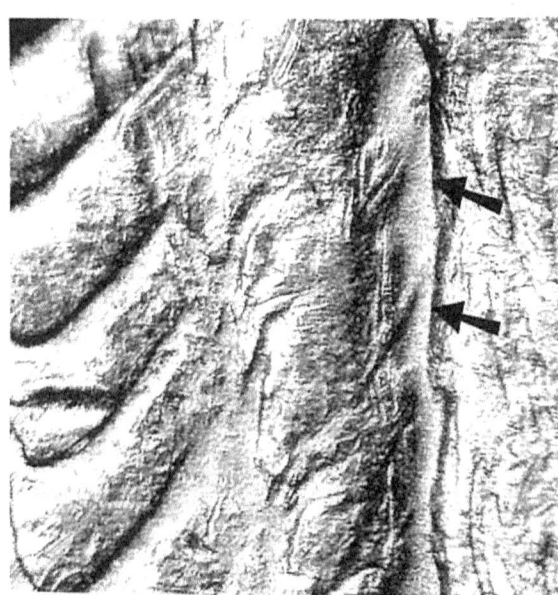

Figure 64 VAM 168/169 Engraved Bars

Figure 65 VAM 117 Engraved Vertical Bar

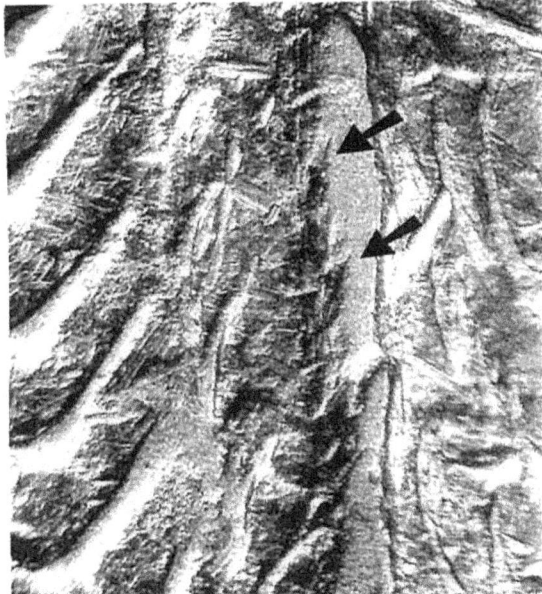

Figure 66 VAM 117 Engraved Vertical Bars

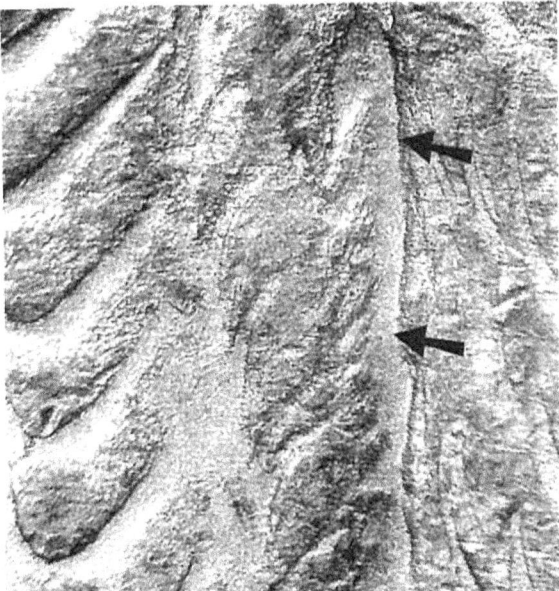

Figure 67 VAM 165 Engraved Diagonal Bars

Figure 68 VAM 143/145 Engraved Lines

Figure 69 VAM 123 Engraved Wing Feather

Figure 70 VAM 189 Engraved Wing Feathers

Figure 71 VAM 80 Normal Unpolished
Wing-Leg Feather

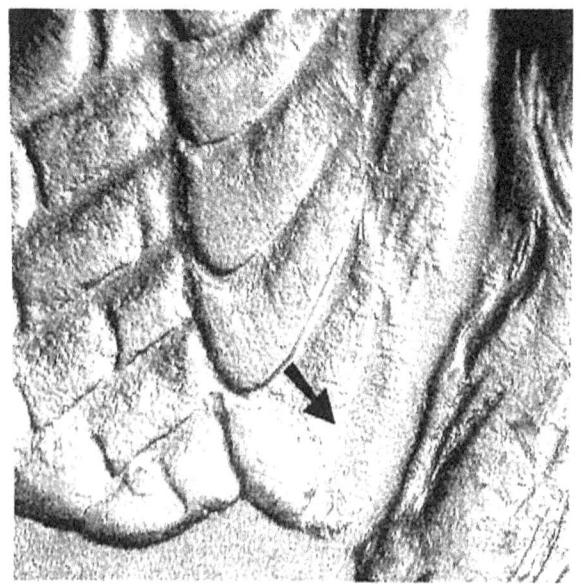

Figure 72 VAM 114 Typical Over Polished
Wing-Leg Feather

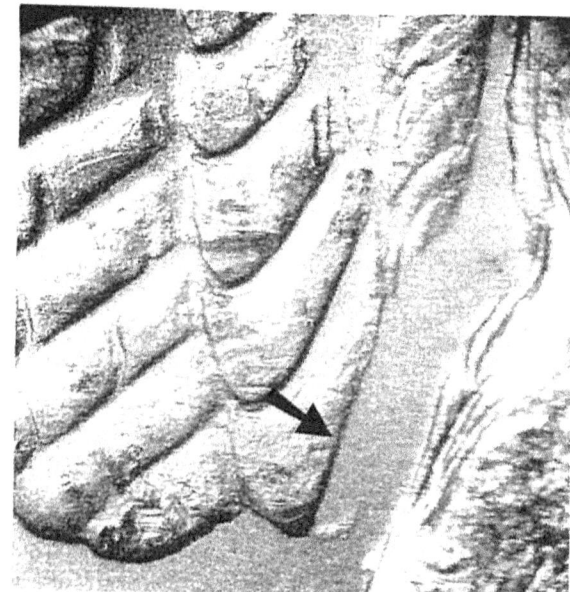

Figure 73 VAM 116 Very Over Polished
Wing-Leg Feather

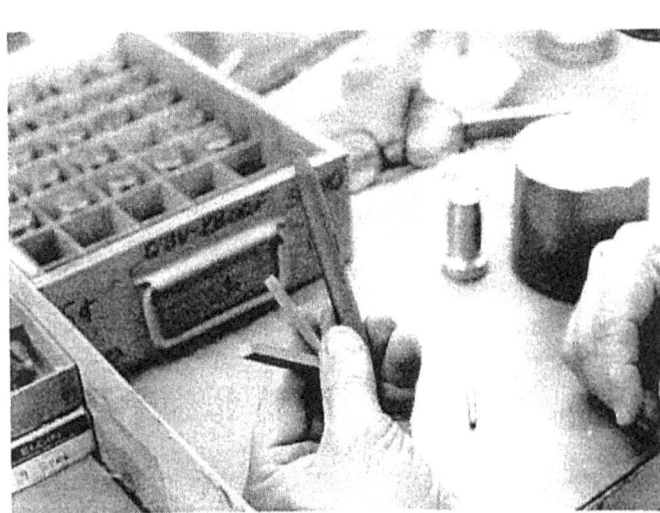

Figure 74 Die Touch-up Tools, 1970 s

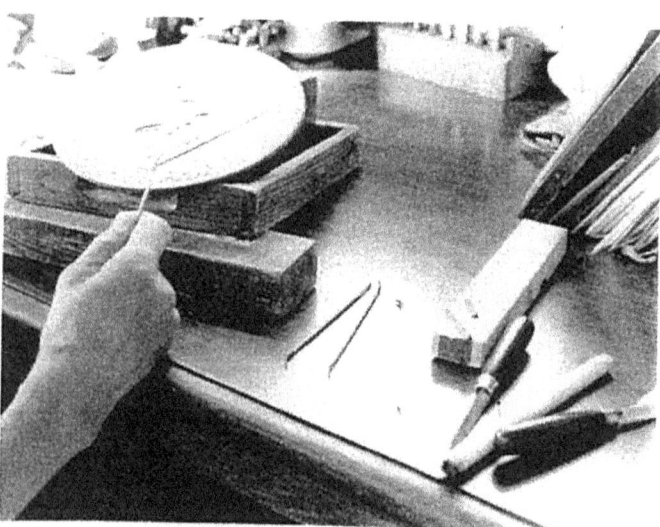

Figure 75 Engraving Tools for Galvano Touch-up, 1970 s

DESIGN TYPES/SUB-TYPES GUIDELINES

The obverse and reverse design types and sub-types are summarized below for the 1878 P 7TF varieties. These designs are discussed in greater detail in the VAM book. The **detailed descriptions and photographs for each 7TF die variety combination** are provided later in this Guide. These can be used for the extensive examination of specific varieties or for confirmation purposes. However, it is sufficient for attribution purposes to just focus on some key design features to aid in die variety identification.

Dr. Roland Girardet has drawn up some accompanying excellent illustrations that *summarize these key design features* for the obverse and reverse Morgan dollar design types. These illustrations cover all the major obverse and reverse Morgan dollar design. Only the type B and C reverses and type I, II/I, II and III obverses need to be considered for the 1878 P 7TF varieties.

7TF REVERSES

B– *Parallel* top arrow feather (PAF) or reverse of 78 type.

B^1**– *Long*** center arrow shaft of nock (refer to VAM's 70– 86). (See Figure 76.)

B^2**– *Short*** center arrow shaft or nock (refer to VAMs 100- 199-2). (See Figure 77.)

B^2**a–** Normal reverse die with complete unbroken In God We Trust (IGWT). There will also be some raised metal of a feather at junction of eagle's right wing and leg (refer to VAM's 100– 134).

B^2**b–** The o in God of IGWT is partially *open* on upper left side from hub break. Remainder of IGWT will be unbroken (refer to VAM's 140– 146). (See Figure 78.)

B^2**c–** Top right serif of r in Trust of IGWT motto is partially *broken* and at a lower level than rest of t. This may include open o in God or an over polished area in junction between eagle's right wing and leg but **broken r takes precedence** in listing (refer to VAM 's 160– 189). (See Figure 79.)

B^2**d–** IGWT motto is slightly *doubled* (refer to VAM 190). (See Figure 80.)

B^2**e–** Bottom of D in DOLLAR is partially or completely *broken* (refer to VAM's 195 & 195A). (See Figure 81.)

B^2**f–** Normal B^2a reverse except area in junction between eagle's right wing and leg is *over polished* with no discernable raised metal of a feather (refer to VAM's 196– 199-2). (See Figure 82.)

Note: B^2g, B^2h, B^2i, B^2j, B^2k, B^2l, B^2m & B^2n are individual die varieties.

C– *Slanted* top arrow feather (SAF) or reverse of 79 type (refer to VAMs 200- 232) .

C^1**– *Shallow*** and ***rounded*** feather end next to eagle's right leg not connected to wing on left (refer to VAM's 200- 203). (See Figure 83.)

C^2**–** Not as shallow and rounded feather end next to eagle's right leg extending to junction of next left two feathers. Added *raised line* between this feather and leg (refer to VAM's 210– 215). (See Figure 84.)

C^3**– *Raised*** and ***square*** feather end next to eagle's right leg (refer to VAM's 220- 232). (See Figure 85.)

OBVERSES

I– *Evenly* divided ear rear with *thin long* ear fill (refer to VAM's 70 & 100). (See Figure 86.)

II– *Unevenly* divided ear rear with *blunt* ear fill and without lines in wheat leaves (refer to VAM's 130- 134, 146, 185- 189, 190, 195, 197, 210, 221- 229.1). (See Figure 87.)

A common sub-type is II 2 with broken point of fourth right star. (See Figure 88.)

II/I– I obverse re-hubbed with II obverse hub. *Short pointed* inner ear fill, *evenly* divided ear rear and without lines in wheat leaves (refer to VAM's 79- 84, 110- 123, 140- 145, 160- 171, 198- 199-1, 200, 201 & 220). (See Figure 89.)

III– *Unevenly* divided ear rear, *large blunt* ear fill, *lines* in wheat leaves.

    III^1– Wheat leaf end *well below* bottom of R in LIBERTY, point of Liberty head neck above middle of denticle (refer to VAM's 203 & 215). (See Figure 90.)

    III^2– Wheat leaf end *close* to bottom of R in LIBERTY, point of Liberty head neck above space between denticles (refer to VAM's 230- 232). (See Figure 91.)

Figure 76 VAM 81 B^1 Long Nock or Center Arrow Shaft   Figure 77 VAM 111 B^2 Short Nock or Center Arrow Shaft

 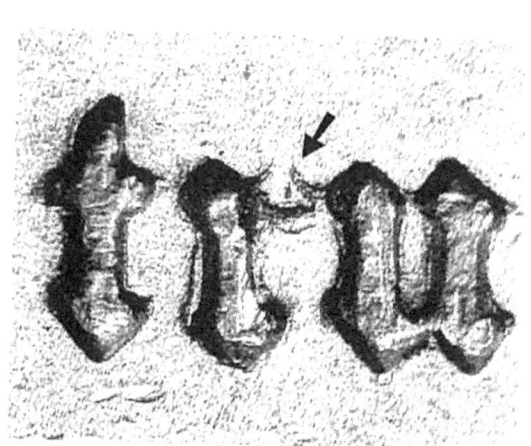

Figure 78 VAM 141 B^{2}b Open o in God   Figure 79 VAM 163 B^{2}c Broken r

Dollar – Morgan: 1878-1921 Design Types: <u>Obverse</u>

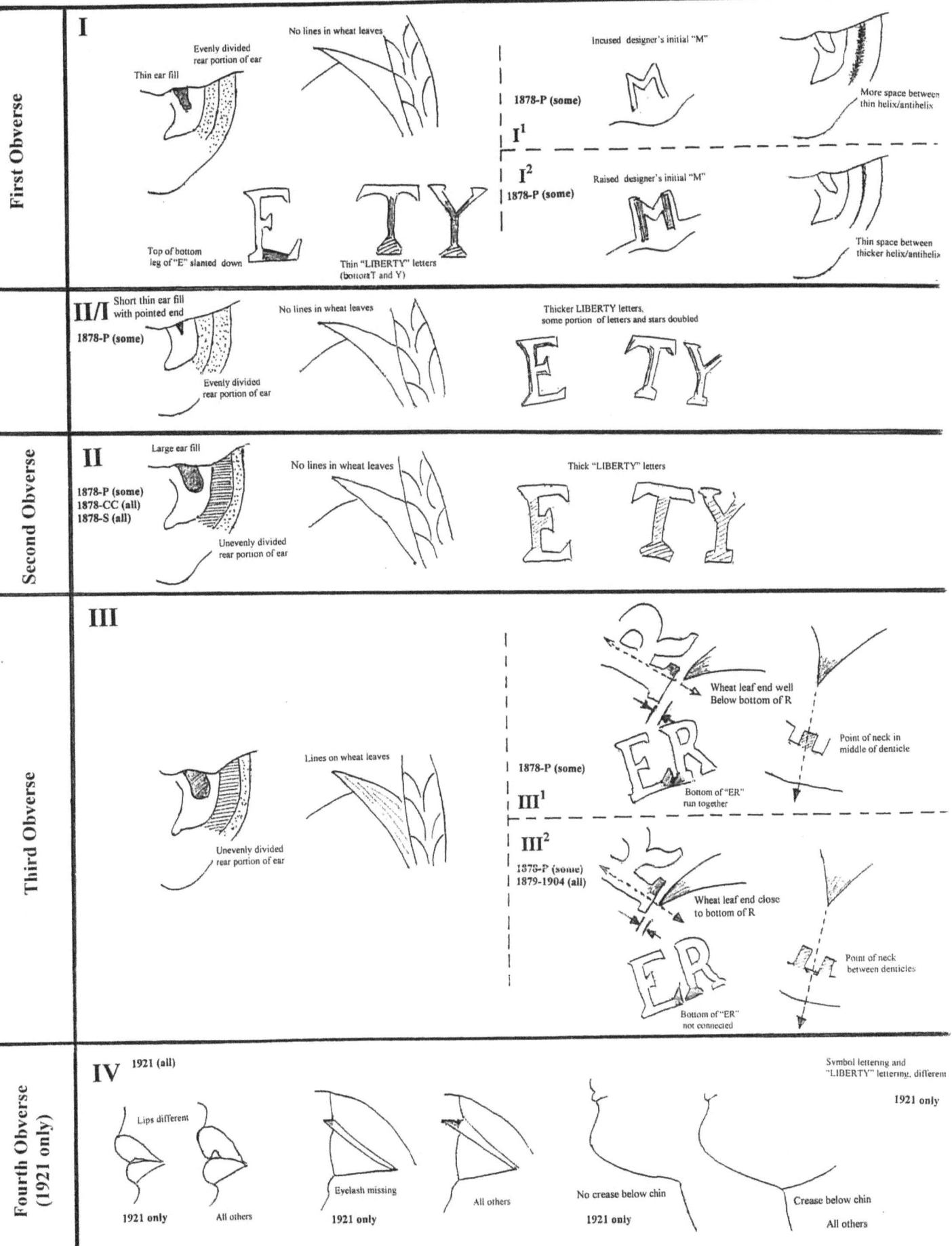

First Obverse

I

Thin ear fill

Evenly divided rear portion of ear

No lines in wheat leaves

Incused designer's initial "M"

1878-P (some)

I¹

I²

1878-P (some)

Raised designer's initial "M"

More space between thin helix/antihelix

Thin space between thicker helix/antihelix

Top of bottom leg of "E" slanted down

Thin "LIBERTY" letters (bottom T and Y)

Second Obverse

II/I

Short thin ear fill with pointed end

1878-P (some)

Evenly divided rear portion of ear

No lines in wheat leaves

Thicker LIBERTY letters, some portion of letters and stars doubled

II

1878-P (some)
1878-CC (all)
1878-S (all)

Large ear fill

No lines in wheat leaves

Thick "LIBERTY" letters

Unevenly divided rear portion of ear

Third Obverse

III

Unevenly divided rear portion of ear

Lines on wheat leaves

Wheat leaf end well Below bottom of R

Point of neck in middle of denticle

1878-P (some)

III¹

Bottom of "ER" run together

III²

1878-P (some)
1879-1904 (all)

Wheat leaf end close to bottom of R

Point of neck between denticles

Bottom of "ER" not connected

Fourth Obverse (1921 only)

IV 1921 (all)

Symbol lettering and "LIBERTY" lettering, different

1921 only

Lips different

1921 only

All others

Eyelash missing

1921 only

All others

No crease below chin

1921 only

Crease below chin

All others

Dollar – Morgan: 1878-1921   Design Types: **Reverse**

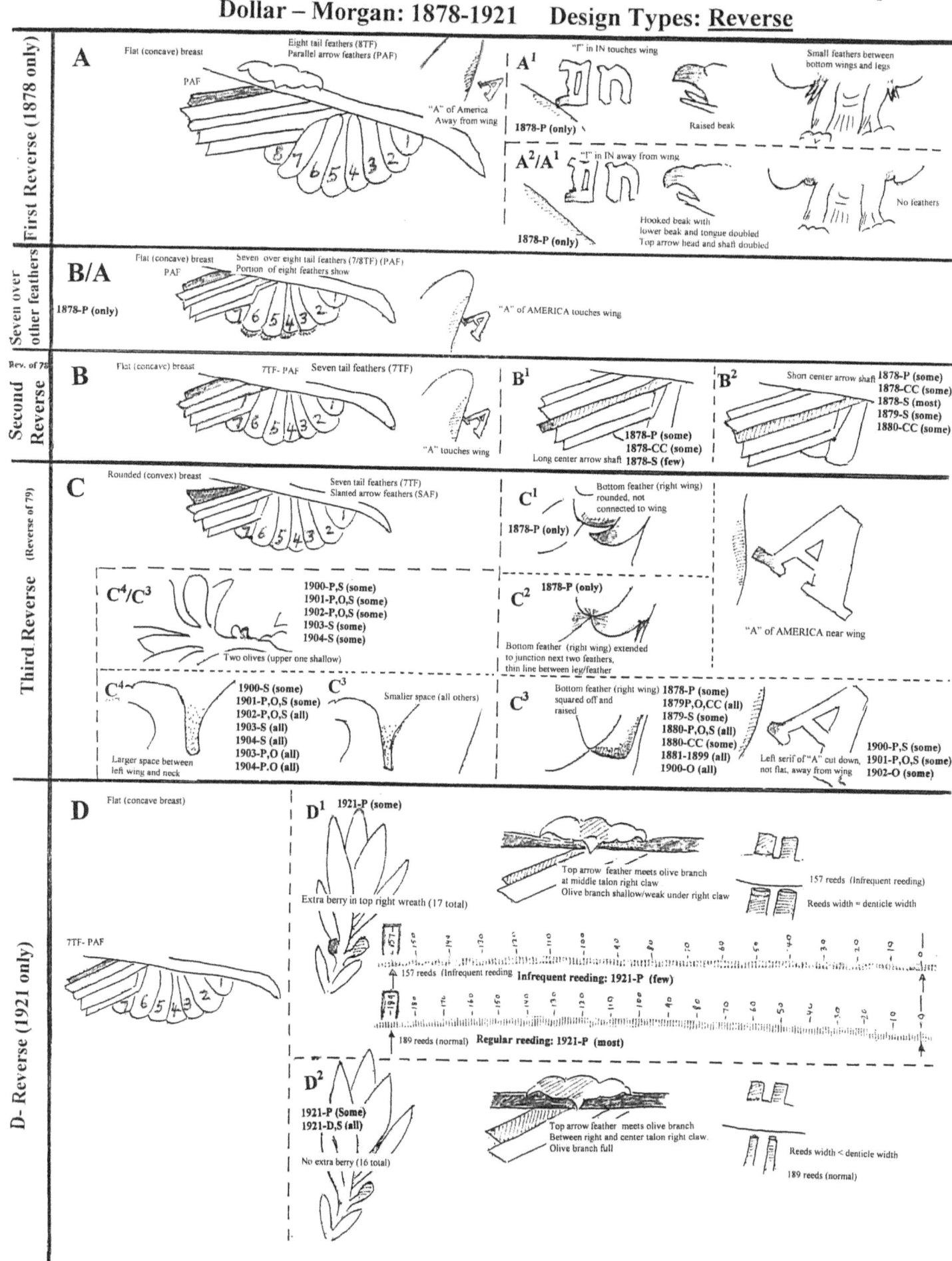

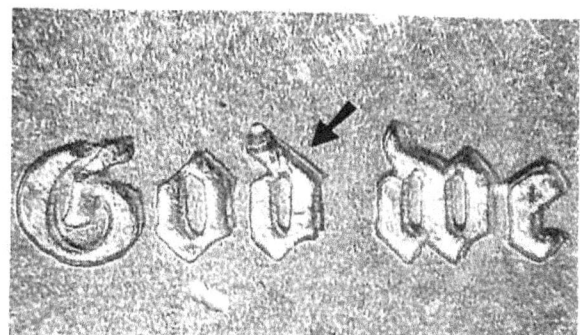

Figure 80 VAM 190 B^{2}d Doubled Motto

Figure 81 VAM 195 B^{2}e Broken D Bottom

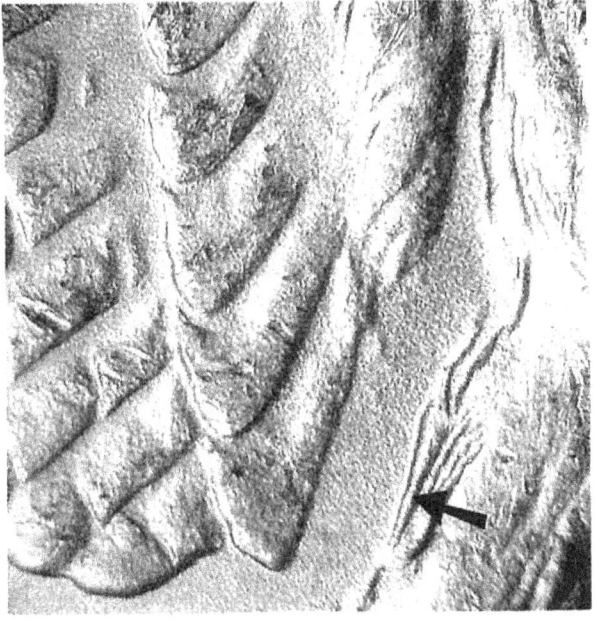

Figure 82 VAM 197 B^{2}f Missing Wing Feather

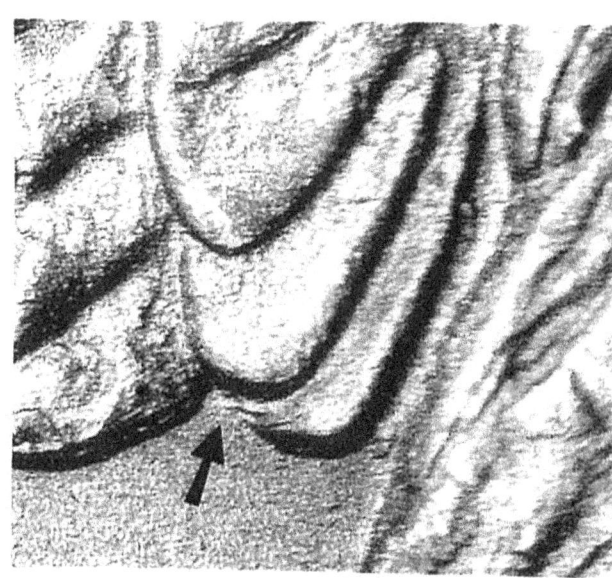

Figure 83 VAM 202 C^{1}Shallow Feather Next to Leg

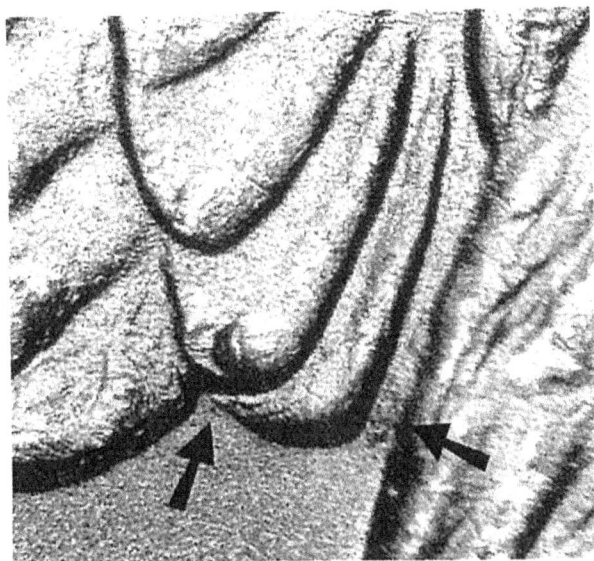

Figure 84 VAM 210 C^2 Line Next to Leg

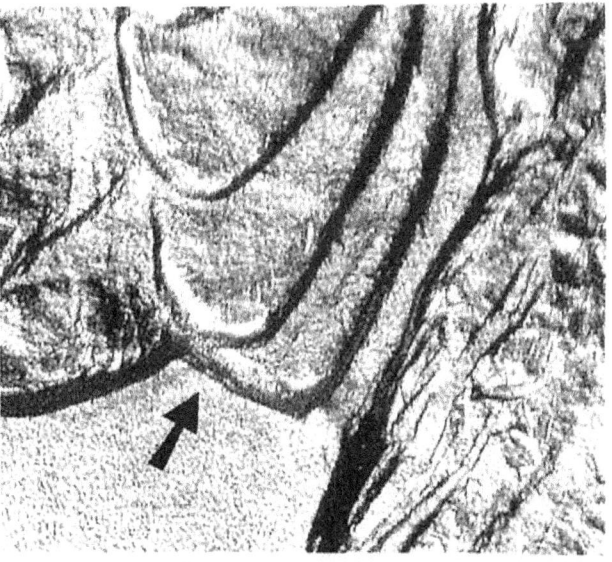

Figure 85 VAM 224 C^3 Square Raised Feather Next to Leg

Figure 86 VAM 70 I Long Thin Inner Ear Fill

Figure 87 VAM 195 II Blunt End Inner Ear Fill

Figure 89 VAM 82 II/I Pointed Inner Ear Fill

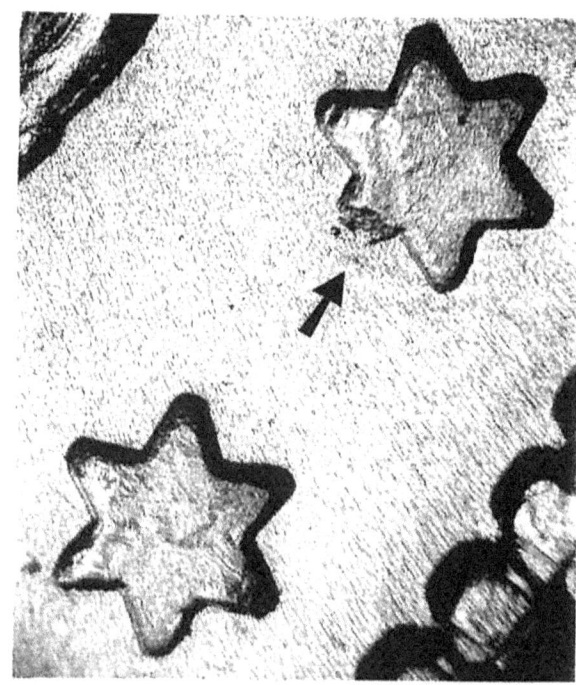

Figure 88 VAM 197 Broken 4th Rt. Star

Figure 90 VAM 202 III¹ Wheat Leaf End Well Below R

Figure 91 VAM 231 III² Wheat Leaf End Close to R

TOP 30 1878 P 7TF DIE VARIETIES

This section presents the Top 30 collectible 1878 P 7TF die varieties out of the currently known 79 die varieties and 42 sub–varieties. Some of the selections are subjective and collectors may have their own favorite die varieties. Obvious ones to include are the Top 100, Hot 50 and Hit List 40 die varieties, strongly doubled dies, ones with unique and interesting features, and the not–so–obvious scarce and rare die varieties. The Top 30 die varieties should aid collectors in focusing their studying and collecting of 1878 P 7TF varieties. Collectors are encouraged to explore the other varieties. It was difficult to pare down a listing to only 30 varieties because the 1878 P 7TF has a large number of doubled dies and hub breaks. The Philadelphia Mint experienced problems in 1878 to prepare satisfactory working dies and had time pressures to strike the required number of coins per month.

The **Top 100** 1878 P 7TF die varieties include VAMs 70 with type I obverse that has a strongly doubled motto, 100 with a type I obverse, 115/198 with strongly tripled cotton bolls and doubled date and stars, 117/141 with strongly tripled second right star and an engraved wing feather for 141, 171/220 with strongly tripled R and doubled cotton bolls, 203 with the early "trial" type III obverse and type C reverse, and 223 with washed out L in LIBERTY and doubled reverse of hub doubling.

The **Hot 50** 1878 P 7TF die varieties include VAMs 79 with doubled cotton leaves and disconnected olive leaf, 145/162 with broken N and M on hub, 169 with strongly quadrupled stars, 170 with strongly doubled date, stars, and UR and 187 with unusual shifted and doubled R.

The **Hit List 40** 1878 P 7TF die varieties include VAMs 116, A, B, C doubled P, 123 spiked eye, 166 tripled eye, 188 polished L, 189 re-engraved wing and 224 low reed count.

Next are some of the many **dual hub obverse II/I doubled dies**. Out of the 33 used with the 7TF reverse dies, seven were already included as Top 100 and Hot 50 varieties. Other selected ones include VAMs 116 with doubled P, L, R and B, 118 with shifted P and doubled ear, 120 with doubled P–R and spikes below eyelid, 121 with doubled E, P, U and R, 1 & 3 three right stars and R that looks like an I over R, 122 with doubled first right star and alligator eye, 123 with doubled R and U–M and seventh left star, 163 with large shift on U and doubled M, 166 with a spiked P and tripled eyelid and 167 with a spiked P and doubled U's.

There are also eight dies with **touch–up engraving** on the missing feather between the eagle's right wing and leg or body. The strongest is VAM 189 with lines and bars to fill in the missing feather. Another fairly strong engraved wing feather is VAM 141 with some vertical bars. VAM 146 has a couple vertical bars engraved in that area as does VAM 123 with vertical bars engraved. The others have less visible bars or only lines between the wing-body.

Several varieties are included as Top 30 because of their unusual nature. VAM 84A has the only **partial clashed 'E'** below the eagle's tail feathers for the 1878 varieties. VAM 188 has an over polished die with the weak **washed out L** in LIBERTY also of the Top 100 VAM 223. VAM 203A has fairly strong **clashed letters** of n, w, st and M. VAM 225A has strong **denticle impressions** below the eagle's tail feathers.

Another category is the **scarce** to **rare** die varieties. Heading the list is VAM 123, which is rare in all grades. Others listed because of the II/I dual hub doubling and are also scarce are VAMs 116, 118, 120, 121, 166 and 167. The VAM 188 is also scarce. Although the doubling on VAMs 226 and 229 is not especially strong, they are among the apparently scarcest of the C reverse types as is VAM 227. The apparent scarcity of the varieties will likely change as more are collected.

The Top 30 1878 P 7TF die varieties are each given a number of **Desirability Stars** from one to five, with five being the most desirable. The desirability number of stars is automatically five for the Top 100 and Hot 50 varieties since they are widely collected with available price guides. The desirability stars for the other Top 30 1878 P 7TF die varieties is somewhat subjective. One of the factors is the **visibility** of the feature and how strong it is relative to other varieties of the same kind for 1878 P 7TF and other Morgan dollar dates. A second factor is the **uniqueness** of the variety kind that is only found on the 1878 P 7TF varieties. A third factor is the **rarity** of the variety. The scarcity and rarity of many of the 1878 P 7TF varieties may not yet be well established because of the past lack of knowledge and interest in some of the varieties.

The chart presented below lists the Top 30 1878 P 7TF die varieties in order of the VAM number as selected by the author. In some cases, the obverse or reverse die is also found on another die combination variety as indicated by a second VAM number with a slash. Obverse or reverse die designations are included for each VAM number along with the main feature of each variety and the number of desirability stars assigned.

There are 16 1878 P 7TF die varieties with five desirability stars, eight with four stars and six with three stars. Most other 1878 P 7TF die varieties included in this Guide have three or less desirability stars. There are a large number of five desirability stars, 16, because of the eight **Top 100** and five **Hot 50** varieties that automatically have five stars. The three others with five stars include VAM 123 because of it's **rarity**, VAM 189 because of it's strong **engraved wing feather** and VAM 203A because of the many **clashed letters** and because the parent variety, 203, is a Top 100. The number of desirability stars is only a rough guide since collectors may have their own set of favorite varieties.

TOP 30 1878 P 7TF DIE VARIETIES

VAM Variety #	Die Designations	Feature	Desirability
70	$I^2$12 • B^1a	Doubled RIB, Type I obverse (**Top 100**)	★★★★★
79	II/I 35 • B^1a	Disconnected olive leaf, doubled leaves (**Hot 50**)	★★★★★
84A	II/I 12 • B^1e	Clashed die partial 'E' below tail feathers	★★★★
100	$I^1$10 • B^2a	Type I obverse (**Top 100**)	★★★★★
115/198	II/I 17 • B^2a/B^2f	Tripled cotton bolls, doubled date & stars (**Top 100**)	★★★★★
116	II/I 18 • B^2a	Doubled P, L, R & B scarce (**Hit List 40**)	★★★★
117/141	II/I 19 • B^2k/B^2i	Tripled second rt star, eng wing feather (**Top 100**)	★★★★★
118	II/I 20 • B^2a	Shifted P, doubled ear scarce	★★★★
120	II/I 31 • B^2a	Doubled P-R, spikes below eyelid scarce	★★★★
121	II/I 38 • B^2a	Doubled E, P, U & R, 1 & 3 right stars scarce	★★★★
122	II/I 36 • B^2a	Doubled first right star, alligator eye	★★★
123	II/I 40 • B^2a	Doubled R & U-M, eng wing feather rare (**Hit List 40**)	★★★★★
145/162	II/I 25 • B^2l/B^2c	Broken N & M, engraved lines (145) (**Hot 50**)	★★★★★
146	II 2 • B^2j	Engraved wing feather	★★★★
163	II/I 26 • B^2c	Shifted U, doubled M	★★★
166	II/I 29 • B^2c	Spiked P, tripled eyelid scarce (**Hit List 40**)	★★★★
167	II/I 30 • B^2c	Spiked P, doubled U's scarce	★★★
169	II/I 32 • B^2n	Quadrupled stars, eng wing feather (**Hot 50**)	★★★★★
170	II/I 33 • B^2c	Doubled UR and date (**Hot 50**)	★★★★★
171/220	II/I 34 • B^2c/C^3b	Tripled R, doubled cotton bolls & cap (**Top 100**)	★★★★★
187	II 5 • B^2c	Doubled R (**Hot 50**)	★★★★★
188/223	II 6 • B^2c/C^3c	Washed out L (223 **Top 100**)(188 **Hit List 40**)	★★★★★
189	II 1 • B^2g	Engraved wing feather (strong) (**Hit List 40**)	★★★★★
203	III^1 2 • C^1b	Short wheat leaf, early C reverse (**Top 100**)	★★★★★
203A	III^1 2 • C^1b	Clashed die letters n, w, st , M	★★★★★
223	II 6 • C^3c	Washed out L, doubled lower rev hub (**Top 100**)	★★★★★
224	II 1 • C^3a	Normal obverse & rev (low reeding count) (**Hit List 40**)	★★★
225A	II 2 • C^3c	Denticle impressions below tail feathers	★★★★
226	II 1 • C^3c	Doubled lower reverse hub scarce	★★★
229	II 2 • C^3a	Doubled right wreath & AMERICA scarce	★★★

SCARCE 1878 P 7TF DIE VARIETIES

This section is to aid the collector in their search for some of the scarce 1878 P 7TF die varieties. The prices realized and apparent scarcity of these varieties and others can change over time as more of the varieties are found, or they continue to be elusive. But at the time of this Guide revision, these highlighted scarce varieties were selling for many hundreds to well over $1,000 in circulated condition and for a thousand to many thousands in uncirculated, if they could be found at all as uncirculated. The VAM 123 is in a class of its own with prices of thousands in any grade because of its rarity.

The following describes some of the key identifiers, along with photographs for these currently scarce varieties.

VAM 116 Doubled, P, L, R & B, 1, 3, 4 & 6 left stars and 1-4 right stars. 1 in date doubled at top right. *Key identifiers*– Pronounced bulge on right of P top loop and small die chip behind eye with vertical line up to hair. (See Figures 92 & 93) *Note:* Not to be confused with same obverse VAM 140 which has open o in God. Has die gouges, very over polished and missing feather at eagle's right wing–leg on later die states 116A, B & C.

VAM 118 Doubled bottom serifs of P, top right serif of left U and top inside of R upper loop in PLURIBUS plus 3, 4 & 7 left stars and 1 & 2 right stars. Slightly doubled right inside of the ear. *Key identifier*– Shallow die chip in lower opening of cap fold. (See Figures 94 & 95) *Note:* Not to be confused with same obverse VAM 160 which has broken r in Trust.

VAM 120 Doubled bottom serifs of P, left and right sides of R in PLURIBUS, right side of second U in UNUM, all left and first three right stars. *Key identifier*– Three close spikes below eyelid front. (See Figures 96 & 97) *Note:* Not to be confused with same obverse VAM 168 which has broken r in Trust and partially open o in God.

VAM 121 Doubled E, P, U & R and 1 in date at top right. *Key identifier*– Tiny die chip in front of eye with broad raised area below eyelid front. (See Figures 98 & 99)

VAM 123 Doubled top and bottom left side of R with bottom right serif missing. Doubled bottom left edge of top left serif of U and M in UNUM and seventh left star. Engraved feather at wing–body. *Key identifiers*– Bottom right serif missing on R and strongly doubled seventh left star. (See Figures 100 & 101)

VAM 166 Doubled E-PLUR, all left stars and first right star, 1 in date at top right. *Key identifier*– Two bars below eyelid front. (See Figures 102 & 103)

VAM 167 Doubled bottom left side of P, shifted U and doubled bottom of R in PLURIBUS. Second U in UNUM slightly doubled on the right side. *Key identifier*– Beveled left inside of 8 lower loop. (See Figures 104 & 105)

VAM 188 Die over polished with weak L in LIBERTY and wheat leaf above L is shortened. *Key identifier*– Weak L. (See Figure 106) *Note:* VAM 223 has same obverse die of washed out L but with C reverse instead of B reverse of VAM 188.

VAM 226 Hub doubled die of lower reverse with doubled tops of serifs of A next to star in AMERICA combined with normal II 1 obverse without broken point on fourth right star. *Key identifier*– Diagonal polishing lines tops of ERT in LIBERTY.

VAM 227 Normal II 1 obverse with normal C³a reverse. Diagonal polishing line though O in OF with reeding count of 176. (See Figure 107) Second reverse die has slight doubling of two leaves at top of left wreath with reeding count of 175. *Key identifier*– Second reverse has small die chip on third left wreath cluster.

VAM 229 II 2 obverse. Some doubled leaves in each cluster of right wreath and bottom inside letters of AMERICA towards rim. *Key identifier*– Die chip at top of forehead. (See Figures 108 & 109)

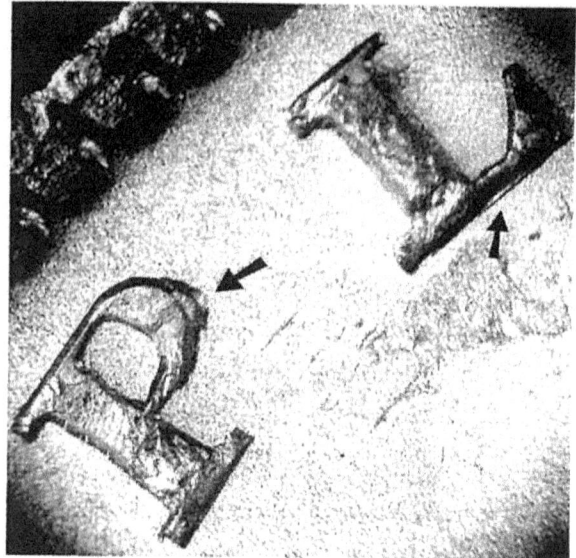

Figure 92 VAM 116 Doubled PL

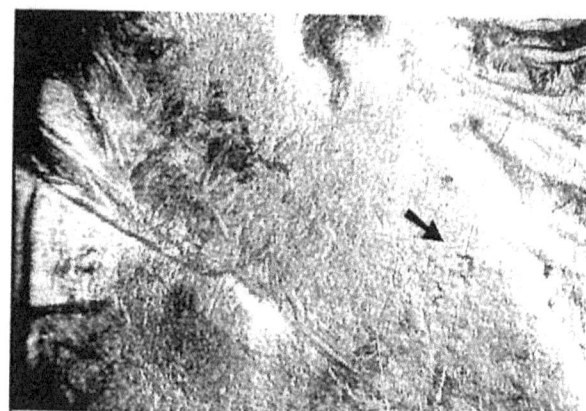

Figure 93 VAM 116 Die Chip & Line

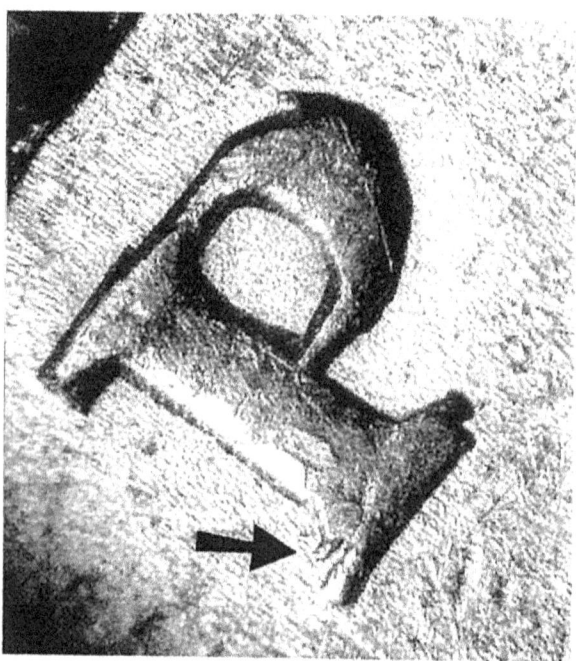

Figure 94 VAM 118 Shifted P

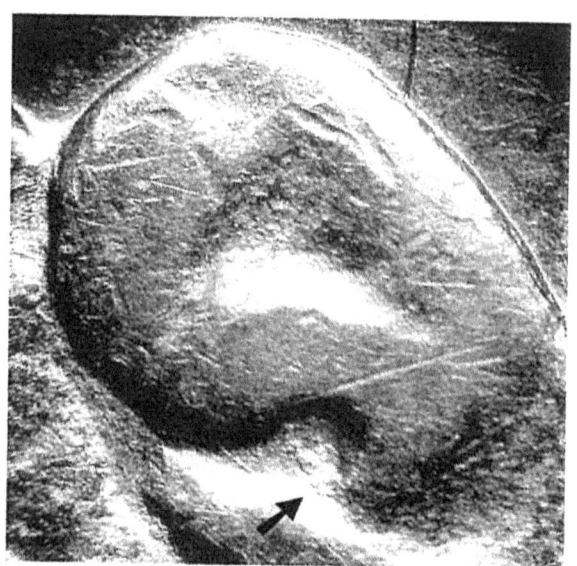

Figure 95 VAM 118 Die Chip Cap Fold

Figure 96 VAM 120 Doubled P

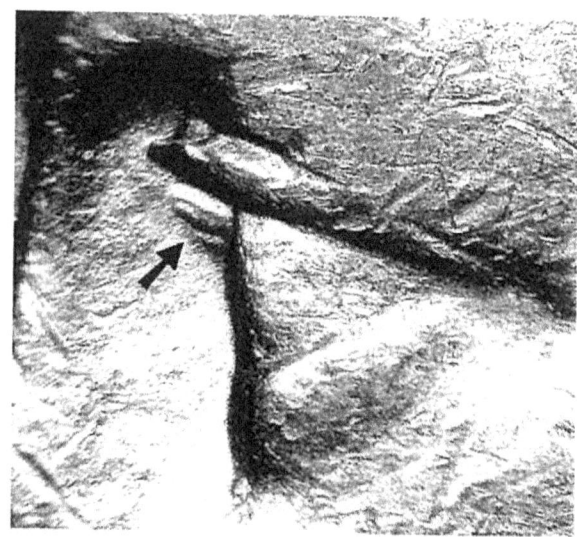

Figure 97 VAM 120 Spikes Below Eyelid

Figure 98 VAM 121 Doubled P

Figure 99 VAM 121 Die Chip Eye Front

Figure 100 VAM 123 Doubled Seventh Left Star

Figure 101 VAM 123 Doubled R

Figure 102 VAM 166 Spiked P

Figure 103 VAM 166 Bars Under Eyelid

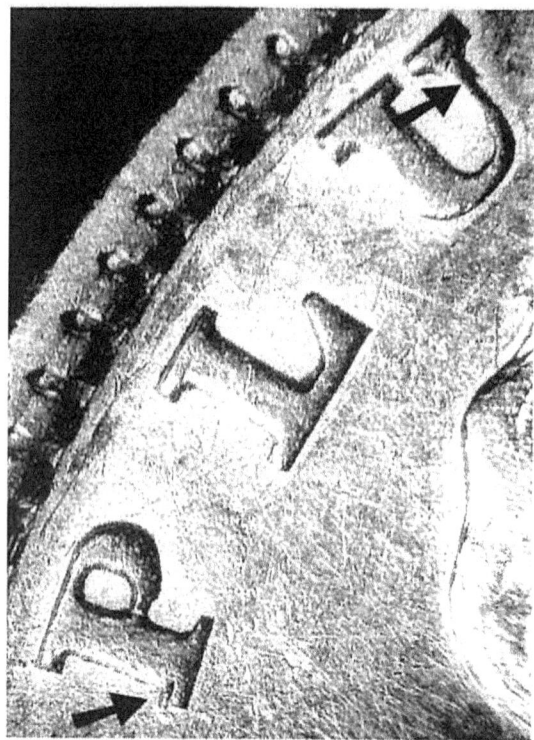

Figure 104 VAM 167 Spiked P

Figure 105 VAM 167 Beveled Inside 8

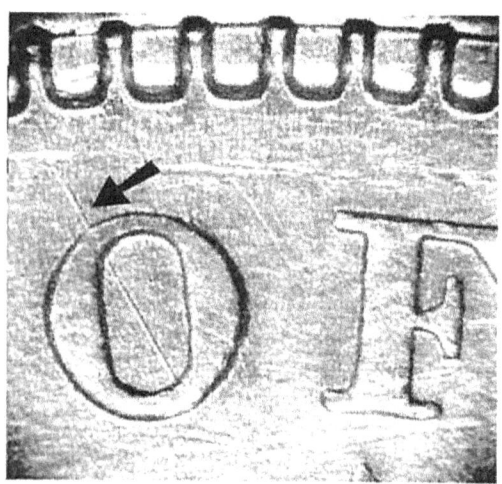

Figure 107 VAM 227 Polishing Line Thru O

Figure 106 VAM 188/223 Washed Out L

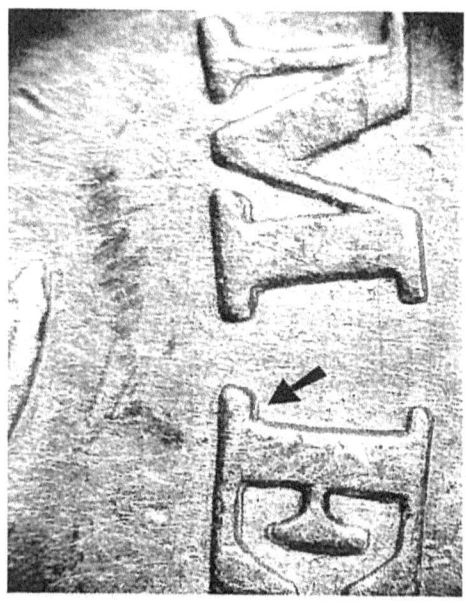

Figure 108 VAM 229 Doubled AMERICA

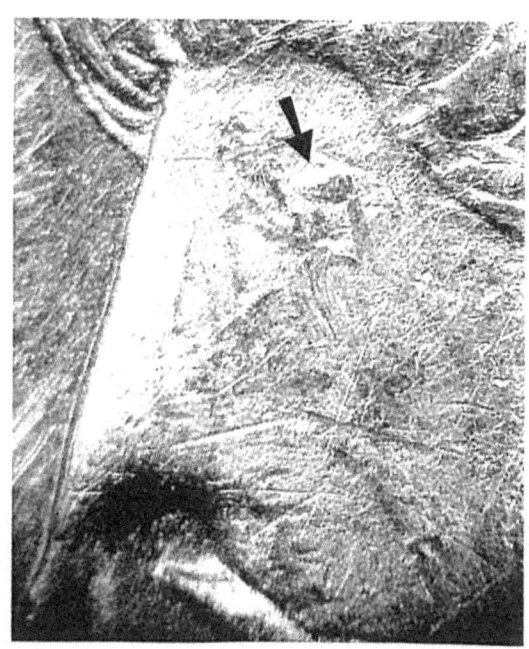

Figure 109 VAM 229 Die Chip on Forehead

HIGH INTEREST 1878 P 7TF VARIETIES

There are 33 dual hub, II/I, obverse dies known for the 1878 P 7TF. They account for the majority of the strongly doubled obverse dies that have a relatively high interest factor. These include strongly doubled stars, motto letters and date digits as well as tripled and quadrupled stars and doubled and tripled cotton bolls and leaves. There also appears some isolated doubled letters such as an apparent I over R and an isolated star that is strongly doubled or tripled that are likely the result of touching up with individual punches.

The descriptions and definitions of the Interest and Rarity Factors are given in the VAM book. The Interest Factor varies from I-1 for a normal die variety that is common to I-5 that is an outstanding die variety with prime interest to variety collectors because of strong features and/or rarity.

There are nine **Top 100** 1878 P 7TF varieties included in the booklet, *The Top 100 Morgan Dollar Varieties; the VAM Keys,* 1996, by Michael Fey & Jeff Oxman plus six **Hot 50** varieties included in the book, *SSDC Official Guide to the Hot 50 Morgan Dollar Varieties,* 2000, by Jeff Oxman. These are automatically assigned I-5 because of their being widely collected, interesting die features and established price guides. There are nine **Hit List 40** varieties included in the book, *Official Guide To The Morgan Dollar Hit List 40,* 2009, by Jeff Oxman that have I-4 or I-5.

The **Top 100** 1878 P 7 TF varieties are **VAMs 70** Doubled RIB, **100** Type I Obverse, **115** Tripled Blossoms, **117 & 141** Tripled Star, **171 & 220** Tripled R, **203** Short Leaf and **223** Washed Out L.

The **Hot 50** 1878 P 7TF varieties are **VAMs 79** Disconnected Leaf, **145 & 162** Broken N & M, **169** Quadrupled Stars, **170** Doubled Date and **187** Doubled R.

The **Hit List 40** 1878 P 7TF varieties are **VAMs 116, A, B, C** Doubled P, **123** Spiked Eye, **166** Tripled Eye, **188** Polished L, **189** Re-Engraved Wing, **222A** Face Chip, **224** Low Reed Count, **227-1** and **228B** Slashed O.

Some of the 1878 P 7TF have amazing strongly doubled and tripled obverse dies that are considered shifts in design rather than just doubling. The later years of the Morgan dollar varieties seldom have such large shifts of the obverse design. The following summarizes the main features of the high Interest Factor dies of I-5 and 4 but not considering their apparent rarity in all cases. Only the VAM numbers are given for the I-3 varieties.

Interest Factor 5

VAM 70	$I^2 12$ obverse with large shift in RIB letters plus only one of two known earlier I obverse for 1878 P 7TF. VAM 70 has B^1 reverse.
VAM 79	II/I 35 obverse with part of nostril missing and slightly doubled hair, cotton bolls and leaves on right side. VAM 79 has B^1 reverse.
VAM 85	II/I 6 obverse with doubled LIBERTY, wheat leaves and grains. VAM 85 has a B^1 type reverse and is rare.
VAM 100	$I^1 10$ obverse with doubled motto letters, most left stars and all right stars. Slightly doubled date.
VAMs 115 & 198/199-1	II/I 17 obverse with tripled right edge of cotton bolls and leaves.
VAMs 117 & 141	II/I 19 obverse with amazing strong single tripled second right star. Also has doubled eye, tripled eyelid and doubled tops of cotton leaves. Both 117 and 141 reverses have engraved wing feather bars.
VAM 123	II/I 40 obverse with doubled R & U-M and seventh left star. Engraved wing– body bars. Very rare.
VAMs 145 & 162	II/I 25 obverse with broken lower serifs of N & M in UNUM.
VAM 169	II/I 32 obverse with strong quadrupled 1-5 left stars with large shifts on 2-4 and 6 & 7 left stars tripled. Reverse has engraved wing-body bars shared with 168.
VAM 170	II/I 33 obverse with strong doubling at top of date digits.
VAM 170A	Die chips Phrygian cap.

VAM 187	II 5 obverse with unusually strong doubling on R in PLURIBUS and N in UNUM.
VAMs 171 & 220	that share the II/I 34 obverse, Tripled R, Shifted Liberty Head Back. The R in PLURIBUS is strongly tripled at lower left. It looks as if an I was punched several times on top of the R left vertical bar to strengthen it. Entire back of the Liberty head is also strongly doubled including cotton bolls and leaves, cap upper loop and bottom edge, all hair below cap and right inside of ear. This is the strongest doubled or shifted II/I obverse and is similar in extent of the shift on cotton bolls and leaves of 1878 P VAM 44 and 1878 CC VAMs 6, 18 & 24.
VAM 189	II 1 obverse with B^2g reverse that is first known and strongest 1878 P 7TF with added engraved feather lines next to eagle's right leg and between wing–body.
VAM 203	$III^1 2$ obverse with heavy die polishing at top. C^1b reverse has doubled legend and In God letters.
VAM 203A	$III^1 2$ obverse with strongly clashed obverse die with clashed letter n of In from reverse next to Liberty head neck, W of We in hair locks, st of Trust in lower right hair vee and M of designer's initial from obverse above d of God.
VAM 223	II 6 obverse with over polished and washed out L in LIBERTY.

Interest Factor 4

VAM 84A	II/I 12 obverse with washed out L in LIBERTY. Some doubled motto letters and stars. Clashed dies and B^1e reverse with partial 'E' below tail feathers.
VAM 116	II/I 18 obverse with doubled P, L, R & B and some left and right stars. Scarce variety. Later dies states of 116A, B & C have gouges and over polished feather at eagle's right wing and leg.
VAM 118	II/I 20 obverse with doubled P, U & R, some left and right stars and right inside of ear. Scarce variety.
VAM 121	II/I 38 obverse with strongly doubled 1 & 3 right stars and E, P, U & R.
VAM 122	II/I 36 obverse with strongly doubled PLURI motto letters and first right star.
VAM 146	II 2 obverse with slightly doubled Liberty head profile. B^2j reverse with engraved wing feather bar.
VAM 163	II/I 26 obverse with shifted U at top as a slanted bar of first U in PLURIBUS. M in UNUM also has a large shift.
VAM 166	II/I 29 obverse with double E PLUR and all left stars. Two bars under front of eyelid. Scarce variety.
VAM 188	II 6 obverse with over polished and washed out L in LIBERTY.
VAM 200	II/I 39 obverse with broken N & M in UNUM.
VAM 201	II/I 35 obverse with part of nostril missing and slightly doubled hair, cotton bolls and leaves on right side. VAM 201 has C^1 reverse.
VAM 215	III^1 1 obverse with C^2a reverse. Proofs.
VAM 224	II 2 obverse. Has edge reeding count of 168 which is second lowest of Morgan dollar series behind some 1921 P with 157.
VAM 225A	II 2 obverse. C^3c reverse with four raised dots of denticle impressions below tail feathers.

Interest Factor 3

VAMs 80, 82, 83, 84, 86, 110, 111, 112A, 119, 120, 133, 134, 140, 140A, 142, 143, 144, 144A, 160, 161, 165, 167, 168, 190, 190A, 196, 196A, 202, 202A, 210, 210A, 210B, 221A, 222B, 226, 226A, 227, 228A & 229.

DIE ATTRIBUTION PROCEDURES

Presented in this section are some attribution steps, key features and identifiers that are to aid in the attribution of the 1878 P 7TF die varieties.

The **first** attribution aid is an **1878 P 7TF Summary Chart**. Presented for all known 76 1878 P 7TF VAM die varieties, in numerical order, are the obverse and reverse die designations, some die features, their availability and number of desirability stars. The availability is given in a scale of six terms from common to rare. Desirability is ranked with one to five stars as previously discussed in the Top 30 1878 P 7TF Die Varieties section. This Summary Chart is useful for obtaining concise information on each variety, but it is not as useful for attributing an unknown variety.

A **second** attribution aid is the **1878 P 7TF Die Combinations Summary Chart**. Columns are provided for the die varieties that fall under the reverse design types and sub-types. The B design type with parallel top arrow feather is divided into the B^1 long nock or center arrow shaft and the B^2 short center arrow nock. A column listing is provided for the B^1 long nock die combinations with short feature description noted for each one. The B^2 short nock reverse is broken down into the main reverse designations of B^2a thru B^2h that include normal, open o in God, broken r in Trust, doubled motto, broken D in DOLLAR, missing wing feather and doubled legend. The C design type with slanted top arrow feather is divided into the C^1, C^2 & C^3 sub-types. The C^3 reverse is further divided in to the normal, doubled left reverse, doubled lower reverse and double right wreath. This chart allows some narrowing down of the possibilities by reverse types when attributing an unknown variety. The short die designations and descriptions can further aid in the die and VAM number identification.

A **third** attribution aid are the **grouped** close-up **photographs** of all the 33 known **II/I Dual Hub Obverse Varieties**. These photographs are divided into those with B^1, B^2 and C design reverses. The photographs are useful for quick comparison and identification of the doubled die or other main feature plus a key identifier of each variety.

A **fourth** attribution aid are the two **listings** of **die combinations** for the obverse and reverse dies. These include the charts on **1878 P 7TF Obverse Die Designation to VAM Number** and **1878 P 7TF Reverse Die Designation to VAM Number.** These listings are useful for quickly determining the obverse and reverse die designations of the VAM varieties and for checking if specific obverse or reverse dies occur for multiple VAM number varieties. Also presented are the known or estimated die progression sequences for the obverse and reverse dies where they occur with multiple pairings.

A **fifth** attribution aid are the detailed **Descriptive Listings** for each VAM variety. These include for each VAM number, in numerical order, the obverse and reverse die designation with descriptions, reeding count, Interest Factor of 1 thru 5, and Rarity Factor of 1 thru 5 as described in the VAM book.

A **sixth** attribution aid are the enlarged **photographs** of each obverse and reverse die variety at the back of the Guide. These photographs are presented in numerical order of VAM number.

The following are some suggested steps for the attribution of the 1878 P 7TF die varieties. These steps will help to quickly narrow down the possible number of varieties to consider when trying to attribute an unknown variety. Unless a specific easily identifiable obverse variety is seen on a coin to be attributed, it is best to **first concentrate on identifying the reverse major and minor design types**. There are fewer reverse 7 TF die varieties than the obverse dies found with them and the reverse design types are usually easier to identify.

1. First determine if top arrow feather is *parallel* for **B design type** or *slanted* for **C design type**.
2. **If B PAF design type reverse,** determine if center arrow shaft or nock is *long and protruding to left* of B^1 type as shown in Figure 110 or *flush left* of B^2 type as shown in Figure 111.
3. **For B^1 design reverse,** with long center arrow shaft or nock, first check to determine if there are protruding TF ends or doubled legs or claws of the so-called 7/8TF which aren't covered in this Guide. There are only 7 die combination varieties and two sub-variety listings with one I and six II/I obverses:
   VAM 70– I type obverse with evenly divided ear rear, with strongly doubled RIB in PLURIBUS.

B^{1}a Middle olive leaves disconnected from branch. (Also 79 B^{1}a)

Note: VAM 79- 86 all have II/I obverses with short and sharp pointed inner ear fill.

VAM 79– II/I 35 Weak nostril from over polished die and doubled lower cotton leaves on right side and ear on right inside. B^{1}g *Key identifier–* Raised metal inside 8's. (Also 201 obverse & 70 B^{1}a)

VAM 80– II/I 6 Doubled wheat leaves and grains. Small die chip at top of eagle's right wing. *Key identifier–* Doubled cap fold. B^{1}b Middle olive leaves disconnected from branch.

VAM 80A– II/I 6 Small die breaks at top left and right of T in STATES.

VAM 81– II/I 7 E doubled on right side of lower right serif, P doubled on left side with short spike on lower left of E PLURIBUS. Die chip on eagle's right wing in middle next to body. *Key identifier–* Lines in cap ribbon. B^{1}c Middle olive leaves disconnected from branch. (Also 82)

VAM 82– II/I 10 First right star strongly doubled. B^{1}c (Also 81) *Key identifier–* Die chip right of lower cotton leaf.

VAM 83– II/I 11 18 Doubled at top right with 1 set high. Vertical die scratch bottom of eagle's left wing. B^{1}d *Key identifier–* Spike at upper inside of ear.

VAM 84– II/I 12 Washed out L in LIBERTY and slanted dash below first 8. B^{1}e Reverse has broken D in DOLLAR. *Key identifier–* Dash below left 8.

VAM 84A– II/I 12 Clashed dies with partial raised 'E' below eagle's tail feathers and partial incuse n of In from reverse next to LIBERTY head neck.

VAM 85– II/I 6 same obverse as VAM 80. B^{1}f *Key identifier–* Vertical thread-like die impression tip eagle's right wing, several raised die chips left side of upper tail feathers.

VAM 86– II/I same obverse as VAM 80. B^{1}h *Key identifiers–* Short die scratches at top of eagle's left wing and at eagle's left leg.

4. **For B^2 design reverse,** with short middle arrow shaft or nock, there are **B^{2}a** dies with *no significant reverse die varieties,* **B^{2}b** dies with *open o in God* from hub break as shown in Figure 112, and **B^{2}c** with a hub break with filled or *broken r in Trust* to form Tiust as shown in Figure 113. There are also a few reverse dies that have *doubled motto* of **B^{2}d** as shown in Figure 114, *broken D in DOLLAR* of **B^{2}e** as shown in Figure 115 and over polished reverse with eagle's *lower right wing missing next to leg* of **B^{2}f** as shown in Figure 116. However, the hub breaks of open o and broken r **take precedent** for variety listings over the latter missing wing feathers since over polished reverse dies are fairly common on B^2 design.

5. **For B^{2}a design of normal reverse,** there are 19 die combination varieties and ten sub-variety listings with one I, 14 II/I and four II obverses:

VAM 100– I type obverse with doubled motto letters, 1-4 & 6 left and all rt. stars, eyelid and date.

VAM 110– II/I 8 Partially broken bottom serifs of N & M in UNUM. *Key identifier–* Broken N & M.

VAM 111– II/I 13 Strongly doubled R in PLURIBUS with bottom shifted down. *Key identifier–* Die scratch lower cotton leaf.

VAM 112– II/I 14 Vertical bar at left inside of top loop of B in PLURIBUS. Doubled 2, 3 left & 1, 3 right stars. *Key identifier–* Vertical bar left side of B upper loop.

VAM 112A– II/I 14 Clashed obverse G.

VAM 113– II/I 15 Doubled N, U & M in UNUM, 2 left and 1, 2 & 5 right stars. Large die flake on cheek in front of ear and die crack thru ear center. *Key identifier–* Die chip on cheek in front of ear.

VAM 114– II/I 16 Doubled R in PLURIBUS with weak lower right serif of left vertical bar, slightly doubled tops of cotton leaves and bolls, 1-6 left and all right stars. *Key identifier–* Over polished lower hair.

VAM 114A– II/I 16 Clashed die with partial incuse t of Trust from reverse in lower hair edge right vee.

VAM 115– II/I 17 Tripled right edges of cotton bolls and leaves. 1 & 7 doubled below upper crossbar. Doubled right outside of ear and all stars. *Key identifier–* Tripled cotton bolls. (Also 198)

VAM 116– II/I 18 Doubled P, L, R, B with large bulge at P right side of top loop. Some doubled stars. Die flake near hairline behind eye with die crack leading to hair. Over polished reverse with gouges on later die states of 116A, B & C. *Key identifier–* Bulge at right of P loop. (Also 140)

VAM 117– II/I 19 Strongly tripled second right star. Doubled E, P, R & 1, 3, 4, 6 left & 1-5 right stars, eye, mouth, chin and right inside of ear. Reverse B^{2}k with engraved bars between eagle's right wing and body. *Key identifier–* Alligator eye. (Also 141 obverse)

VAM 118– II/I 20 Strongly doubled lower right serif of P in PLURIBUS with line extending to right beyond base. Slightly doubled right inside of ear and some left and right stars. *Key identifier–*

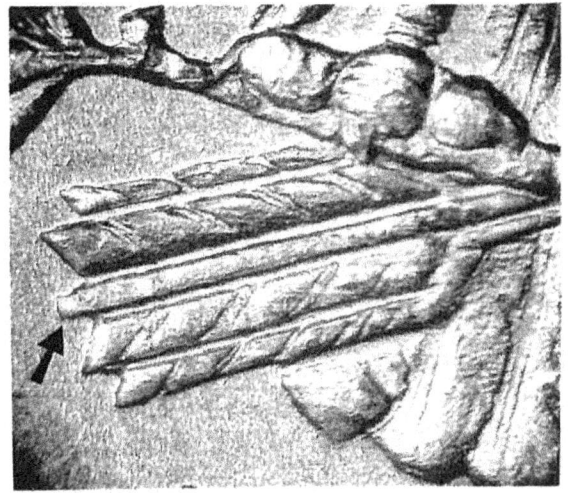

Figure 110 VAM 81 B[1] Long Nock

Figure 111 VAM 111 B[2] Short Nock

Figure 115 VAM 195 B[2]e Broken D Bottom

Figure 112 VAM 141 B[2]b Open o in God

Figure 113 VAM 163 B[2]c Broken r

Figure 116 VAM 197 B[2]f Missing Wing Feather

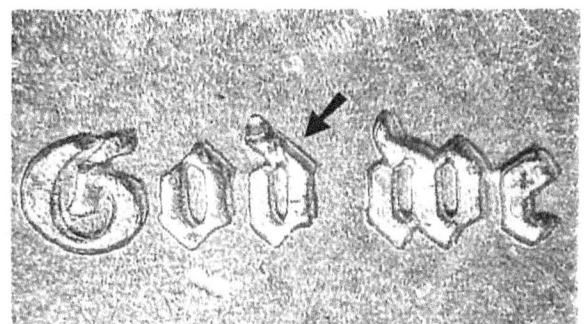

Figure 114 VAM 190 B[2]d Doubled Motto

Die chip below cap fold. (Also 160)

VAM 119– II/I 21 Doubled top right of E in E PLURIBUS and doubled all left stars and ear tripled on right and top inside. *Key identifier*– Doubling at top right corner of E and tripled ear. (Also 161)

VAM 120– II/I 31 Strongly doubled lower right serif of P in PLURIBUS with line even with base end. Three spikes below front of eyelid. Doubled left and 1-3 right stars. *Key identifier*– Three spikes below eyelid. (Also 168)

VAM 121– II/I 38 Strongly doubled E, P, U & R in E PLURIBUS with short bar in upper left inside of R upper loop. Strongly doubled 1 & 3 right stars. *Key identifier*– Tiny die chip front of eye with raised area below eyelid.

VAM 122– II/I 36 Strongly doubled first right star and PLURI. Type I LIBERTY with thin letters. All left and 1, 4-6 right stars doubled. *Key identifier*– Doubled eye front.

VAM 123– II/I 40 Bottom right serif missing from left vertical bar of R in PLURIBUS. Strongly doubled 7 left star. Doubled eyelid in front of eye. Engraved bars at eagle's right wing–leg. *Key identifier*– Doubled seventh left star.

VAM 130– II 1 Normal II obverse without broken point of fourth right star. Multiple dies exist.

VAM 130A– II 1 Die gouge thru lower part of IB. Die chip lower part of Phrygian cap.

VAM 130B– II 1 Semi-circular die gouges in eagle's left wing. Spike above eyelid. (Also 185A obverse)

VAM 130C– II 1 Weak nostril with die breaks at R and top of Phrygian cap.

VAM 131– II 2 Normal II obverse with broken point on fourth right star. Multiple dies exist.

VAM 131A– II 2 Die chip in hair below BE in LIBERTY.

VAM 131B– II 2 Die scratch thru RT in LIBERTY. (Also 195A, 210A)

VAM 131C– II 2 Die scratch thru IB in LIBERTY. Some show clashed dies with partial incuse n of In from reverse next to LIBERTY head neck. (Also 195)

VAM 132– II 3 Same as II 2 but die over polished with missing nostril.

VAM 133– II 4 Same as II 2 but doubled motto letters, wheat leaves on right and top of Phrygian cap.

6. For B²b design reverse with *open o in God*, there are 7 die combination varieties and three sub-varieties listings with 6 II/I and one II 2 obverse.

VAM 140– II/I 18 See VAM 116 above.

VAM 140A– II/I 18 Die scratches lower jaw.

VAM 141– II/I 19 See VAM 117 above. Reverse B²i with engraved wing feather bars.

VAM 141A– II/I 19 Die gouge eagle's left wing tip.

VAM 142– II/I 22 Doubled top of 878, lower lip, nostril, P, R, U & left U & M in UNUM. *Key identifier*– Doubled left U in UNUM. (Also 196)

VAM 142A– II/I 22 Die chips reverse at top right of S OF and eagle's left wing.

VAM 143– II/I 23 Doubled top of first 8 with extra metal in lower loop, P. R, B, left U, 2, 6 & 7 left stars. Short spike below eyelid front. B²l reverse with die scratches in tail feathers and wreath leaves and some engraved lines on wing feathers. *Key identifier*– Spike below eyelid and scratches reverse. (Same reverse die as 145.)

VAM 144– II/I 24 Doubled 3-7 left stars towards rim. Ear slightly doubled at right inside, lower hair, E, R, S and date. Over polished wing feathers and partially open o in God. *Key identifier*– Two die chips on chin.

VAM 144A– II/I 24 Clashed die with faint incuse n of In from reverse next to Liberty head neck.

VAM 145– II/I 25 Broken bottom serifs of N & M in UNUM with bottom right serif of M missing. Doubled P, UR, S, 3 left & 5 right stars and 17. Spike below eyelid. B²l reverse with die scratches in tail feathers and wreath leaves and some engraved lines on wing feathers. (Also 143 reverse) *Key identifier*– Broken N & M.

VAM 146– II 2 Diagonal lines in E, R & Y in LIBERTY and slightly doubled profile. Engraved wing feather bar of B²j reverse and over polished middle of wing. *Key identifier*– Engraved wing feather bars.

7. For B²c design reverse with *broken arm of r in Trust* that is weak or missing, there are 17 die combination varieties and four sub-variety listings with 12 II/I and 5 II obverses.

VAM 160– II/I 20 See VAM 118 above.

VAM 161– II/I 21 See VAM 119 above.

VAM 162– II/I 25 See VAM 145 above.

VAM 163– II/I 26 First U in PLURIBUS strongly doubled at top left as a slanted bar. Doubled E, U, R, M, 7 left & 1. *Key identifier–* Shifted U at upper left serif. (Same reverse die as 167.)

VAM 164– II/I 27 PL doubled on right side and R has notch at top inside of upper loop in PLURIBUS. Doubled B, UNU, 1, 3, 4 right stars. *Key identifier–* Vertical line left end of cap ribbon and 3 spikes between eagle's right wing and body.

VAM 165– II/I 28 P in PLURIBUS has long spike above lower right serif, spike at top right of upper loop and bar above vertical shaft. L in PLURIBUS doubled on right side of vertical shaft. Doubled E PLUR, 1-5 left & 1-5 right stars. B^{2}m reverse with engraved bars between eagle's right wing and body. *Key identifier–* Vertical spike top right of P and vertical bar right side of L.

VAM 166– II/I 29 Thick spike just above P lower right serif and tiny spike at top right of upper loop. Two shallow bars under front of eyelid. Doubled E PLUR, all left & 1 right stars. *Key identifier–* Two bars under eyelid front.

VAM 167– II/I 30 P in PLURIBUS has notch above lower left serif and first U doubled below right side of right top serif. *Key identifier–* Beveled left inside of left 8 loops. (Same reverse die as 163.)

VAM 168– II/I 31 See VAM 120 above. Reverse B^{2}n with engraved bars between eagle's right wing and body and bar at wing--leg. (Same reverse die as 169.)

VAM 169– II/I 32 2-4 left stars strongly quadrupled at top right. Doubled E PLUR left side, 18-8 and eyelid. Doubled/tripled left & 1-5 right stars. *Key identifier–* Strongly quadrupled 2-4 left and doubled 3-5 right stars. (Same reverse die as 168.)

VAM 170– II/I 33 Doubled tops of 1878. Doubled P, U & R in PLURIBUS with U doubled at lower right and R doubled above lower left serif and weak lower right serif of left vertical bar. *Key identifier–* Die chip on neck above M initial.

VAM 170A– II/I33 Die chip Phrygian cap.

VAM 171– II/I 34 Strongly tripled lower left serif of R in PLURIBUS. Strongly doubled Phrygian cap upper loop, bottom of cotton bolls and right leaves, plus all of hair below cap. Doubled P, U, last U, all stars, right inside of ear. *Key identifier–* Tripled lower left serif of R. (Also 220)

VAM 185– II 1 Normal II obverse without broken point on fourth right star. Multiple dies exist.

VAM 185A– II 1 Spike above eyelid. Slight doubling of chin front. (Same obverse 130B)

VAM 185B– II 1 Die scratch thru I–R.

VAM 186– II 2 Normal II obverse with broken point on fourth right star. Multiple dies exist.

VAM 186A– II 2 Short spike above eyelid. Vertical polishing lines in mouth.

VAM 186B– II 2 Very over polished wing. Raised die chips left 8 lower loop.

VAM 187– II 5 Strongly doubled P at top, middle and lower right side. Doubled LURIB & UN. Two spikes below eyelid front.

VAM 188– II 6 Die over polished with L shallow in LIBERTY, shortened wheat leaf above L.(Also 223)

VAM 189– II 1 Normal II obverse. B^{2}g reverse with added diagonal feather lines engraved in lower inside of eagle's right wing next to leg and at wing–body. Broken r in Trust.

8. For B^{2}d– h four reverse varieties with *doubled motto, broken D in DOLLAR, missing wing feathers next to eagle's right leg and doubled legend,* there are 8 die combination varieties and three sub-variety listings with four II/I and four II obverses.

VAM 190– II 3 Missing nostril from over polished die. Different die than VAM 132.
    B^{2}d Doubled God We to right. R in Trust not broken.

VAM 190A– II 3 Clashed dies with partial incuse n of In from reverse next to Liberty head neck.

VAM 195– II 2 Diagonal line thru B in LIBERTY. (Same obverse as 131C)
    B^{2}e Bottom of D in Dollar broken away. R in Trust not broken.

VAM 195A– II 2 Diagonal line thru R and top of T in LIBERTY. (Same obverse as 131B, 210A)
    B^{2}e Partially broken D bottom in DOLLAR, r in Trust not broken. Different die than VAM 195.

VAM 196– II/I 22 See VAM 142 above. B^{2}f Die over polished with part of eagle's lower right wing missing next to leg. R in Trust not broken.

VAM 196A– II/I 22 Clashed dies with partial incuse n of In from reverse next to Liberty head neck and incuse st of Trust in right hair vee of Liberty head lower hair edge.

VAM 197– II 7 Doubled UR-BUS UNU at top inside. (Also 134) B^{2}f Feathers completely missing next to eagle's right leg. R in Trust not broken. Different die than VAMs 196, 198 & 199-2.

VAM 198– II/I 17 See VAM 115 above. B^{2}f Missing wing feathers. R in Trust not broken.

VAM 199– (Same as VAM 164)

VAM 199-1–– (Same as VAM 198)

VAM 134– II 7 Slightly doubled UR-BUS UNU at top inside. (Also 197) B²h Doubled STATE AMERICA, right star and some right wreath leaves towards coin center. R in Trust not broken.

9. If <u>C SAF design type reverse</u>, determine if *wing feather next to eagle's right leg is rounded, shallow* and not connected to wing on left of **C¹**, is *shallow* with *thin line between eagle's right leg and first wing feather* of **C²** or *squared off and raised* of **C³** reverse.

10. <u>For C¹ design reverse</u> with *rounded and shallow wing feather next to eagle's right leg,* as shown in Figure 117, there are four die combination varieties and two sub-variety listings with two minor variations of this reverse combined with two II/I and two minor variations of III¹ obverse.

    VAM 200– II/I 39 Broken serifs of N & M in UNUM. Doubled 1-6 left & 1-3 right stars, E, P, U, S. *Key identifier–* Broken N & M.

        C¹a Slightly doubled inside of legend letters towards rim and tops of In God We Trust.

    VAM 201– II/I 35 See VAM 79 above.

        C¹a Different die than VAMs 200 & 202.

    VAM 202– III¹1 Lines in wheat leaves with left end of wheat leaf below R in line with right side of R vertical shaft. Doubled stars, date and lower hair. (Also 215)

        C¹a Different die than VAMs 200 & 201.

    VAM 202A– Clashed dies with faint partial incuse n of In from reverse next to Liberty head neck.

    VAM 203– III¹2 Heavy die polishing at top with short wheat leaf below R in PLURIBUS.

        C¹b Doubled outside leaves in right wreath, all legend letters towards rim and In God tops.

    VAM 203A– III¹2 Clashed dies with partial incuse n of In from reverse next to Liberty head neck and incuse st of Trust in right hair vee of Liberty head lower hair edge.

11. <u>For C² design reverse</u> with *thin line between eagle's right leg and first wing feather,* as shown in Figure 118, there are only two die combination varieties with II and III¹ obverses and two sub-variety listings.

    VAM 210– II 2 Vertical polishing line thru Y in LIBERTY. C²a reverse.

    VAM 210A– II 2 Diagonal line thru R and top of T in LIBERTY.

    VAM 210B– II 2 Diagonal line thru middle of I and lower part of B in LIBERTY. Some show clashed dies with partial incuse n of In from reverse next to Liberty head neck and incuse st of Trust in right hair vee of Liberty head lower hair edge.

    VAM 215– III¹1 See VAM 202 above. C²a reverse. Proofs.

12. <u>For C³ design reverse</u> with *squared off and raised wing feather next to eagle's right leg,* as shown in Figure 119, there are 13 variety combinations and eight sub-variety listings with four minor variations of this reverse combined with one II/I, five II and three III² obverses.

    VAM 220– II/I 34 See VAM 171 above.

        C³b Hub doubling of UNITED STATES, left wreath leaves with strong doubling on left inside U.

    VAM 221– II 1 Die chip on forehead front on some specimens.

        C³b See VAM 220 above. (Different die) Multiple obverse & reverse dies exist.

    VAM 221A– Four raised dots of denticle impressions left of wreath bow.

    VAM 222– II 2 C³b See VAM 220 above. (Different die)

    VAM 222A– II 2 Die chips above & below Liberty head lips.

    VAM 222B– II 2 Vertical die gouge at base of left cotton boll & thin die scratch from boll to near Y in LIBERTY. Die gouge thru front wheat leaf. (Also 228A)

    VAM 222C– II 2 Spikes above and below eyelid front.

    VAM 222D– II 1 Over polished lower hair.

    VAM 223– II 6 See VAM 188 above.

        C³c Hub doubling on outside edges of left and right wreath & tops of serifs of A next to star in AMERICA. Double polishing lines inside wreath bow.

    VAM 224– II 2 C³c See VAM 223 above. (Different die) Double polishing lines between eagle's legs on right side.   Edge– Second lowest edge reeding count of 168 of Morgan dollar series.

    VAM 225– II 2 Faint short spike below eyelid front. C³c See VAM 223 above. (Different die)

    VAM 225A– C³a Four raised dots below middle tail feathers from denticle impressions.

    VAM 226– II 1 C³c See VAM 223 above. (Different die)

    VAM 226A– II 1 Clashed obverse n.

VAM 227– II 1 C³a Normal C³ reverse without any significant doubling. Coins with 176 reeds have a long diagonal die polishing line thru O in OF. Coins with 175 reeds have slight doubling of top leaves in left wreath.

VAM 228– II 2 C³a Heavy horizontal polishing lines thru wreath bow on some specimens. Multiple dies.

VAM 228A– II 2 Vertical die gouge at base of left cotton boll & thin die scratch from boll to near Y in LIBERTY. Die gouge thru front wheat leaf. (Same die as VAM 222B.)

VAM 228B– II 2 Long diagonal die polishing line thru O in OF. (Same die as one of VAM 227.)

VAM 229– II 2 Die chip on forehead. C³b Some doubled leaves in right wreath and bottom inside of AMERICA.

VAM 229.1– II 8 Slightly doubled top of Phrygian cap, LIBERTY, hair front and US UNUM. C³a reverse.

VAM 230– III²1 Long wheat leaf with weak lines close to bottom of R in PLURIBUS. Left edge of wheat leaf below R in line with middle part of T vertical shaft.

C³a Normal C³ reverse without any significant doubling. Multiple dies exist.

VAM 231– III²2 Slightly tripled stars, date & motto letters towards rim. Vertical polishing lines below eyelid front.

C³c See VAM 223 above. (Different die) Three polishing lines above lower right wreath ribbon.

VAM 232– III²3 Right stars sextupled towards rim. U's of PLURIBUS doubled at bottom inside. Top of Phrygian cap doubled.

C³b See VAM 220 above. (Different die) Diagonal scratch from top of right end of olive branch.

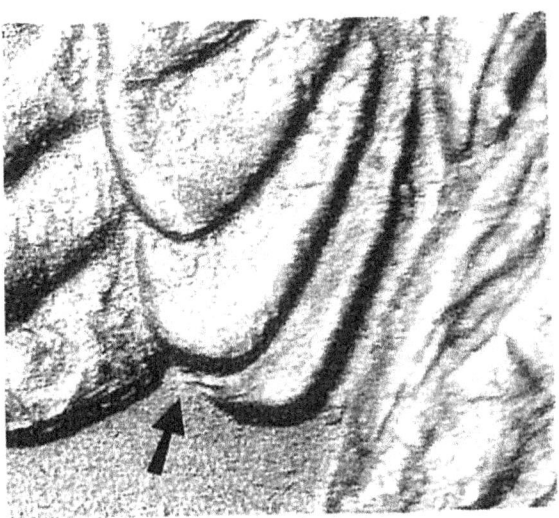

Figure 117 VAM 202 C¹ Shallow Feather
Next to Leg

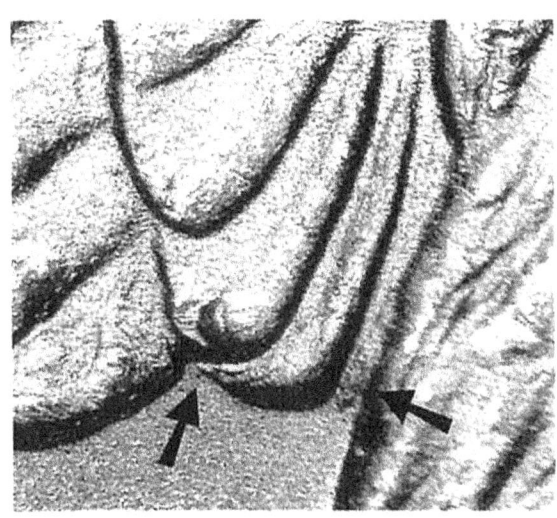

Figure 118 VAM 210 C² Line Next to Leg

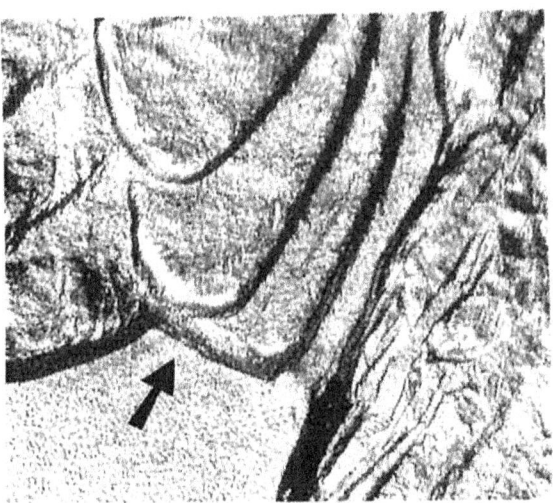

Figure 119 VAM 224 C³ Square Raised Feather
Next to Leg

TF= Tail Feathers   Dbld= Doubled

Availability Terms:

Common: Readily available variety likely seen at even the smallest local coin show.

Available: A little bit harder to find than common. May take a couple small shows or a larger one to locate.

Somewhat Scarce: Could take several visits to larger shows to locate. Some premium for attributed coins.

Scarce: Could take months of searching even at larger shows to locate. Larger premium for attributed coins.

Very Scarce: Difficult to locate even at larger local or regional shows. Premium could be substantial for attributed coins depending on desirability of variety.

Rare: Thought to have such a low population that years of searching regional and national shows may be required to "Cherry Pick". Attributed coins should bring a substantial premium.

VAM #	Die Designations / Key Features	Availability	Desirability
B Reverse with Parallel Top Arrow Feather			
B¹ Long nock reverse			
70	I²12 obverse Strongly doubled RIB in PLURIBUS. B¹a reverse Middle olive leaves disconnected from branch. (Also 79)	Available	★★★★★
79	II/I 35 Weak nostril from over polished die and doubled lower cotton leaves on right side and ear on rt. inside. (Also 201) *Key identifier*– Raised metal inside 8's. B¹g (Also 70)	Available	★★★★★
80	II/I 6 Dbld wheat leaves and grains. B¹b Middle olive leaves disconnected from branch. Lines below TF. Small die chip at top of eagle's rt. wing. *Key identifier*– Dbld cap fold.	Available	★★★
80A	II/I 6 B¹b Breaks at top left & rt of rt T in STATES.	Somewhat scarce	★★★
81	II/I 7 E dbld rt. side of lower right serif, P on left side with short spike on lower left. B¹c Middle olive leaves disconnected from branch. Die chip on eagle's rt. wing in middle next to body. (Also 82) *Key identifier*– Lines in cap ribbon.	Available	★★
82	II/I 10 First right star strongly doubled. Doubled E, P, R, B, S, U & N. B¹c (Also 81) *Key identifier*– Die chip right of lower cotton leaf.	Available	★★★
83	II/I 11 18 doubled at top right with 1 set high. Motto doubled. B¹d Normal *Key identifier*– Spike at upper inside of ear.	Available	★★★
84	II/I 12 Washed out L in LIBERTY, slanted dash below first 8. B¹e Broken D in DOLLAR. Over polished eagle's left wing & TF. *Key identifier*– Dash below left 8.	Available	★★★
84A	II/I 12 B¹e Clashed dies with partial raised 'E' below eagle's tail feathers and partial incuse n of In from reverse next to LIBERTY head neck.	Somewhat scarce	★★★★
85	II/I 6 B¹f *Key identifiers*– Vertical thread-like die impression top of eagle's right wing, die chips left side upper tail feathers.	Rare	★★★★
86	II/I 6 B¹h *Key identifiers*– Short die scratches top eagle's left wing and eagle's left leg.	Scarce	★★★★
B² Short nock reverse			
B²a Normal reverse			
100	I¹10 Doubled motto, 1-4 & 6 left stars, all rt. stars, eyelid front & date.	Available	★★★★★
110	II/I 8 Partially broken bottom N & M serifs. Some doubled left & rt. stars. *Key identifier*– Broken N & M.	Available	★★★
111	II/I 13 Strongly doubled R in PLURIBUS with bottom shifted down. Doubled 7 left & 1 rt. stars. *Key identifier*– Die scratch lower cotton leaf.	Available	★★★
112	II/I 14 Vertical bar at left inside of top loop of B in PLURIBUS. Doubled 2, 3 left & 1, 3 rt. stars. *Key identifier*– Vertical bar left side of B upper loop.	Available	★★★
112A	II/I 14 Clashed obverse G.	Scarce	★★★
113	II/I 15 Doubled N, U & M in UNUM 2, left & 1, 2 &5 rt. stars. Large die flake on cheek in front of ear & die crack thru ear center. *Key identifier*– Die flake on cheek in front of ear.	Available	★★★
114	II/I 16 Doubled R in PLURIBUS with weak lower right serif of left vertical bar, slightly dbld tops of cotton leaves and bolls, 1-6 left & all rt. stars. *Key identifier*– Over polished lower hair.	Available	★★
114A	II/I 16 Clashed die with partial incuse t of Trust from reverse in lower hair edge right vee.	Available	★★
115	II/I 17 Tripled right edges of cotton bolls & leaves. Dbld date with 1 & 7 dbld below upper crossbar. Dbld rt. inside of ear, all stars. (Also 198) *Key identifier*– Tripled cotton bolls.	Somewhat scarce	★★★★★
116	II/I 18 Dbld P, L, R, B & bulge at P rt. side top loop. Dbld 1, 3, 4, 6 left & 1-4 rt. stars. Die flake hairline behind eye & die crack to hair. (Also 140) *Key identifier*– Bulge at rt. of P loop.	Scarce	★★★★
116A,B,C	II/I 18 Die gouges on reverse and over polished wing– leg feather.	Scarce	★★★★

| 117 | II/I 19 Strongly tripled second right star. Dbld E, P, R & 1, 3, 4, 6 left & 1-5 rt. stars, eye front, mouth, chin & rt. inside of ear. (Also 141) *Key identifier*– Alligator eye. **B²k** Engraved bars at wing-body. | Somewhat scarce | ★★★★★ |

| 118 | II/I 20 Strongly doubled lower right serif of P with line extending to rt. beyond base. Dbld right inside of ear, 3, 4, 7 left & 1, 2 rt. stars. (Also 160) *Key identifier*– Die chip below cap fold. | Scarce | ★★★★ |

| 119 | II/I 21 Doubled top right of E in E PLURIBUS, all left stars and ear tripled rt. and top inside. (Also 161) *Key identifier*– Doubling at top right corner of E and tripled ear. | Available | ★★★ |

| 120 | II/I 31 Strongly dbld lower rt. serif of P with line even with base end. Dbld left & 1-3 rt. stars. Three spikes below front of eyelid. (Also 168) *Key identifier*– Three spikes below eyelid. | Scarce | ★★★★ |

| 121 | II/I 38 Strongly doubled E, P, U & R with short bar in upper left inside of R upper loop & 1 & 3 rt. stars. *Key identifier*– Tiny die chip eye front, raised area below eyelid. | Scarce | ★★★★ |

| 122 | II/I 36 Strongly doubled first right star and PLURI. Type I LIBERTY with thin letters. All left & 1, 4-6 rt. stars doubled. *Key identifier*– Doubled eye front. | Somewhat scarce | ★★★ |

| 123 | II/I 40 Bottom right serif missing from left vertical bar of R. Strongly doubled 7 left star. Doubled eyelid in front of eye. **B²o** Engraved wing–leg feather. *Key identifier*– Doubled seventh left star. | Rare | ★★★★★ |

130	II 1 Normal without broken point of fourth right star. Multiple dies exist.	Available	★
130A	II 1 Die gouge thru lower part of IB. Die chip lower part of Phrygian cap.	Available	★★
130B	II 1 Spike above eyelid. Semi-circular die gouges in eagle's left wing. (Same obverse 185A)	Scarce	★★
130C	II 1 Die breaks at R and above Phrygian cap.	Scarce	★★
131	II 2 Normal with broken point on fourth right star. Multiple dies exist.	Available	★
131A	II 2 Die chip in hair below BE in LIBERTY.	Somewhat scarce	★★
131B	II 2 Die scratch thru RT in LIBERTY. (Same obverse 195A, 210A)	Available	★★
131C	II 2 Die scratch thru IB in LIBERTY. Some show clashed dies with partial incuse n of In from reverse next to LIBERTY head neck. (Same obverse 195)	Available	★★
132	II 3 Same as II 2 but die over polished with partial missing nostril.	Available	★★
133	II 4 Same as II 2 but with dbld motto letters, wheat leaves on rt. and top of Phrygian cap.	Available	★★★

B²b Reverse with Open o in God

| 140 | II/I 18 Dbld P, L, R, B & bulge at P rt. side top loop. Dbld 1, 3, 4, 6 left & 1-4 rt. stars. Die flake at hairline behind eye & die crack to hair. (Also 116, 199-2) *Key identifier*– Bulge at rt. of P loop. | Available | ★★★ |

| 140A | II/I 18 Die scratches lower reverse. | Available | ★★★ |

| 141 | II/I 19 Strongly tripled second rt. star. Dbld E, P, R & 1, 3, 4, 6 left & 1-5 rt. stars, eye front, mouth, chin & rt. inside of ear. (Also 117) Reverse **B²i** Engraved wing feather bars. *Key identifiers*– Alligator eye & engraved wing feather. | Available | ★★★★★ |

| 141A | II/I 19 Die gouge eagle's left wing tip. | Somewhat scarce | ★★★★★ |

| 142 | II/I 22 Doubled tops of 878, lower lip, nostril, P, R, U & left U & M in UNUM. (Also 196) *Key identifier*– Doubled left U in UNUM. | Available | ★★★ |

| 142A | II/I 22 Die chips top reverse at top rt. of S OF & eagle's left wing. | Somewhat scarce | ★★★ |

| 143 | II/I 23 Dbld 8 top left & metal in lower loop, P, R, B, left U, 2, 6 & 7 left stars. Spike below eyelid front. **B²l** Die scratches TF & wreath leaves & engraved lines at wing-body. (Also 145) *Key identifiers*– Spike below eyelid & scratches. | Available | ★★★ |

| 144 | II/I 24 Doubled 3-7 left stars, ear at rt. inside, lower hair, E, R, S & date . Over polished wing feathers and partially open o in God. *Key identifier*– Two die chips on chin. | Available | ★★★ |

| 144A | II/I 24 Clashed die with faint incuse n of In from reverse next to Liberty head neck. | Available | ★★★ |

| 145 | II/I 25 Broken bottom serifs of N & M. Dbld P, UR, S, 3 left & 5 rt. stars & 17. Spike below eyelid front. (Also 162) **B²l** Die scratches TF & wreath leaves & engraved lines at wing-body. (Also 143) *Key identifier*– Broken N & M. | Somewhat scarce | ★★★★★ |

| 146 | II 2 Diagonal lines in E, R & Y in LIBERTY and slightly dbld profile. **B²j** Engraved wing feather bar, over polished middle of wing. Open o in God. *Key identifier*– Eng wing feather. | Available | ★★★★ |

B²c Reverse with Broken r Arm in Trust

| 160 | II/I 20 Strongly doubled lower right serif of P with line extending to rt. beyond base. Dbld right inside of ear, 3, 4, 7 left & 1, 2 rt. stars. (Also 118) *Key identifier*– Die chip below cap fold. | Available | ★★★ |

| 161 | II/I 21 Doubled top right of E in E PLURIBUS, all left stars and ear on rt. and top inside. (Also 119) *Key identifier*– Doubling at top right corner of E. | Available | ★★★ |

| 162 | II/I 25 Broken bottom serifs of N & M. Dbld P, UR, S, 3 left & 5 rt. stars & 17. Spike below eyelid front. (Also 145) Over polished wing feathers. *Key identifier*– Broken N & M. | Available | ★★★★★ |

| 163 | II/I 26 First U in PLURIBUS strongly doubled at top left as a slanted bar. Dbld E, U, R, M, 7 left star & 1. *Key identifier*– Shifted U at upper left serif. (Same rev 167.) | Available | ★★★ |

| 164 | II/I 27 PL dbld on rt. side & notch at top inside of R upper loop. Dbld B, UNU, 1, 3, 4 rt. stars. | Available | ★★ |

Very weak feather next to eagle's rt. leg. *Key identifier*– Vertical line left end of cap ribbon & 3 spikes between eagle's rt. wing & body.

165	**II/I 28** Dbld E PLUR, 1-5 left & 1-5 rt. stars. Long spike above P lower rt. serif, spike at top rt. of upper loop. *Key identifier*– Vertical spike top rt. of P and vertical bar rt. side of L. **B²m** Engraved bars at wing-body.	Available	★★★
166	**II/I 29** Dbld E PLUR, all left & 1 rt. stars. Thick spike just above P lower rt. serif, spike at top rt. upper loop. Two shallow bars under front of eyelid. *Key identifier*– Two bars under eyelid front.	Scarce	★★★★
167	**II/I 30** Notch above P lower left serif, first U dbld below rt. side of rt. top serif & bottom of B. Second U in UNUM dbld on rt. side. *Key identifier*– Beveled left inside left 8 loops. (Same rev 163.)	Scarce	★★★
168	**II/I 31** Strongly doubled lower rt. serif of P with line even with base end. Dbld left & 1-3 rt. stars. Three spikes below front of eyelid. (Also 120) Reverse **B²m** Engraved bars wing-body. (Also 169 rev.) *Key identifier*– Three spikes below eyelid.	Somewhat scarce	★★★
169	**II/I 32** Dbld E PLUR left side. Dbld/tripled left & 1-5 rt. stars. 2-4 left stars strongly quadrupled at top rt. Dbld 18-8 & eyelid. *Key identifier*– Strongly quadrupled 2-4 left & dbld 3-5 rt. stars. (Also 168 rev.)	Somewhat scarce	★★★★★
170	**II/I 33** Doubled tops of 1878, all stars, P, U & R with U dbld at lower rt. and R above lower left serif & weak lower rt. serif of left vertical bar. *Key identifier*– Die chip on neck above M initial.	Available	★★★★★
170A	**II/I 33** Die dots and chips at cap and right cotton leaf.	Available	★★★★★
171	**II/I 34** Strongly tripled lower left serif of R. Strongly dbld cap upper loop, bottom of cotton bolls and rt. leaves, all hair below cap. Dbld P, U, last U, all stars, rt. inside ear (Also 220) *Key identifier*– Tripled lower left serif of R.	Somewhat scarce	★★★★★
185	**II 1** Normal II obverse without broken point on fourth right star. Multiple dies exist.	Available	★
185A	**II 1** Short spike above eyelid. Slight doubling chin front. (Same obverse 130B)	Available	★★
185B	**II 1** Die scratches thru I–R.	Available	★★
186	**II 2** Normal II obverse with broken point on fourth right star. Multiple dies exist.	Available	★
186A	**II 2** Short spike above eyelid. Vertical polishing lines mouth.	Available	★★
186B	**II 2** Raised die chips left 8 lower loop. Very over polished wing.	Available	★★
187	**II 5** Doubled LURIB and UN. R strongly doubled at top, middle and lower right side. Bottom serif of N strongly doubled at top left. Two spikes below eyelid front.	Somewhat scarce	★★★★★
188	**II 6** Die over polished with L weak & shallow in LIBERTY & shortened wheat leaf above L. (Also 223)	Very scarce	★★★
189	**II 1** Normal. **B²g** Diagonal lines engraved at wing–leg & wing–body. First reported & strongest 1878 P 7TF engraved wing feathers. Broken r in Trust.	Somewhat scarce	★★★★★

B²d–h Reverse with Doubled Motto, Broken D, Missing Feathers, Doubled Legend

190	**II 3** Missing nostril from over polished die. Different die than VAM 132. **B²d** Doubled God We to right and eagle's left wing at top. R in Trust not broken.	Available	★★★
190A	**II 3** Clashed dies with partial n next to Liberty head neck.	Somewhat scarce	★★★
195	**II 2** Diagonal line thru IB in LIBERTY. (Same obverse as 131C) **B²e** Bottom of D in Dollar broken away. R in Trust not broken.	Available	★★★
195A	**II 2** Diagonal line thru R and top of T in LIBERTY. (Same obverse as 131B, 210A) **B²e** Partially broken bottom of D in DOLLAR. R in Trust not broken. Different die than VAM 195.	Available	★★
196	**II/I 22** Doubled tops of 878, lower lip, nostril, P, R, U & left U & M in UNUM. (Also 142) *Key identifier*– Doubled left U in UNUM. **B²f** Die over polished with part of eagle's lower right wing missing next to leg. R in Trust not broken.	Available	★★★
196A	**II/I 22** Clashed dies with partial incuse n of In from reverse next to Liberty head neck and incuse st of Trust in right hair vee of Liberty head lower hair edge.	Available	★★★
197	**II 7** Slightly doubled UR-BUS UNU at top inside and right stars. (Also 134) **B²f** Feathers completely missing next to eagle's right leg. R in Trust not broken. Different die than VAMs 196, 198 & 199-2	Available	★★
198	**II/I 17** Tripled right edges of cotton bolls and leaves. Dbld date with 1 & 7 dbld below upper crossbar. Dbld rt. inside of ear, all stars. (Also 115) *Key identifier*– Tripled cotton bolls. **B²f** Missing wing feathers. R in Trust not broken. Different die than VAMs 196, 197 & 199-2.	Somewhat scarce	★★★★★
199	Same as VAM 164		
199-1	Same as VAM 198		
134	**II 7** Slightly doubled UR-BUS UNU at top inside and right stars. (Also 197) **B²h** Slightly doubled STATES AMERICA, right star & some leaves in rt. wreath towards coin center. R in Trust not broken.	Somewhat scarce	★★★

C Reverse with Slanted Top Arrow Feather

C¹ Reverse with Rounded Shallow Feather Next to Eagle's Right Leg

200 II/I 39 Broken serifs N & M in UNUM. Dbld 1-6 left & 1-3 rt. stars, E, P, U, S. *Key identifier*– Available ★★★
Broken N & M. **C¹a** Slightly dbld inside of legend letters towards rim & tops of In God We Trust.

201 II/I 35 Weak nostril from over polished die & dbld lower cotton leaves on right side & ear on Available ★★★
rt. inside. (Also 79) *Key identifier*– Raise metal inside 8's. **C¹a** Different die than VAMs 200 & 202.

202 III¹1 Lines in wheat leaves with left end of wheat leaf below R in line with right side of R Available ★★★
vertical shaft. Dbld stars, date & lower hair. **C¹a** Different die than VAMs 200 & 201.

202A III¹1 Clashed dies with partial n next to Liberty head neck. Available ★★★

203 III¹2 Heavy die polishing at top with short wheat leaf below R in PLURIBUS. Available ★★★★★
C¹b Doubled outside leaves in right wreath, all legend letters towards rim and In God tops.

203A III¹2 Clashed dies with partial incuse n of In from reverse next to Liberty head neck Somewhat scarce ★★★★★
and incuse st of Trust in right hair vee of Liberty head lower hair edge.

C² Reverse with Shallow Feather & Line Next to Eagle's Right Leg

210 II 2 Vertical polishing line thru Y in LIBERTY. **C²a** Reverse Available ★★★

210A II 2 Diagonal line thru R and top of T in LIBERTY. Available ★★★

210B II 2 Diagonal line thru middle of I & lower part of B in LIBERTY. Some show clashed dies Available ★★★
with partial incuse n of In from rev. next to neck & incuse st of Trust in rt. hair vee of lower hair edge.

215 III¹1 Obverse Same die as VAM 202. **C²a** Reverse Proofs. Rare ★★★

C³ Reverse with Square Raised Feather Next to Eagle's Right Leg

220 II/I 34 Strongly tripled lower left serif of R. Strongly dbld cap upper loop, bottom of Somewhat scarce ★★★★★
cotton bolls & rt. leaves, all hair below cap. Dbld P, U, last U, all stars, rt. inside ear (Also 171)
Key identifier– Tripled lower left serif of R. **C³b** Hub doubling of UNITED STATES & some left
wreath leaves with strong doubling on left inside of U.

221 II 1 Die chip on forehead front on some specimens. **C³b** See VAM 220 above. (Different die) Available ★★
Multiple obverse & reverse dies exist.

221A II 1 **C³b** Denticle impressions left of wreath bow. Available ★★

222 II 2 **C³b** See VAM 220 above. (Different die) Somewhat scarce ★★

222A II 2 Die chips above & below Liberty head lips. Somewhat scarce ★★

222B II 2 Vertical die gouge at base of left cotton boll & thin die scratch from boll to near Somewhat scarce ★★★
Y in LIBERTY. Die gouge thru front wheat leaf. Same die as VAM 228A.

222C II 2 Spikes above and below eyelid front. Somewhat scarce ★★

222D II 2 Over polished lower hair. Scarce ★★

223 II 6 Die over polished with L weak & shallow in LIBERTY & shortened wheat leaf Available ★★★★★
above L. (Also 188) **C³c** Hub doubling on outside edges of left & rt. wreath & tops of
serifs of A next to star in AMERICA. Double polishing lines inside wreath bow.

224 II 2 **C³c** See VAM 223 above. (Different die) Double polishing lines between eagle's legs Available ★★★
on rt. side. **Edge**– Second lowest edge reeding count of 168 of Morgan dollar series.

225 II 2 Faint short spike below eyelid front or behind eye. **C³c** See VAM 223 above. (Different die) Available ★★

225A II 2 **C³a** Four raised dots below middle tail feathers from denticle impressions. Available ★★★★

226 II 1 **C³c** See VAM 223 above. (Different die) Scarce ★★★

226A II 1 **C³c** Clashed obverse n. Somewhat scarce ★★★

227 II 1 **C³a** Normal reverse without any significant doubling. Coins of 176 reeds have long Very scarce ★★★
diagonal die polishing line thru O in OF. Same die as VAM 228B. Coins of 175 reeds have
slight doubling of top leaves in left wreath.

228 II 2 **C³a** Horizontal polishing lines thru wreath bow on some specimens. Multiple dies. Somewhat scarce ★★

228A II 2 Vertical die gouge at base of left cotton boll & thin die scratch from boll to near Y Somewhat scarce ★★★
in LIBERTY. Die gouge thru front wheat leaf. Same die as VAM 222B.

228B II 2 **C³a** Long diagonal die polishing line thru O in OF. Same die as one of VAM 227. Scarce ★★

229 II 2 Die chip on forehead. **C³d** Some dbld leaves in rt. wreath & bottom inside of AMERICA. Scarce ★★★

229.1 II 8 Slightly doubled top of Phrygian cap, LIBERTY, hair front and US UNUM. **C³a** reverse Available ★★

230 III²1 Long wheat leaf with weak lines close to bottom of R in PLURIBUS. Left edge of wheat Available ★★
leaf below R in line with middle part of T vertical shaft.
C³a Normal reverse without any significant doubling. Multiple dies exist.

231 III²2 Slightly tripled stars, date & motto letters towards rim. Vertical polishing lines below Available ★★
eyelid front. **C³c** See VAM 223 above. (Different die) Three fine polishing lines above lower rt. ribbon.

232 III²3 Rt. stars sextupled towards rim. U's of PLURIBUS dbld at bottom inside. Top of Phrygian Available ★★
cap dbld. **C³b** See VAM 220 above. (Different die) Diagonal scratch from top of rt. end of olive branch.

1878 P 7TF DIE COMBINATIONS SUMMARY

(Number designates VAM variety)   November 2010

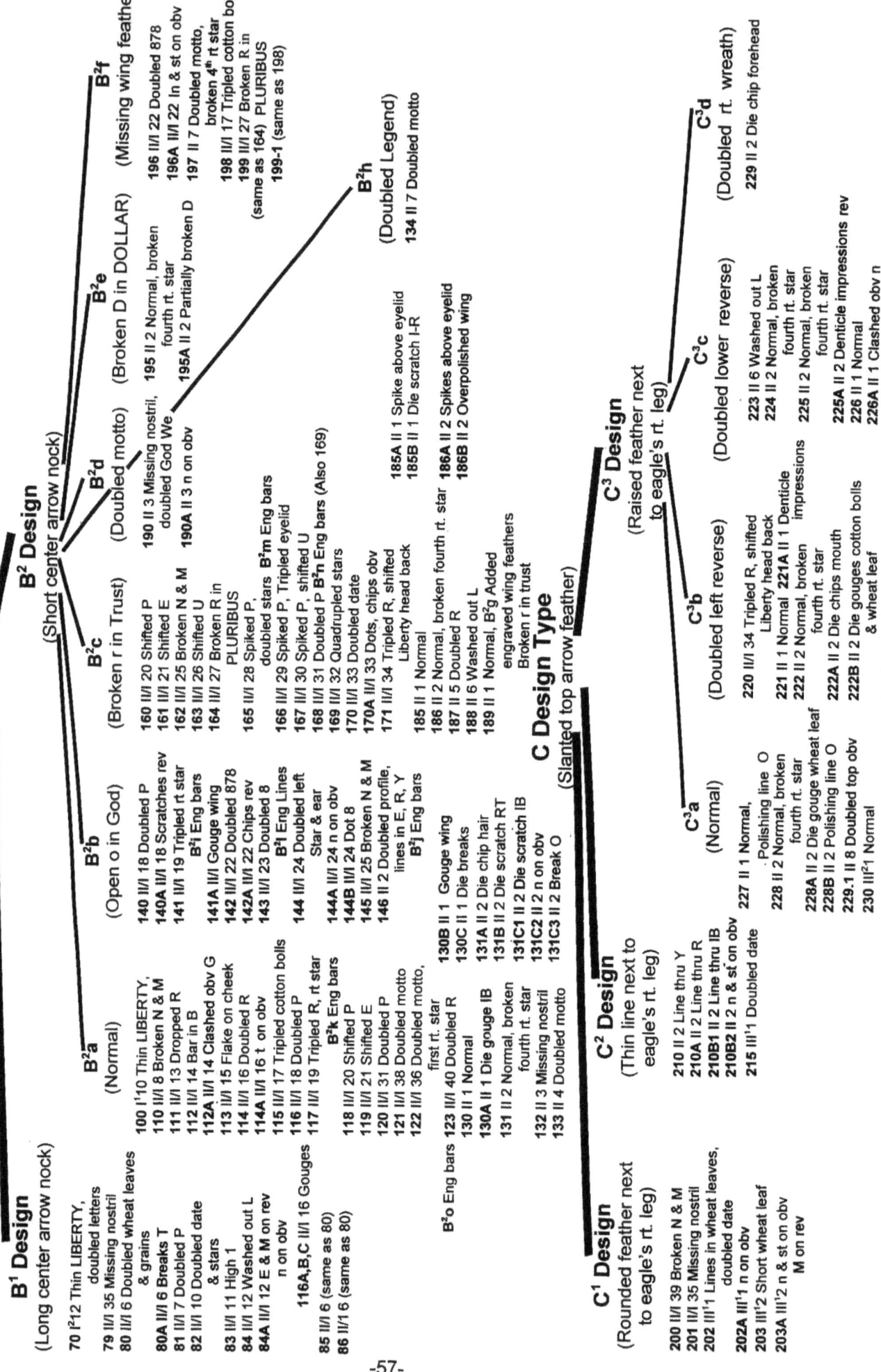

B Design Type
(Parallel top arrow feather)

B¹ Design
(Long center arrow nock)

70 I²12 Thin LIBERTY, doubled letters
79 II/I 35 Missing nostril
80 II/I 6 Doubled wheat leaves & grains
80A II/I 6 Breaks T
81 II/I 7 Doubled P
82 II/I 10 Doubled date
112A II/I 14 Clashed obv G & stars
83 II/I 11 High 1
84 II/I 12 Washed out L
84A II/I 12 E & M on rev n on obv

116A,B,C II/I 16 Gouges

85 II/I 6 (same as 80)
86 II/I 6 (same as 80)

B² Design
(Short center arrow nock)

B²a (Normal)
100 I¹10 Thin LIBERTY, doubled letters
110 II/I 8 Broken N & M
111 II/I 13 Dropped R
112 II/I 14 Bar in B
113 II/I 15 Flake on cheek
114 II/I 16 Doubled R
114A II/I 16 t on obv
115 II/I 17 Tripled cotton bolls
116 II/I 18 Doubled P
117 II/I 19 Tripled R, rt star

B²k Eng bars
118 II/I 20 Shifted E
119 II/I 21 Shifted E
120 II/I 31 Doubled P
121 II/I 38 Doubled motto
122 II/I 36 Doubled motto, first rt. star

B²o Eng bars
123 II/I 40 Doubled R
130 II 1 Normal
130A II 1 Die gouge IB
131 II 2 Normal, broken fourth rt. star
132 II 3 Missing nostril
133 II 4 Doubled motto

B²b (Open o in God)
140 II/I 18 Doubled P
140A II/I 18 Scratches rev
141 II/I 19 Tripled rt star

B²i Gouge wing
141A II/I Gouge wing
142 II/I 22 Doubled 878
142A II/I 22 Chips rev
143 II/I 23 Doubled 8

B²l Eng Lines
144 II/I 24 Doubled left Star & ear
144A II/I 24 n on obv
144B II/I 24 Dot 8
145 II/I 25 Broken N & M
146 II 2 Doubled profile, lines in E, R, Y

B²j Eng bars
130B II 1 Gouge wing
130C II 1 Die breaks
131A II 2 Die chip hair
131B II 2 Die scratch RT
131iC1 II 2 Die scratch IB
131C2 II 2 n on obv
131C3 II 2 Break O

B²c (Broken r in Trust)
160 II/I 20 Shifted P
161 II/I 21 Shifted E
162 II/I 25 Broken N & M
163 II/I 26 Shifted U
164 II/I 27 Broken R in PLURIBUS
165 II/I 28 Spiked P, doubled stars
166 II/I 29 Spiked P, Tripled eyelid
167 II/I 30 Spiked P, shifted U
168 II/I 31 Doubled P
169 II/I 32 Quadrupled stars
170 II/I 33 Doubled date
170A II/I 33 Dots, chips obv
171 II/I 34 Tripled R, shifted Liberty head back
185 II 1 Normal
186 II 2 Normal, broken fourth rt. star
187 II 5 Doubled R
188 II 6 Washed out L
189 II 1 Normal, B²g Added engraved wing feathers Broken r in trust

B²m Eng bars   B²n Eng bars (Also 169)

185A II 1 Spike above eyelid
185B II 1 Die scratch I-R
186A II 2 Spikes above eyelid
186B II 2 Overpolished wing

B²d (Doubled motto)
190 II 3 Missing nostril, doubled God We
190A II 3 n on obv

B²e (Broken D in DOLLAR)
195 II 2 Normal, broken fourth rt. star
195A II 2 Partially broken D

B²f (Missing wing feather)
196 II/I 22 Doubled 878
196A II/I 22 In & st on obv
197 II 7 Doubled motto, broken 4th rt star
198 II/I 17 Tripled cotton bolls
199 II/I 27 Broken R in PLURIBUS (same as 164)
199-1 (same as 198)

B²h (Doubled Legend)
134 II 7 Doubled motto

C Design Type
(Slanted top arrow feather)

C¹ Design
(Rounded feather next to eagle's rt. leg)

200 II/I 39 Broken N & M
201 II/I 35 Missing nostril
202 III¹1 Lines in wheat leaves, doubled date
202A III¹1 n on obv
203 III¹2 Short wheat leaf
203A III¹2 n & st on obv M on rev

C² Design
(Thin line next to eagle's rt. leg)

210 II 2 Line thru Y
210A II 2 Line thru R
210B1 II 2 Line thru IB
210B2 II 2 n & st on obv
215 III¹1 Doubled date

C³ Design
(Raised feather next to eagle's rt. leg)

C³a (Normal)
227 II 1 Normal, Polishing line O
228 II 2 Normal, broken fourth rt. star
228A II 2 Die gouge wheat leaf
228B II 2 Polishing line O
229.1 II 8 Doubled top obv
230 III²1 Normal

C³b (Doubled left reverse)
220 II/I 34 Tripled R, shifted Liberty head back
221 II 1 Normal
221A II 1 Denticle impressions
222 II 2 Normal, broken fourth rt. star
222A II 2 Die chips mouth
222B II 2 Die gouges cotton bolls & wheat leaf
222C II 2 Spiked eye

C³c (Doubled lower reverse)
223 II 6 Washed out L
224 II 2 Normal, broken fourth rt. star
225 II 2 Normal, broken fourth rt. star
225A II 2 Denticle impressions rev
226 II 1 Normal
226A II 1 Clashed obv n
231 III²2 Tripled stars

C³d (Doubled rt. wreath)
229 II 2 Die chip forehead

B DESIGN TYPE
(Parallel top arrow feather)

B¹ DESIGN
(Long center arrow nock)

✳ Key Identifier

II/I 35 B¹a VAM 79
Doubled Cotton Leaves

II/I 35 B¹a VAM 79 Metal in 8's ✳

II/I 6 B¹b VAM 80
Doubled B & Leaf

II/I 6 B¹b VAM 80 Lines in LIB

II/I 6 B¹b VAM 80 ✳
Doubled Cap Fold

II/I 7 B¹c VAM 81 Spiked Γ

II/I 7 B¹c VAM 81 ✳
Lines in Ribbon

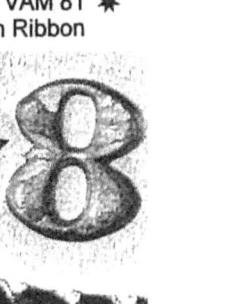

II/I 7 B¹c VAM 81 Doubled
1-2 Left Star

II/I 7 B¹c VAM 81 Doubled Date

II/I 10 B¹c VAM 82 Die Chip ✳

II/I 10 B¹c VAM 82
Doubled 1-2 Rt. Stars

II/I 10 B¹c VAM 82 Doubled 8-8

II/I 11 B¹d VAM 83 Doubled URI

II/I 11 B¹d VAM 83 Doubled 18

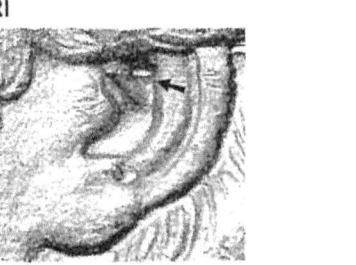

II/I 11 B¹d VAM 83 ✳
Spike in Ear

II/I 12 B¹e VAM 84
Over Polished L & Leaf

II/I 12 B¹e VAM 84 ✳
Dash Below 8

B² DESIGN
(Short center arrow nock)
B²a
(Normal)

✳ Key Identifier

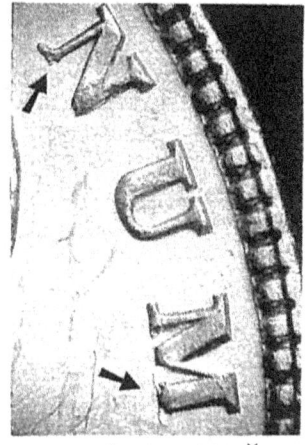

II/I 8 B²a VAM 110 ✳
Broken N & M

II/I 14 B²a VAM 112 ✳
Bar in B

II/I 13 B²a VAM 111 Dropped R

II/I 13 B²a VAM 111 ✳
Die Scratch Leaf

II/I 14 B²a VAM 112
Doubled E

II/I 14 B²a VAM 112
Doubled 1

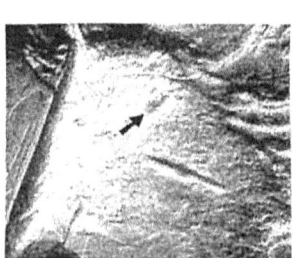

II/I 14 B²a VAM 112
Die Chip Forehead

II/I 14 B²a VAM 112
Die Scratches Leaves

II/I 15 B²a VAM 113 Doubled 8-8

II/I 15 B²a VAM 113 ✳
Die Flake on Cheek

II/I 16 B²a VAM 114 ✳
Over Polished Hair

II/I 16 B²a VAM 114 Doubled R

II/I 17 B²a VAM 115
Doubled Date & Stars
(Also B²f VAM 198)

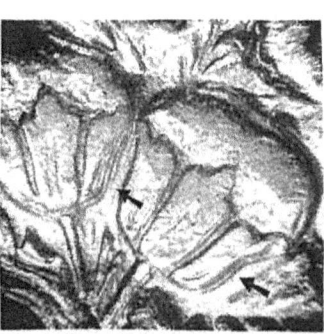

II/I 17 B²a VAM 115 ✳
Tripled Cotton Bolls

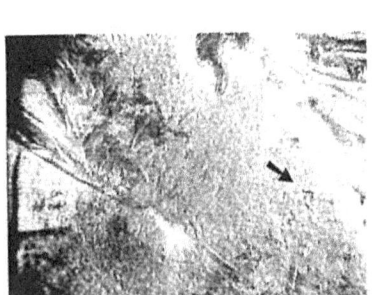

II/I 18 B²a VAM 116
Die Chip & Line
(Also B²b VAM 140)

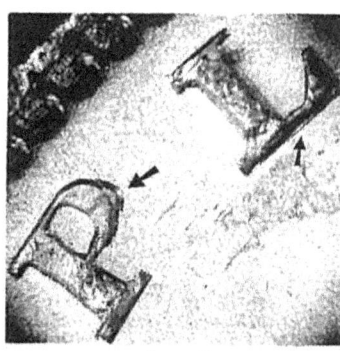

II/I 18 B²a VAM 116 ✳
Doubled PL

B²a
(Normal)

✳ Key Identifier

II/I 19 B²a VAM 117
Tripled Second Rt. Star

II/I 19 B²a VAM 117 Doubled P
(Also B²b VAM 141)

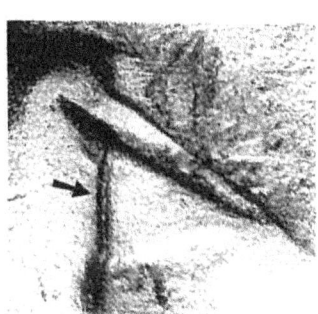
II/I 19 B²a VAM 117 Alligator Eye ✳

II/I 20 B²a VAM 118 Shifted P
(Also B²c VAM 160)

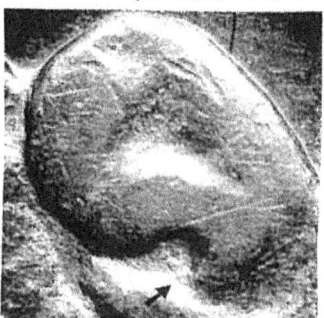
II/I 20 B²a VAM 118 ✳
Die Chip Cap Fold

II/I 21 B²a VAM 119 ✳
Tripled Ear

II/I 21 B²a VAM 119
Shifted E
(Also B²c VAM 161)

II/I 31 B²a VAM 120 Doubled P
(Also B²c VAM 168)

II/I 31 B²a VAM 120 Doubled R

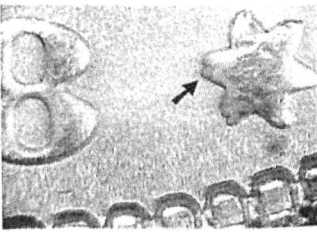
II/I 36 B²a VAM 122
Doubled Rt. Star

II/I 36 B²a VAM 122
Doubled Motto

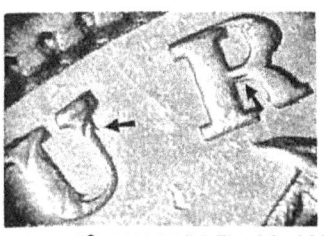
II/I 38 B²a VAM 121 Doubled UR

II/I 31 B²a VAM 120 ✳
Spikes Below Eyelid

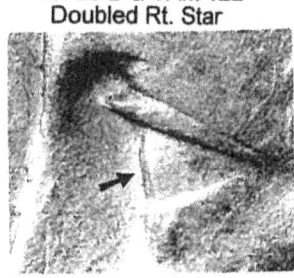
II/I 36 B²a VAM 122 ✳
Doubled Eye Front

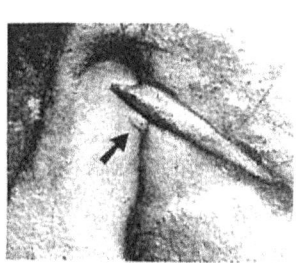
II/I 40 B²a VAM 123 Spiked Eye

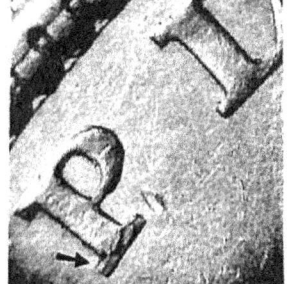
II/I 38 B²a VAM 121
Doubled P

II/I 38 B²a VAM 121 ✳
Die Chip Eye Front

II/I 40 B²a VAM 123 ✳
Doubled Seventh Left Star

II/I 40 B²a VAM 123 Doubled R

-60-

 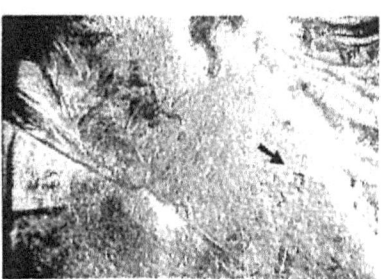 

II/I 18 B²b VAM 140 Doubled PL II/I 18 B²b VAM 140 Die Chip & Line II/I 19 B²b VAM 141 Doubled P II/I 19 B²b VAM 141 ✳
(Also B²a VAM 116) (Also B²a VAM 117) Alligator Eye

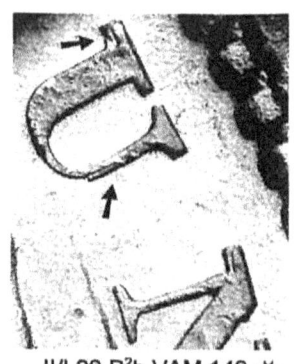  

II/I 22 B²b VAM 142 ✳ II/I 22 B²b VAM 142 II/I 22 B²b VAM 142
Doubled U M Split Serif Doubled 8-8, Tripled 7
(Also B²f VAM 196)

II/I 19 B²b VAM 141
Tripled Second Rt. Star

II/I 23 B²b VAM 143 ✳ II/I 23 B²b VAM 143
Spiked Eye Doubled Seventh Left Star

 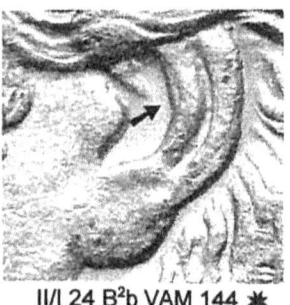

II/I 24 B²b VAM 144
Doubled Left Stars & E

II/I 24 B²b VAM 144 ✳
Doubled Ear

  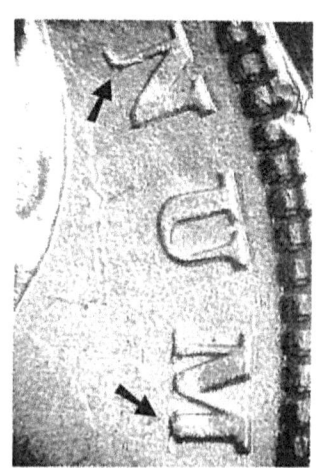

✳ II/I 24 B²b VAM 144 II/I 24 B²b VAM 144 Doubled Date II/I 25 B²b VAM 145 Doubled 1-7 II/I 25 B²b VAM 145 ✳
Die Chips Chin (Also B²c VAM 162) Broken N & M

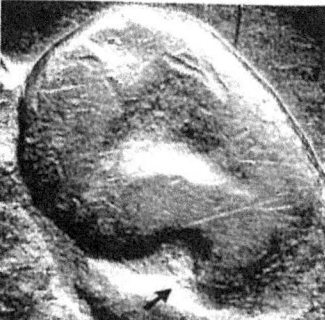

I/I 20 B²c VAM 160 Shifted P
(Also B²a VAM 118)

II/I 20 B²c VAM 160 ✳
Die Chip Cap Fold

II/I 21 B²c VAM 161 Shifted E
(Also B²a VAM 119)

II/I 21 B²c VAM 161 ✳
Tripled Ear

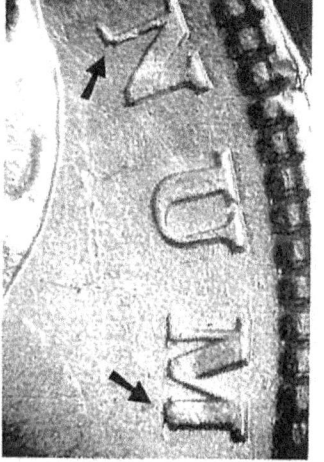

II/I 25 B²c VAM 162 ✳
Broken N & M

II/I 25 B²c VAM 162 Doubled 1-7
(Also B²b 145)

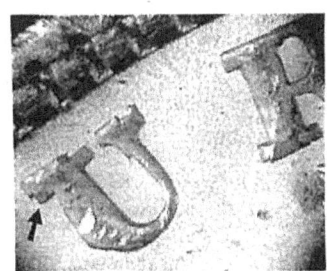
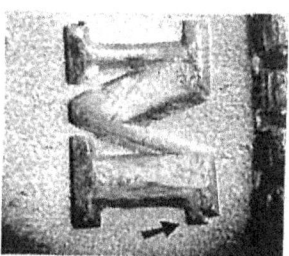

✳ II/I 26 B²c VAM 163 Shifted U

II/I 26 B²c VAM 163
Doubled M

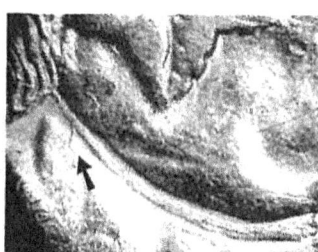

II/I 27 B²c VAM 164
Doubled PL

II/I 27 B²c VAM 164
Broken R

II/I 27 B²c VAM 164 ✳
Line Cap Ribbon

II/I 28 B²c VAM 165 ✳
Doubled PL

II/I 28 B²c VAM 165 Doubled UR

II/I 29 B²c VAM 166 Spiked P

II/I 29 B²c VAM 166 ✳
Bars Under Eyelid

B²c
(Broken r in Trust, takes precedence)

✳ Key Identifier

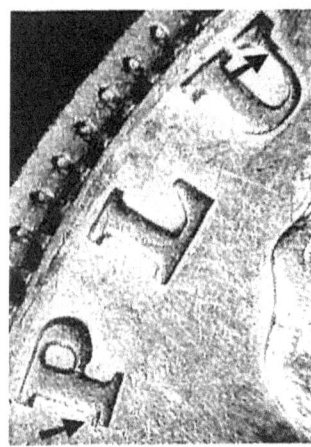

II/I 30 B²c VAM 167 Spiked P

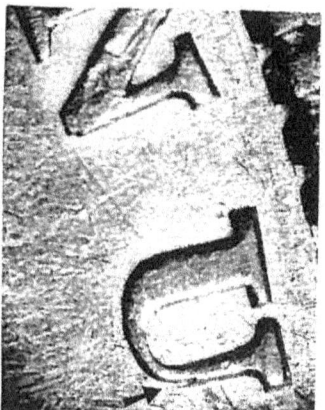

II/I 30 B²c VAM 167 Doubled U

II/I 30 B²c VAM 167 ✳
Beveled Inside 8

II/I 31 B²c VAM 168 Doubled P

II/I 31 B²c VAM 168 Doubled R
(Also B²a VAM 120)

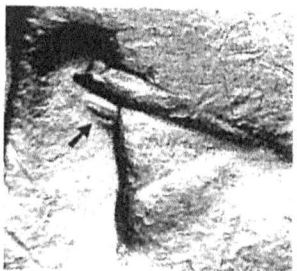

II/I 31 B²c VAM 168 ✳
Spikes Below Eyelid

II/I 32 B²c VAM 169
Die Chip Cotton Leaf

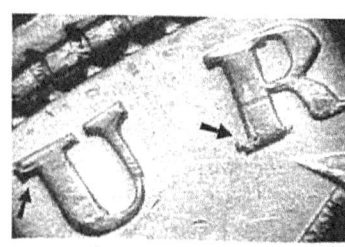

II/I 33 B²c VAM 170 Doubled UR

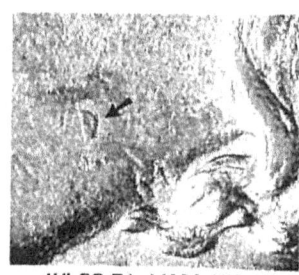

II/I 33 B²c VAM 170 ✳
Die Chip Neck

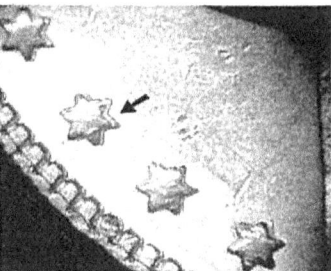

II/I 32 B²c VAM 169
Quadrupled Left Stars

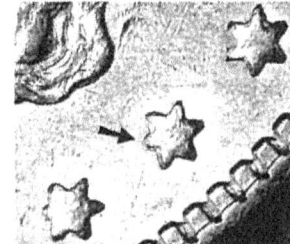

II/I 32 B²c VAM 169 ✳
Doubled 3-5 Rt. Stars

II/I 33 B²c VAM 170 Doubled Date

II/I 34 B²c VAM 171 Doubled P
(Also C³b VAM 220)

II/I 34 B²c VAM 171 ✳
Tripled R

II/I 34 B²c VAM 171
Doubled Cotton Bolls, Cap

B²f
(Missing wing feather)

* Key Identifier

II/I 17 B²f VAM 198
Doubled Date & Stars

II/I 17 B²f VAM 198 *
Tripled Cotton Bolls

(Also B²a VAM 115)

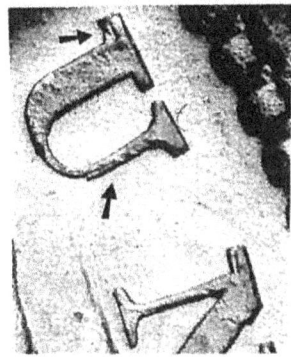  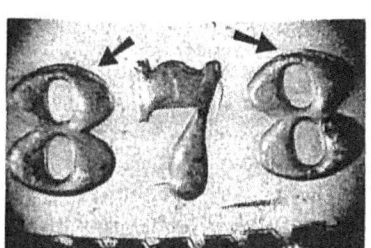

II/I 22 B²f VAM 196 *
Doubled U

II/I 22 B²f VAM 196
M Split Serif
(Also B²b VAM 142)

II/I 22 B²f VAM 196
Doubled 8-8, Tripled 7

C DESIGN TYPE
(Slanted top arrow feather)

  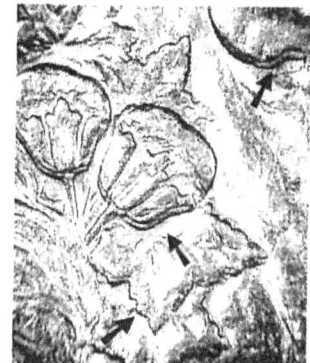

II/I 34 C³b VAM 220 Doubled P
(Also B²c VAM 171)

II/I 34 C³b VAM 220 *
Tripled R

II/I 34 C³b VAM 220
Doubled Cotton Bolls, Cap

  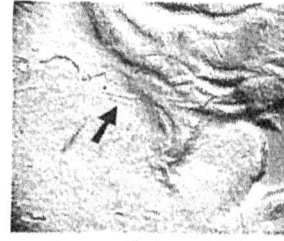 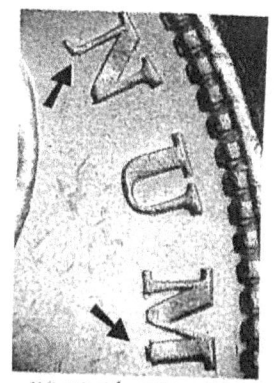

II/I 35 C¹a VAM 201
Doubled Cotton Leaves
(Also B¹a VAM 79)

II/I 35 VAM 201 C¹a Metal in 8's *

II/I 39 C¹a VAM 200
Double Lines Ear Front

II/I 39 C¹a VAM 200 *
Broken N & M

1878 P 7TF OBVERSE DIE DESIGNATIONS TO VAM NUMBER

Die	VAMs	Die	VAMs
I¹10	100 (2 dies)	II 1	All different dies 130, 130A, 130B, 130C,
I²12	70		185, 185B, 189, 221, 226, 226A, 227-2
II/I 1	15 (8TF)	II 1	Same dies 130B, 185A & 221A, 227-1
II/I 2	19, 18, 20 (8TF)	II 2	All different dies 131, 131A, 146, 186, 186A,
II/I 3	21, 43 (8TF & 7/8TF)		186B, 195, 210, 210B, 222, 222A, 222C,
II/I 4	16 (8TF)		222D, 224, 225, 225A, 228(7 dies), 228B, 229
II/I 5	17, 42 (8TF & 7/8TF)	II 2	Same dies 131C, 195
II/I 6	22 (8TF), 80 , 80A, 85, 86	II 2	Same dies 131B, 195A, 210A
II/I 7	81 (7TF), 33, 30 (7/8TF)	II 2	Same dies 222B, 228A
II/I 8	40, 31 (7/8TF), 110	II 3	132, 190 (different dies), 190A
II/I 9	38 (7/8TF)	II 4	133
II/I 10	82	II 5	187
II/I 11	83	II 6	Same dies 188, 223
II/I 12	84, 84A	II 7	Same dies 134, 197
II/I 13	111	II 8	229.1
II/I 14	112, 112A	III¹1	Same dies 202, 215
II/I 15	113	III¹2	203, 203A
II/I 16	114, 114A	III²1	230 (4 different dies)
II/I 17	115, 198	III²2	231
II/I 18	140, 140A, 116, 116A,B,C	III²3	232
II/I 19	117, 141, 141A		
II/I 20	118, 160		
II/I 21	119, 161		
II/I 22	142, 142A, 196, 196A		
II/I 23	143		
II/I 24	144, 144A		
II/I 25	145, 162		
II/I 26	163		
II/I 27	164		
II/I 28	165		
II/I 29	166		
II/I 30	167		
II/I 31	120, 168		
II/I 32	169		
II/I 33	170, 170A		
II/I 34	171, 220		
II/I 35	79, 201		
II/I 36	122		
II/I 37	44 (7/8TF)		
II/I 38	121		
II/I 39	200		
II/I 40	123		

1878 P 7TF REVERSE DIE DESIGNATIONS TO VAM NUMBER

Die	VAMs
B^{1}a	70
B^{1}b	80, 80A
B^{1}c	Same dies 82, 81
B^{1}d	83
B^{1}e	84, 84A
B^{1}f	85
B^{1}g	79
B^{1}h	86
B^{2}a	All different dies 100-116, 118-122, 130-133
B^{2}b	All different dies 140, 140A, 141, 142, 144
B^{2}c	All different dies 160-162, 164, 170, 170A, 171, 185, 186, 188, 189
B^{2}c	Same dies 166, 187
B^{2}c	Same dies 167, 163
B^{2}d	190, 190A
B^{2}e	Different dies 195, 195A
B^{2}f	All different dies 196, 197, 198
B^{2}g	189
B^{2}h	134
B^{2}i	141
B^{2}j	146
B^{2}k	117
B^{2}l	143, 145
B^{2}m	165
B^{2}n	168, 169
B^{2}o	123
C^{1}a	All different dies 200, 201, 202
C^{1}b	203, 203A
C^{2}a	Same dies 210, 210A, 210B
C^{2}a	215 different die?
C^{3}a	All different dies 227-2, 228(7 dies), 228A, 229.1, 230 (4 dies known)
C^{3}a	Same dies 227-1, 228B
C^{3}b	All different dies 220, 221, 222, 222A, 222B, 222C, 222D, 232
C^{3}c	All different dies 223, 224, 225, 226, 226A, 231
C^{3}d	229

B Reverse 78 (Parallel Arrow Feather)

B¹ Reverse, Long Center Arrow Nock

70   **I²12 • B¹a (Doubled Letters)**   (180)   I-5   R-4

Obverse I²12– Doubled motto with R, I and B having large shift at bottom and UM tripled on right side. All stars on right tripled at bottom. 878 in date doubled. First 8 doubled at top inside of both loops and at bottom outside of lower loop. 7 doubled below upper crossbar and at bottom left and upper right of vertical shaft. Second 8 doubled at top inside and bottom outside of lower loop and tripled at lower left outside of upper loop. Nostril slightly over polished. Front of neck slightly doubled.

Reverse B¹a– Earlier type B¹ reverse, 7 TF parallel arrow feather at top, with long center arrow shaft or nock. Die over polished with left three leaves disconnected from olive branch and middle of eagle's right and left wing missing. *Die marker–* Curved polishing line in wreath bow.

79   **II/I 35 • B¹g (Missing Nostril, Doubled Cotton Leaves)**   (180)   I-5   R-4

Obverse II/I 35– Slightly doubled LIBERTY shifted left. Doubled 2 thru 7 left stars and first three right stars. Lower part of Liberty head nostril partially missing from over polished die. R of PLURIBUS doubled at top inside of upper loop. Hair, cotton bolls & leaves doubled on rt. side. Ear slightly doubled on rt. inside. *Key identifier–* Metal in loops of both 8's. (Also 201)

Reverse B¹g– Different die than VAM 70. Die over polished with left three leaves disconnected from olive branch and middle of eagle's right and left wing missing. Die chip at top of right wreath. *Die marker–* Vertical polishing line on lower middle tail feathers.

80   **II/I 6 • B¹b (Doubled LIBERTY, Wheat Leaves & Grains, Disconnected Leaves)**   (180)   I-3   R-4

Obverse II/I 6– Doubled last four letters in LIBERTY shifted down. First three letters have polishing lines. Slightly doubled E PLURIBUS UNUM at left top serifs. Doubled 2 & 3 left stars and 3 & 4 right stars. Doubled tops of wheat leaves and grains, cotton leaves and bolls and Phrygian cap top loop. 878 slightly doubled. First 8 doubled on left inside of upper loop. 7 doubled at top right of shaft. Second 8 doubled on left and bottom inside of upper loop and bottom inside of lower loop. Shallow over polished ear. *Key identifier–* Doubled cap fold.

Reverse B¹b– Die over polished with last three leaves slightly disconnected from olive branch. Diagonal lines in field below tail feathers. *Die marker--* Small die chip on eagles's right wing at top next to body.

80A   **II/I 6 • B²b (Doubled LIBERTY, Wheat Leaves, Disconnected Leaves, Die Breaks T)** (180)   I-3   R-5

Reverse B²b– Die cracks at top of all legend letters with die breaks at top left and right of T and left of N in UNITED.

81   **II/I 7 • B¹c (Doubled P)**   (180)   I-2   R-4

Obverse II/I 7– Type II LIBERTY with thick letters. Doubled E, P and R in PLURIBUS. Doubled 187 in date with 1 doubled on left of shaft, 8 on top surface and 7 on left of top serif. All left stars and first three right doubled. Area around nose and lips over polished. Fine diagonal polishing line through R in LIBERTY. *Key identifier–* Lines in cap ribbon.

Reverse B¹c– Die over polished with last three leaves disconnected from olive branch and blank spots in middle of both eagle's wings. *Die marker--* Die chips on eagle's right wing in middle next to body and top of inner feathers. (Also 82)

82   **II/I 10 • B¹c (Doubled Date & Stars)**   (180)   I-3   R-4

Obverse II/I 10– Doubled LIBERTY shifted up. Doubled E, P R, B, S, U and N in motto. Doubled 1, 2, 3 and 5 right stars with first one very strong; doubled 1-6 left stars on left side. Doubled 1 on right side, both 8's doubled over center of top loop. *Key identifier–* Die chip right of lower cotton leaf. (B¹c reverse also 81)

83   **II/I 11 • B¹d (High 1)**   (180)   I-3   R-4

Obverse II/I 11– Doubled LIBERTY shifted left; all letters in E PLURIBUS UNUM doubled. Doubled 1, 2, 5 and 6 left stars and 1-4 right stars. 1 in date doubled on right side and set high. First 8 doubled at top right outside and left outside of upper loop and bottom inside of lower loop. 7 doubled slightly on left side of left top serif and right side on left lower serif. Lower part of nostril weak from over polishing. *Key identifier–* Spike at upper inside of ear.

Reverse B¹d– Over polishing of die in middle of eagle's left wing. *Die marker–* Thin vertical die scratch at bottom of eagle's left wing.

84   **II/I 12 • B¹e (Washed Out L, Broken D)**   (180)   I-3   R-4

Obverse II/I 12– Slightly doubled LIBERTY shifted left, with surface around L and right wheat leaf flat and detail not brought out. Missing nostril. Doubled E, P, L, U, R, B and S in E PLURIBUS. Doubled 1-4, 6 & 7 left stars and all right stars. Slanted dash below left 8 with die chip at top left inside of upper loop on some specimens. *Key identifier–* Dash below left 8.

Reverse B¹e– D of DOLLAR broken at bottom with just two lines remaining. *Die marker–* Die chip on eagle's right wing, sixth feather down and also next to body. Die over polished with blank areas in eagle's left wing and tail feathers.

84A(revised)   **II/I 12 • B¹e (Washed Out L, Broken D, Clashed Obverse n, Reverse E & M)** (180)   I-4   R-5

Obverse II/I 12– Strongly clashed die with partial incuse n of In from reverse showing next to Liberty head neck.

Reverse B¹e– Clashed die with partial raised E from obverse LIBERTY below eagle's tail feathers on left side. Vertical bar and middle serif of E show. Also has raised designer's initial M from obverse showing above d of God. Late die states show die chip at top of right wreath.

85   **II/I 6 • B¹f (Dbld LIBERTY, Wheat Leaves & Grains, "7" Rev., Thread-Like Die Impression Wing) (?)**   I-5   R-6

Obverse II/I 6– Earlier die state than VAM 80.

Reverse B¹f– Short vertical thread-like die impression at tip of eagle's right wing and short horizontal one at top right of upper tail feathers. Die slightly over polished with left three leaves disconnected from olive branch and small blank spot in middle of eagle's left wing. *Die marker–* Several raised die chips at left side of upper tail feathers. "7" on right leg of A in STATES. Die likely had very short life because early die polished proof-like state has peripheral die crack all around die.

86   **II/I 6 • B¹h (Dbld LIBERTY, Wheat Leaves & Grains, Disconnected Leaves)**   (180)   I-3   R-6

Obverse II/I 6– Earlier die state than VAM 80.

Reverse B¹h– Die over polished with left three leaves disconnected from olive branch and middle of eagle's left wing missing. *Die marker–* Numerous fine short die scratches at top of eagle's left wing just below st and at eagle's left leg.

B²a Normal Reverse

100-1   I¹10 • B²a (Doubled Obverse Motto)   **(180)   I-5   R-4**
  Obverse I¹10– Doubled E PLURIBUS UNUM and 1-4 & 6 left stars and all right stars towards rim. Eyelid slightly doubled below front. Date slightly doubled with 1 doubled below crossbar, first 8 at top inside and left outside of upper loop, 7 at top right and below crossbar and second 8 at lower left outside of upper loop.
  Reverse B²a– Later type B² reverse with shorter center arrow shaft of nock. Die 1– *Die markers*– Diagonal die scratch in top opening of A in DOLLAR, small semi-circular die impression line on outside of tenth outer feather from bottom of eagle's right wing and a few light horizontal polishing lines inside wreath bow.

100-2   I¹10 • B²a (Doubled Obverse Motto)   **(180)   I-5   R-4**
  Obverse I¹10– Earliest die state.
  Reverse B²a– Die 2– *Die markers*– Fine horizontal die polishing line on second inner feather from bottom of eagle's left wing and on sixth outer feather from bottom of eagle's right wing. Over polished flat area in middle of eagle's left wing. No lines in wreath bow or in A of DOLLAR.

110(revised) II/I 8 • B²a (Broken N & M)   **(180)   I-3   R-4**
  Obverse II/I 8– Type II LIBERTY with thick letters. Doubled P-U-B on top left, second U on right and S at bottom of fully struck specimens. Partially broken bottom serifs of N & M in UNUM. Doubled left stars and 1, 3, 4 & 5 right stars. Doubled date with doubled 1 & 7 at top right, first 8 on surface of both loops, 7 at lower edge of crossbar and right 8 at bottom outside of lower loop on fully struck specimens. *Key identifier*– Broken N & M.
  Reverse B²a– Shallow die gouge across eagle's right leg.

111   II/I 13 • B²a (Dropped R)   **(193)   I-3   R-5**
  Obverse II/I 13– Slightly doubled LIBERTY (L, I & B only). Doubled U and R in PLURIBUS with R dropped down. Doubled 7 left star and 1 right star. *Key identifier*– Die scratch lower cotton leaf.

112   II/I 14 • B²a (Bar in B)   **(194)   I-2   R-4**
  Obverse II/I 14– Type II LIBERTY. Vertical bar at left inside of top loop of B in PLURIBUS. Doubled 2 and 3 left stars and 1 and 3 right stars. 1 and 7 in date doubled at top right. *Key identifier*– Vertical bar left side of B upper loop.

112A   II/I 14 • B²a (Bar in B, Clashed Obverse G)   **(193)   I-3   R-6**
  Obverse II/I 14– Clashed die with partial incuse G of God from reverse showing next to Liberty head neck.

113   II/I 15 • B²a (Flake on Cheek)   **(194)   I-2   R-4**
  Obverse II/I 15– Type II LIBERTY. Doubled N, U and M in UNUM. Doubled 2 left star and 1, 2 and 5 right stars. Both 8's in date doubled at top left outside. Die crack thru ear center and large die flake on cheek. *Key identifier*– Die flake on cheek in front of ear.
  Reverse B²a– R in Trust a little weak with triangle on horizontal part. Feather next to eagle's right leg weak from over polishing.

114   II/I 16 • B²a (Doubled R and Stars)   **(178)   I-2   R-4**
  Obverse II/I 16– Slightly doubled LIBERTY. Doubled P, R and B in PLURIBUS. Doubled first six left stars and all right stars. Tops of cotton leaves and bolls slightly doubled and right side of wheat leaves. *Key identifier*– Over polished lower hair.

114A   II/I 16 • B²a (Doubled R and Stars, Clashed Obverse t)   **(178)   I-2   R-5**
  Obverse II/I 16– Clashed die with faint partial incuse t of Trust from reverse showing in right hair vee of lower hair edge. Die over polished in hair above date.
  Reverse B²a– Die over polished with flat spot in middle of eagle's left wing and right wing slightly separated from leg. Small die chip in middle of eagle's breast. Different die than for VAM 114.

115   II/I 17 • B²a (Doubled Date, Tripled Cotton Bolls)   **(194)   I-5   R-5**
  Obverse II/I 17– Doubled I, B, E, T, T and Y in LIBERTY shifted left with R, T and Y having large shifts. Doubled N, U and M in UNUM. Doubled date with 1 and 7 doubled below upper crossbar and both 8's on lower left outside of upper and lower loop. Tripled right edges of cotton bolls and leaves. Doubled right inside of ear. All right and left stars doubled, some with large shifts. *Key identifier*– Tripled cotton bolls. (Also 198)

116(revised) II/I 18 • B²a (Doubled P & 1-8)   **(189)   I-4   R-7**
  Obverse II/I 18– Type II LIBERTY. Doubled E PL,R, B, left stars, 1-4 right stars. 1 doubled at top right and right 8 doubled at lower left and bottom inside and top left outside of lower loop. Die flake near hair line behind eye with die scratch leading to hair. Two tiny die chips at back of jaw-neck junction. (Also 140 which is earlier die state.) *Key identifier*– Bulge at right of P loop and die flake and line behind eye. Die gouge at rim below third left star.
  Reverse B²a– Fairly full feather between eagle's right wing and leg.

116A   II/I 18 • B²a (Doubled P & 1-8, Die Gouge State 1)   **(189)   I-4   R-6**
  Reverse B²a– Slightly polished die with weakened feather between eagle's right wing and leg. Die gouges added to lower and middle arrow heads, single diagonal gouge on top arrow head, diagonal gouge from end of lower arrow head and on left side of DO. Heavy polishing lines from olive branch tip, and around arrow feathers, olive leaves and in tail feathers. Some specimens show heavy clash mark above arrow heads, but no clash letter transfer.

116B(revised) II/I 18 • B²a (Doubled P & 1-8, Die Gouge State 2)   **(180?)   I-4   R-5**
  Reverse B²a– Heavily polished die with most of feather between eagle's right wing and leg removed except for small bit at bottom. Clash marks and gouges/polishing lines removed in fields. Later die states show vertical die scratch added from bottom of lower arrow head and vertical and horizontal polishing lines around olive.

116C(revised) II/I 18 • B²a (Doubled P & 1-8, Die Gouge State 3)   **(180)   I-4   R-5**
  Reverse B²a– Die further lightly polished with tiny bar remaining of feather between eagle's right wing and leg. Die gouges added to right side of wreath bow, top arrow head and back of top arrow head. Heavy polishing lines added at right side of eagle's left leg, diagonal line in upper tail feathers, two lines in lower right tail feathers and diagonal line above arrow feathers. Small vertical die gouge added at top right outside of wreath bow on late die states.

117   II/I 19 • B²k (Tripled Right Star, Engraved Wing Feathers)   **(194)   I-5   R-5**
  Obverse II/I 19– Doubled LIBERTY shifted right. Doubled E, P & E in E PLURIBUS. Doubled 2, 3 & 4 left stars and 1-5 right stars (number 2 is strongly tripled and is one of the best examples of a tripled star). Incomplete band in cap. Front of eye doubled and

front of eyelid tripled. Doubled mouth, upper chin and right inside of ear. Tops of cotton leaves doubled. P in PLURIBUS strongly doubled. 1 in date is doubled on left side of stem. First 8 doubled at top inside of upper loop and bottom inside of lower loop. Second 8 doubled at bottom outside of lower loop. Thread-like die impression at back of neck. *Key identifier*– Alligator eye. (Also 141)

      Reverse B²k– Thin vertical bar with fine lines on surface engraved between eagle's right wing and leg. Vertical bars with fine lines on surface between eagle's right wing and body and one diagonal die gouge. Die over polished with missing feathers in middle of wings.

118   II/I 20 • B²a (Shifted P, Doubled Ear)   **(194)**   **I-4**   **R-6**

      Obverse II/I 20– Type II LIBERTY. Doubled bottom serif of P, top right serif of first U and top inside of R upper loop in PLURIBUS. Doubled 3, 4 & 7 left stars and 1 and 2 right stars. Slightly doubled right inside of ear. *Key identifier*– Die chip below cap fold. (Also 160)

119   II/I 21 • B²a (Shifted E)   **(193)**   **I-3**   **R-4**

      Obverse II/I 21– Slightly doubled LIBERTY shifted left and up. E in motto doubled on top and bottom right outside. All left stars doubled on left side. Ear tripled on right and top inside. *Key identifier*– Tripled ear and double top right corner of E. (Also 161)

120   II/I 31 • B²a (Doubled P)   **(?)**   **I-3**   **R-6**

      Obverse II/I 31– Type II LIBERTY. Doubled bottom serifs of P and left and right sides of R in PLURIBUS. Doubled right side of second U in UNUM. All left stars and first three right stars doubled. Three spikes below front of eyelid. *Key identifier*– Three spikes below eyelid. (Also 168)

121   II/I 38 • B²a (Doubled Motto)   **(194)**   **I-4**   **R-4**

      Obverse II/I 38– LIBERT in LIBERTY slightly doubled on left side. Strongly doubled 1 and 3 right stars. E, P, U and R in E PLURIBUS strongly doubled. 1 in date slightly doubled at top right. *Key identifier*– Tiny die chip front of eye with raised area below eyelid.

122   II/I 36 • B²a (Doubled Motto and First Right Star, Alligator Eye)   **(194)**   **I-4**   **R-4**

      Obverse II/I 36– Type I LIBERTY slightly doubled to left. Type II ear. Motto letters doubled with PLURI particularly strong. All left stars slightly doubled on left side. Doubled 1, 4, 5 & 6 right stars with large shift on number one. Doubled eye front and Phrygian cap top. *Key identifier*– Doubled eye front.

123(revised)   II/I 40 • B²o (Doubled R & U-M, Stars & Eye, Engraved Wing Feather)   **(194)**   **I-5**   **R-7**

      Obverse II/I 40– Slightly doubled LIBERTY shifted left. Doubled top and lower left outside plus bottom right serif missing from R in PLURIBUS. Doubled lower edge of top left serif of U & M in UNUM. Strongly doubled seventh left star and doubled 1-3 right stars. Left 8 doubled at top inside of upper loop and bottom left outside of lower loop. Right 8 slightly doubled at bottom outside of lower loop. Slightly doubled right inside of ear. Spike below eyelid front. Long polishing line in top of Phrygian cap and multiple polishing lines to right of designer's initial, M, and in hair below cap lower rear.

      Reverse B²o– Feather engraved with several vertical bars and fine lines on them between eagle's right wing and leg. Both wings over polished in middle with flat areas. Rough surfaces on parts of eagle and lower wreath.

130   II 1 • B²a (Normal)   **(180, 194)**   **I-1**   **R-4**

      Obverse II 1– Normal type II obverse with no apparent die breaks or doubling except for slight doubling on right side of 7 (hub defect). 180 reed die has slight tripled to quadrupled 2-6 left stars.

      Reverse B²a– Weak feather next to eagle's right leg on some specimens. Multiple dies exist.

130A   II 1 • B²a (Die Gouge IB, Die Chip Lower Cap)   **(180)**   **I-2**   **R-5**

      Obverse II 1– Horizontal die gouge thru lower part of IB. Die chip in lower part of Phrygian cap.

130B   II 1 • B²a (Spike Above Eyelid, Semi-circular Die Gouges Wing)   **(194)**   **I-2**   **R-5**

      Obverse II 1– Short spike above eyelid front. Slight doubling on chin front. Same die as VAM 185A.

      Reverse B²a– Two nearly semi-circular die gouges on eagle's left wing near neck-wing junction. Over polished die at eagle's right wing-leg junction.

130C1(revised)   II 1 • B²a (Weak Nostril)   **(178)**   **I-2**   **R-4**

      Obverse II 1– Die over polished with slightly weak nostril and gaps in lower hair. *Die 1 markers*– Vertical polishing line above back of cap ribbon and vertical polishing line thru vertical base of Y in LIBERTY. Fourth right star has slightly weak left point but not broken off. *Die 2 marker*– Short die polishing line at top right of R in LIBERTY. No polishing line in Y.

      Reverse B²a– Over polished die with flat area in middle of eagle's left wing and weak feather between eagle's right wing bottom and leg. *Die marker*– Horizontal polishing lines to right of wreath bow. Occurs with obverse Dies 1 & 2.

130C2   II 1 • B²a (Weak Nostril, Break Above Cap)   **(?)**   **I-2**   **R-6**

      Obverse II 1– Die crack from R in PLURIBUS thru wheat leaves over to cap fold and to M in UNUM. Tilted field die bread above Phrygian cap.

130C3   II 1 • B²a (Weak Nostril, Breaks at R & Above Cap)   **(?)**   **I-2**   **R-6**

      Obverse II 1– Fine die crack thru U and below R in PLURIBUS with displaced field die break below R.

131(revised)   II 2 • B²a (Normal)   **(178, 179, 180, 194)**   **I-1**   **R-2**

      Obverse II 2– Normal type II obverse with broken point off number 4 right star and slight doubling on right side of 7 (hub defect). Some specimens have small spike above eyelid front. Die 1– X polishing lines at left of top cotton leaf and small raised dot below earlobe. (Also VAM 228-3.)

      Reverse B²a– Feathers weakly struck in middle of eagle's left wing and next to eagle's right leg on some specimens. Multiple dies exist. Die 1– Polishing outlines at top of LLAR.

131A   II 2 • B²a (Die Chip in Hair)   **(194)**   **I-2**   **R-5**

      Obverse II 2– Die chip in hair below BE in LIBERTY on late die states. Thin die scratch in front of die chip down to forehead. Thin long horizontal die scratches from bottom of eye front, eye socket and nostril. Worm-like die scratch thru Y in LIBERTY. Heavy vertical die scratch in space between curls behind neck.

131B   II 2 • B²a (Die Scratch Thru RT)   **(179)**   **I-2**   **R-5**

      Obverse II 2– Heavy diagonal die scratch thru R and top of T in LIBERTY. (Same die as VAM 195A)

131C1   II 2 • B²a (Die Scratch Thru IB)   **(180)**   **I-2**   **R-5**

      Obverse II 2– Heavy diagonal die scratch thru B and bottom of I in LIBERTY. Slightly doubled bottom of PL and left side of R. (Same die as VAM 195.)

131C2   II 2 • B²a (Die Scratch Thru IB, Clashed Obverse n)   (180)   I-2   R-5
     Obverse II 2– Faint partial incuse n next to neck from reverse In on some specimens.
131C3   II 2 • B²a (Die Scratch Thru IB, Clashed Obverse n, Die Break O)   (179)   I-2   R-6
     Reverse B²a– Later die state has die crack at top of STATES OF with break at top right of O and small displaced field at right side of
        second S in STATES.
132(revised)   II 3 • B²a (Missing Nostril)   (179, 180)   I-2   R-4
     Obverse II 3– Same as II 2 but die has been over polished with most of nostril missing. *Die 1 marker*– Curvy die scratch at back of cap
        above ribbon and slightly doubled bottom of E. Different die than VAM 190, but several dies exist.
     Reverse B²a– *Die 1 marker*– Fine horizontal polishing lines in wreath bow.
133(revised)   II 4 • B²a (Doubled Motto)   (194)   I-3   R-4
     Obverse II 4– Same as II 1 but with slightly doubled LIBERTY to left, wheat leaves on right, top of Phrygian cap and E PLURIBUS
        UNUM towards rim and extra metal at top right of P.
     Reverse B²a– Fine raised dots and fine polishing lines on eagle's wings with polished splotches in middle of eagle's left wing.

B²b Reverse with Open o in God

140(revised)   II/I 18 • B²b (Doubled P & 1-8, Partially Open O, Over Polished Wings)   (189)   I-3   R-5
     Obverse II/I 18– Latest die state after use with VAM 116 with fine die crack from 1-2 left stars to 18.
     Reverse B²b– Same as B²a but with hub break which causes open upper part of o in God (this example is only partially open showing
        initial stage of hub break). Die 2– Die over polished with areas of wing feathers and eagle's right wing missing next to leg. Earliest
        die state which was later used with VAM 144.
140A   II/I 18 • B²b (Doubled P & 1-8, Partially Open O, Die Scratches Reverse)   (180)   I-3   R-4
     Obverse II/I 18– Earliest die state before use with VAM 116.
     Reverse B²b– Partial open o in God. Die 1– Vertical die scratches inside both legs, on and below arrow heads, left of wreath bow,
        around top olive leaf cluster and top of inner feathers of eagle's right wing.
141(revised)   II/I 19 • B²i (Tripled Rt. Star, Engraved Wing Feather)   (194)   I-5   R-4
     Reverse B²i– Feather with three vertical bars and fine lines on them engraved between eagle's right wing and leg. Open o in God.
141A   II/I 19 • B²i (Tripled Right Star, Engraved Wing Feather, Die Gouge Wing Tip)   (194)   I-5   R-5
     Reverse B²i– Short shallow diagonal die gouge from upper side of eagle's left wing tip. Scattered light polishing lines in lower fields.
142   II/I 22 • B²b (Doubled 8-8, Tripled 7)   (179)   I-3   R-4
     Obverse II/I 22– Doubled LIBERTY shifted left. Doubled P, R, U, U and M in PLURIBUS UNUM. Doubled top of 878 in date and
        right side of 7 vertical shaft. Lower lip and nostril doubled. (Also 196)
     Reverse B²b– Feather weak in middle of eagle's left wing.
142A   II/I 22 • B²b (Doubled 8-8, Tripled 7, Die Chips Top Reverse)   (179)   I-3   R-6
     Reverse B²b– Die cracks thru tops of ATES OF AMERICA with die chips at top right of S OF and eagle's left wing.
143(revised)   II/I 23 • B²l (Doubled 8, Scratches in Tail Feathers, Engraved Lines Wing Feathers)   (180)   I-3   R-4
     Obverse II/I 23– Doubled LIBERTY shifted left. Doubled P, R and B in PLURIBUS and left U in UNUM. Doubled 2, 6 & 7 left stars
        and top outside of left 8 in date with extra metal inside bottom loop. Short spike below eyelid front.
     Reverse B²l– Extensive polishing die scratches in eagle's tail feathers and in leaves to left and right of wreath bow. Two thin engraved
        bars with fine lines on surface between eagle's right wing and leg. Fine vertical engraving lines on feathers between eagle's right
        wing and body. (Same die as VAM 145.)
144   II/I 24 • B²b (Doubled LIBERTY, Date & Left Stars & Ear)   (180)   I-3   R-4
     Obverse II/I 24– All letters slightly doubled to left in LIBERTY. Slightly doubled top right of E and R has notch at top inside of upper
        loop, and S doubled at bottom of upper and lower serifs in E PLURIBUS. Ear slightly doubled at right inside. Left stars and 1-4
        right stars doubled towards rim and doubled lower hair and lower lip. Date doubled with 1 slightly doubled at top right of left
        bottom crossbar. First 8 and 7 doubled at top outside. Second 8 doubled at left inside of upper loop and top right outside of lower
        loop. Nostril is weak. *Key identifier*– Two small die chips on chin on some specimens and horizontal die scratch in wheat leaves
        and in hair above eye..
     Reverse B²b– Die over polished with areas of wing feathers and eagle's right wing missing next to leg. Partial open o in God.
144A   II/I 24 • B²b (Doubled LIBERTY, Date, Left Stars & Ear, Clashed Obverse n)   (180)   I-3   R-5
     Obverse II/I 24– Clashed die with edge of faint partial incuse n of In from reverse next to Liberty head neck.
144B (Eliminated, likely planchet flaw or gas bubble.)
145   II/I 25 • B²l (Broken N and M, Scratches in Tail Feathers, Engraved Lines Wing Feather)   (180)   I-5   R-4
     Obverse II/I 25– Type II LIBERTY. Doubled P, UR, and S in PLURIBUS. Broken bottom serifs of N and M in UNUM with bottom
        right serif of M completely gone. Doubled 3 left star and 5 right star. 1 and 7 in date doubled on right side with 1 slanted to left.
        Spike below eye front. *Key identifier*– Broken N & M.
     Reverse B²l– (Same die as VAM 143.)
146(revised)   II 2 • B²j (Line in E, R & Y, Doubled Profile, Engraved Wing Feather)   (194)   I-4   R-4
     Obverse II 2– Same as II 2 but with thin diagonal die scratch thru bottom of E, two thru top of R and one thru middle of Y in
        LIBERTY. Slightly doubled Liberty head profile on lips, chin and upper neck.
     Reverse B²j– Feather with single vertical bar and lines on it engraved between eagle's right wing and leg. Middle of eagle's wing over
        polished with missing feathers. Open o in God. *Key identifier*– Engraved wing feather.

B²c Reverse with Broken r Arm in Trust

160   II/I 20 • B²c (Shifted P)   (194)   I-3   R-5
     Reverse B²c– Same as B²a but with hub break which causes die fill on arm or broken r in Trust to produce Tiust. A hub break since
        variety appears on many dies of 1878 P 7TF, 1878 S and 1879 S with reverse of 78.
161   II/I 21 • B²c (Shifted E)   (194)   I-3   R-4
     Reverse B²c– Eagle's left wing slightly over polished in middle.

162 II/I 25 • B²c (Broken N and M)   (180)   I-5   R-5
Reverse B²c– Die over polished with weak feathers in both eagle's wings and next to eagles' right leg.

163 II/I 26 • B²c (Shifted U)   (194)   I-4   R-4
Obverse II/I 26– Slightly doubled LIBERTY (L, I, B & T only) shifted to left. Doubled E, U, R and M in E PLURIBUS UNUM (U and M are particularly large shifts). Doubled 7 left star. Doubled 18 in date with 1 doubled at top right and first 8 doubled at left inside of upper loop. *Key identifier*– Shifted U at upper left serif.
Reverse B²c– Slightly weak feathers in eagle's left wing and next to eagle's right leg. Long die scratch from top of left wreath thru upper tail feathers down to wreath above A. (Also 167.)

164(revised) II/I 27 • B²c (Broken R in PLURIBUS)   (180)   I-2   R-4
Obverse II/I 27– Slightly doubled LIBERTY (I, B and T only) shifted to left. Doubled 1, 3 & 4 right stars. Doubled P, L, R and B in PLURIBUS on right side and UNU letters below upper serifs. *Key identifier*– Vertical line left end of cap ribbon.
Reverse B²c– Very weak feathers next to eagle's right leg from over polished die. Three short horizontal die spikes between eagle's right wing and body.

165(revised) II/I 28 • B²m (Spiked P, Doubled Motto, Engraved Wing Feathers)   (180)   I-3   R-4
Obverse II/I 28– Type II LIBERTY. Doubled E- PLUR and S in E PLURIBUS. Doubled 1-5 left stars and 1-5 right stars. *Key identifier*– Vertical spike top right of P and vertical bar right side of L.
Reverse B²m– Diagonal bars with fine lines on surface engraved between eagle's right wing and body. Weak feathers next to eagle's right leg and middle of wings from over polished die.

166 II/I 29 • B²c (Spiked P, Tripled Eyelid)   (193)   I-4   R-6
Obverse II/I 29– Type II LIBERTY. Doubled E-PLUR of E PLURIBUS. All left stars and first right star doubled. Two bars under front of eyelid. 1 in date slightly doubled at top right. *Key identifier*– Two bars under eyelid front.
Reverse B²c– Weak feathers in middle of eagle's left wing. (Also 187.)

167 II/I 30 • B²c (Spiked P, Shifted U)   (194)   I-3   R-6
Obverse II/I 30– Type II LIBERTY. Doubled bottom left side of P, shifted U and doubled bottom of R in PLURIBUS. Second U in UNUM slightly doubled on right side. *Key identifier*– Beveled left inside of left 8 loops.
Reverse B²c– Weak feathers in middle of eagle's left wing and next to eagle's right leg. No long die scratch from wreath. (Also 163.)

168(revised) II/I 31 • B²n (Doubled P, Engraved Wing Feathers)   (193)   I-3   R-6
Reverse B²n– Vertical and diagonal bars with fine lines on surface engraved between eagle's right wing and body. Thin vertical bar with fine lines on surface engraved between eagle's right wing and leg. Weak feathers in middle of eagle's left wing from over polished die. Also has partially open o in God. (Also 169.)

169 II/I 32 • B²n (Quadrupled Stars)   (193)   I-5   R-4
Obverse II/I 32– Doubled LIBERTY shifted to left. E PLUR-B doubled on left side, S doubled at bottom and UNUM doubled at top. First five left stars quadrupled with 2-4 having very large shifts; 6 and 7 left stars tripled. 1-3 and 5 right stars doubled and 4 right star tripled. Doubled 18-8 with doubled 1 at top right, left 8 at right inside and left outside of upper loop and right 8 at top inside of lower loop. Slight doubling below eyelid front. *Key identifier*– Strongly quadrupled 2-4 left and doubled 3-5 right stars.
Reverse B²n– Also has partially open o in God. Weak feathers in middle of eagle's left wing and next to eagle's right wing. (Also 168.)

170 II/I 33 • B²c (Doubled Date)   (193)   I-5   R-4
Obverse II/I 33– Doubled LIBERTY shifted slightly to left. Doubled E, P, U and R in E PLURIBUS. All left stars slightly doubled at top and all right stars doubled. Date doubled with tops of 1878 showing greatest shift. Slightly doubled ear at right inside. Die chip on lower neck. *Key identifier*– Die chip on neck above M initial.
Reverse B²c– Weak feathers in middle of eagle's left wing and next to eagle's right wing.

170A II/I 33 • B²c (Doubled Date, Die Chips Phrygian Cap)   (193)   I-5   R-6
Obverse II/I 33– Rusted die with raised dots at top of Phrygian cap with two large die chips above right cotton leaf.

171 II/I 34 • B²c (Tripled R, Shifted Liberty Head Back)   (193)   I-5   R-6
Obverse II/I 34– Doubled LIBERTY to left. Doubled P, U and last U, tripled R in PLURIBUS. Doubled 1, 3 and 6 left stars and 1, 3 and 4 right stars. Large doubled shift on back of Liberty head including bottom of cotton balls and right leaves, Phrygian cap upper loop and bottom edge of cap, all of hair below cap and right inside of ear. One of strongest doubled II obverse Liberty head comparable to doubled cotton balls and leaves of 1878 P VAM 44 and 1878 CC VAMs 6, 18 & 24. *Key identifier*– Tripled lower left serif of R. (Also 220)

185 II 1 • B²c (Broken R)   (193)   I-2   R-3
Reverse B²c– Some also with over polished in space between eagle's wing and leg. Multiple dies exist.

185A II 1 • B²c (Spike Above Eyelid)   (193)   I-2   R-5
Obverse II 1– Short spike above eyelid front. Slight doubling on chin front. (Also 130B)

185B II 1 • B²c (Die Scratch Thru I-R)   (193)   I-2   R-5
Obverse II 1– Heavy diagonal die scratch thru lower part of I and another short one at top of R in LIBERTY.

186 II 2 • B²c (Broken R)   (193)   I-2   R-3
Reverse B²c– Some also with open o in God and some with over polished wings. Multiple dies exist.

186A II 2 • B²c (Broken R, Spike Above Eyelid)   (?)   I-2   R-6
Obverse II 2– Short spike above eyelid front. Three vertical polishing lines in mouth and some raised metal at left inside of both 8's upper loop and at top inside of first 8 lower loop.

186B II 2 • B²c (Broken R, Very Over Polished Wing)   (?)   I-2   R-5
Obverse II 2– Some raised die chips in lower loop of first 8.
Reverse B²c– Eagle's left wing very over polished with missing feathers in center and lower inside.

187 II 5 • B²c (Doubled R)   (193)   I-5   R-4
Obverse II 5– Same as II 1 except doubled letters LURIB in PLURIBUS and UN in UNUM. R strongly doubled at top, middle and lower right side. Bottom serif of N doubled strongly at top left. Two spikes below eyelid front.

188 II 6 • B²c (Washed Out L)   (193)   I-4   R-6
Obverse II 6– Same as II 1 except die is polished down so L in LIBERTY is weak and wheat leaf above L is shortened. (Also 223)

189 II 1 • B²g (Added Engraved Wing Feather)   (193)   I-5   R-6
Reverse B²g– Same as B²c with broken r in Trust but with die over polished with original feathers missing on eagle's right wing next to

leg and center of eagle's left wing. Diagonal feather lines engraved in missing feather area next to eagle's right leg with two upper lines bent in middle. Broad line at top of engraved area extending up to middle of wing. First known die of Philadelphia Mint adding wing feathers to 7 tail feather reverse.

B²d-h Reverses with Doubled Motto, Broken D, Missing Feathers, Dbld Legend

190	II 3 • B²d (Missing Nostril, Doubled Motto)	(179)	I-3	R-4

Obverse II 3– Missing nostril from over polished die. Different die than VAM 132.

Reverse B²d– Same as B²a but with doubled God and We to right, eagle's left wing feathers at top and top edge of eagle's right wing. Wings over polished in center. R in Trust not broken.

190A	II 3 • B²d (Missing Nostril, Doubled Motto, Clashed Obverse n)	(179)	I-3	R-5

Obverse II 3– Clashed die with faint partial incuse n of In from reverse next to Liberty head neck.

195	II 2 • B²e (Broken D)	(179)	I-2	R-3

Obverse II 2– Diagonal die scratch line thru B and bottom of I in LIBERTY. Slightly doubled bottom of PL and left side of R. Curved die polishing line to right of right cotton boll. (Same die as VAM 131C)

Reverse B²e– Bottom of D in DOLLAR completely broken. R in Trust not broken.

195A	II 2 • B²e (Broken D)	(179)	I-2	R-3

Obverse II 2– Diagonal die scratch line thru R and top of T in LIBERTY. Several small raised die chips in front of ear. (Same die as VAM 131B, 210A)

Reverse B²e– Same as B²a but with partially broken bottom of D in DOLLAR. Some specimens show die over polished with last three leaves disconnected from olive branch.

196	II/I 22 • B²f (Doubled 878, Missing Feathers)	(179)	I-3	R-4

Reverse B²f– Same as B²a but with die over polished with part of eagle's lower right wing missing next to leg. R in Trust not broken.

196A	II/I 22 • B²f (Doubled 878, Missing Feathers, Clashed Die In & st)	(179)	I-3	R-5

Obverse II/I 22– Strong die clash marks with partial incuse In of In from reverse showing next to Liberty head neck and partial incuse st of Trust from reverse showing in right hair vee of lower hair edge.

197	II 7 • B²f (Doubled UR-BUS UNU, Missing Feathers)	(180, 194)	I-2	R-4

Obverse II 7– Slightly doubled UR-BUS UNU at top inside of letters towards coin center. (Also 134)

Reverse B²f– Feather completely missing next to eagle's right leg. R in Trust not broken. Different die than VAMs 196, 198 & 199-2.

198	II/I 17 • B²f (Doubled Date, Tripled Cotton Bolls, Missing Feathers)	(194)	I-5	R-5

(Same as VAM 199-1)

Reverse B²f– Missing wing feather. R in Trust not broken.

199	II/I 27 • B²f (Broken R in PLURIBUS, Missing Feathers)	(180)	I-2	R-4

(Same as VAM 164)

199-1	II/I 17 • B²f (Doubled Date, Tripled Cotton Bolls, Missing Feathers)	(194)	I-5	R-5

(Same as VAM 198)

199-2 (Eliminated, became VAMs 116B & C.)

134(revised)	II 7 • B²h (Doubled UR-BUS UNU, Reverse Legend)	(180)	I-3	R-5

Obverse II 7– Slightly doubled UR-BUS UNU at top inside of letters and right stars towards coin center. *Die markers*– Fine horizontal polishing line thru top of right wheat leaf and raised dot on top right serif on E. (Also 197)

Reverse B²h– Slightly doubled STATES AMERICA, right star and some leaves in top two clusters of right wreath towards coin center. *Die markers:* Early die state shows only heavy die polishing line looped around olive branch right end and a few above R in DOLLAR and last A in AMERICA. Later die states have added fine isolated die polishing lines above NE D, below tail feathers and arrow heads. R in Trust not broken and o in God not open.

C Reverse 79 (Slanted Arrow Feather)

C¹ Reverse, Rounded Feather Next to Eagle's Right Leg

200(revised)	II/I 39 • C¹a (Broken N and M, Doubled Reverse Legend Letters)	(179, 194)	I-4	R-6

Obverse II/I 39– Serifs of N and M in UNUM broken similar to II/I 25. Type II LIBERTY. First six stars on left and first three stars on right doubled. 1 doubled at top right as a notch. Slightly doubled E P-U-S at top right and first U in UNUM at top and lower right. *Key identifier*– Broken N & M.

Reverse C¹a–Left serif of A in AMERICA almost touches eagle's wing, with bottom of letter serifs slanting down and to left. Inner side of right serif of A is cut off square. Slanted arrow feather at top. Bottom inside feather of eagle's right wing next to leg is rounded and not connected to wing on left. Leaves of right wreath doubled on outside, lower inside of legend letters doubled towards rim and tops of In God We Trust letters doubled. Die chip on D in UNITED. *Die marker*– Small die chip on inside end of fourth outside feather from bottom of eagle's left wing.

201(revised)	II/I 35 • C¹a (Missing Nostril, Doubled Cotton Leaves & Legend Letters)	(179)	I-4	R-6

Reverse C¹a– Die chip on D of DOLLAR. *Die marker*– Shallow horizontal die scratch from right tail feather to olive branch.

202(revised)	III¹1 • C¹a (Lines in Wheat Leaves, Doubled Date & Reverse Legend)	(180)	I-3	R-5

Obverse III¹1– Lines in all wheat leaves, with more detail in cotton boll tops than type II obverse. Thin vertical bars of LIBERTY letters. Complete ribbon line at bottom of Phrygian cap. Date slightly doubled at top inside of upper and lower loops of 8's and left sides of 1 and 7 shafts. All left and right stars doubled towards coin center. Lower hair doubled.

Reverse C¹a– Die chip on D in UNITED. *Die marker*– Two diverging polishing lines in space left of eagle's left leg.

202A	III¹1 • C¹a (Lines in Wheat Leaves, Doubled Date, Clashed Obv n, Rev M)	(180)	I-3	R-5

Obverse III¹1– Clashed die with faint partial incuse n of In from reverse next to Liberty head neck.

Reverse C¹a– Clashed die with faint raised designer's initial M from obverse showing above W in We.

203(revised) III^{1}2 • C^{1}b (Short Wheat Leaf, Doubled Reverse Lettering) (179) I-5 R-6
    Obverse III^{1}2– Same as III^{1}1, but with heavy die polishing at top. Wheat leaf below R is short, well below the R, and contains lines. Wheat grains are well separated, with long wheat leaf between the stalks. Bottom serifs are thin in motto. Bottom of E and R run together in LIBERTY.
    Reverse C^{1}b– Doubled outside of leaves of right wreath, all legend letters towards rim, In God tops and wing tips feathers. Doubling stronger than C^{1}a. No die chip on D in UNITED. *Die marker*– Some horizontal die polishing lines at bottom of eagle's right wing.

203A(rev) III^{1}2 • C^{1}b (Short Wheat Leaf, Dbld Peripheral Letters, Clashed Obv n, W, st, Rev M) (179) I-5 R-7
    Obverse III^{1}2– Strongly clashed die with almost full incuse n of In from reverse next to Liberty head neck, partial incuse W of We from reverse in space between hair locks at right of designer's initial M and partial incuse st of Trust from reverse showing in right hair vee of lower hair edge.
    Reverse C^{1}b– Clashed die with raised designer's initial M from obverse showing above d of God.

C^2 Reverse, Thin Line Next to Eagle's Right Leg

210(revised) II 2 • C^{2}a (Line Through Y, Extra Feather) (194) I-3 R-6
    Obverse II 2– Vertical polishing line through Y in LIBERTY.
    Reverse C^{2}a– Same as C^{1}a except that inner serif of left A in AMERICA is thinner. No doubling of right wreath, legend or motto letters. Bottom feather of eagle's right wing extends to junction of next two feathers, and a thin line is present between eagle's right leg and first wing feather. *Die marker*– Long diagonal die scratches thru eagle's right two tail feathers down to right wreath and another scratch from bottom of arrow feathers to left side of wreath bow.

210A(revised) II 2 • C^{2}a (Line Through R) (179) I-3 R-5
    Obverse II 2– Diagonal line through R and top of T in LIBERTY.
    Reverse C^{2}a– *Die marker*– Small die chip between left two tail feathers.

210B1 II 2 • C^{2}a (Line Through IB) (194) I-3 R-5
    Obverse II 2– *Die markers*– Diagonal line through the middle of I and lower part of B in LIBERTY and curving downwards from B into hair and extending up from I across wheat leaf. Horizontal die scratch on lower lip and tiny die chip at bottom right of nose.
    Reverse C^{2}a– Same as VAM 210A with small die chip between left two tail feathers.

210B2 II 2 • C^{2}a (Line Through IB, Clashed Obverse n & st) (194) I-3 R-6
    Obverse II 2– Raised dots on Liberty head face and neck from rusted die. Heavy die clash marks with partial incuse n of In from reverse next to Liberty head neck and partial incuse st of Trust from reverse showing in right hair vee of lower hair edge.

215 III^{1}1 • C^{2}a (Doubled Date, Extra Feather) (?) I-4 Proof

C^3 Reverse, Square Feather Next to Eagle's Right Leg

Type II & II/I Obverse with C^{3}b Reverse with Doubled Left Reverse

220 II/I 34 • C^{3}b (Tripled R, Shifted Liberty Head Back, Doubled Left Reverse) (176) I-5 R-6
    Reverse C^{3}b– Left serif of A is cut down so it is not flat on top and away from wing. Bottom of serif is not slanting. Bottom feather of eagle's right wing is squared off and raised. Hub doubling of UNITED STATES at bottom inside with left inside strong on U of UNITED, I of In at top, top right edge of eagle's right wing, and left edge of some leaves in left wreath. This is normal reverse design used for most of the Morgan silver dollars series, except for hub doubling which also appears on some 1879 O & S dies.

221-1 II 1 • C^{3}b (Cut Down A, Doubled Left Reverse, Doubled B) (193) I-2 R-3
    Obverse II 1– Die 1– Some specimens show die chip dot on forehead front. Doubled bottom of B in PLURIBUS. Extra metal at top inside of lower loop of left 8 and couple polishing lines at front of eyelid.
    Reverse C^{3}b– Same hub doubling but different die. Several obverse and reverse dies. Die 1– Vertical polishing line in space to left of eagle's right leg.

221-2 II 1 • C^{3}b (Cut Down A, Doubled Left Reverse, Polishing Line Cotton Leaf) (193) I-2 R-3
    Obverse II 1– Die 2– Diagonal polishing line in hair gap behind neck. Vertical polishing line below right cotton leaf.
    Reverse C^{3}b– Same hub doubling but different die. Several obverse and reverse dies. Die 2– Diagonal polishing lines at top of wing-neck gap.

221A II 1 • C^{3}b (Cut Down A, Doubled Left Rev., Denticle Impressions Wreath Bow) (180) I-3 R-6
    Obverse II 1– Short horizontal die scratch thru middle wheat leaf. (Same die as VAM 227-1.)
    Reverse C^{3}b– Four raised dots in a square to left of wreath bow with lateral spacing of denticle spaces.

222 II 2 • C^{3}b (Cut Down A, Doubled Left Reverse) (176, 178, 193) I-2 R-5
    Reverse C^{3}b– Same hub doubling but different die.

222A II 2 • C^{3}b (Cut Down A, Die Chips Mouth) (178) I-2 R-6
    Obverse II 2– Die chips above and below Liberty head lips.

222B II 2 • C^{3}b (Cut Down A, Die Gouges Cotton Boll & Front Wheat Leaf) (176) I-3 R-6
    Obverse II 2– Vertical die gouge at base of left cotton boll and long thin die scratch from side of left boll to right of Y in LIBERTY. Thick die gouge above LI in LIBERTY thru front wheat leaf. (Same die as VAM 228A)

222C II 2 • C^{3}b (Spiked Eye) (194) I-2 R-6
    Obverse II 2– Short spikes above and below eyelid front.

222D II 2 • C^{3}b (Cut Down A, Over Polished Lower Hair) (193) I-2 R-6
    Obverse II 2– Lower hair edge over polished with gaps showing. Left point of fourth right star almost completely missing. *Die marker*– Diagonal polishing line in Phrygian cap fold.
    Reverse C^{3}b– *Die marker*– Several fine die chips at top of wing-neck gap.

Type II Obverse with C³c Reverse with Doubled Lower Reverse

223(revised) II 6 • C³c (Washed Out L, Doubled Lower Reverse)   (194)   I-5   R-5
Reverse C³c– Hub doubling of outside edges of some leaves in left and right wreath, bottom of bow right ribbon, and tops of serifs of A next to star in AMERICA, L– AR in DOLLAR and right star doubled towards rim on fully struck coins with die not excessively polished. Also appears on some 1879 P & O dies. *Die marker*– Double horizontal polishing lines inside wreath bow.

224(revised) II 2 • C³c (Doubled Lower Reverse, 168 Reed Count)   (168)   I-4   R-5
Reverse C³c– Same hub doubling but different die. *Die marker*– Double horizontal polishing lines between eagle's legs on right side.
Edge– Second lowest edge reeding count of 168 of Morgan dollar series.

225(revised) II 2 • C³c (Doubled Lower Reverse)   (179, 193)   I-2   R-5
Obverse II 2– Faint short spike or thin diagonal polishing lines below eyelid front or behind eye on some specimens.
Reverse C³c– Same hub doubling but different die.

225A II 2 • C³c (Doubled Lower Reverse, Denticle Impressions on Reverse)   (193)   I-4   R-5
Obverse II 2– Faint short spike below eyelid front.
Reverse C³c– Four raised dots below middle tail feathers from impressions of outside of denticles. Spacing between them matches denticle spacing. Short horizontal spikes to right of 1 and 2 tail feathers.

226(revised) II 1 • C³c (Doubled Lower Reverse)   (194)   I-3   R-6
Obverse II 1– Some diagonal polishing lines in tops of ERT in LIBERTY. *Die marker*– Thin diagonal die scratch at left end of cap ribbon.
Reverse C³c– Same hub doubling but different die. *Die marker*– Three short horizontal ticks at outside of eagle's left leg.

226A II 1 • C³c (Doubled Lower Reverse, Clashed Obverse n)   (194)   I-3   R-6
Obverse II 1– Clashed die with faint tick of n of In from reverse next to Liberty head neck.

Type II Obverse with C³a Normal Third Reverse

227–1 II 1 • C³a (Normal Second Obverse, Normal Third Reverse, Line Thru O in OF)   (176)   I-3   R-6
Obverse II 1– Short horizontal die scratch thru middle wheat leaf. (Same die as VAM 221A.)
Reverse C³a– Normal C³ reverse without any significant doubling. Long diagonal die polishing line thru O in OF. (Same die as VAM 228B.)

227–2 II 1 • C³a (Normal Second Obverse, Normal Third Reverse, Die Chip on Wreath)   (175)   I-3   R-6
Obverse II 1– Polishing lines at bottom of LIBERTY letters.
Reverse C³a– Die chip on third cluster from bottom of left wreath. Very slight doubling of two leaves at top of left wreath.

228(revised) II 2 • C³a (Broken Fourth Rt. Star, Normal Third Reverse)   (178, 179, 193)   I-2   R-6
Reverse C³a– Heavy horizontal polishing lines thru wreath bow on some specimens. Multiple dies exist.

228-1 II 2 • C³a (Broken 4ᵗʰ Rt. Star, Normal Third Rev., Die Chip Eyelid)   (193)   I-2   R-6
Obverse II 2– Die 1– Tiny die chip at top of eyelid front.
Reverse C³a– Die 1– Horizontal die scratch in space to left of eagle's right leg.

228-2 II 2 • C³a (Broken 4ᵗʰ Rt. Star, Normal Third Rev., X Polishing lines Cotton Leaf)   (193)   I-2   R-6
Obverse II 2– Die 2– X polishing lines at left of top cotton leaf and small raised dot below earlobe. (Also VAMs 131 Die 1 & 228-3.)
Reverse C³a– Die 1– Same as VAM 228-1.

228-3 II 2 • C³a (Broken 4ᵗʰ Rt. Star, Normal Third Rev., X Polishing lines Cotton Leaf)   (?)   I-2   R-6
Obverse II 2– Die 2– X polishing lines at left of top cotton leaf and small raised dot below earlobe. (Also VAMs 131 Die 1 & 228-2.)
Reverse C³a– Die 2– Some diagonal polishing lines between eagle's upper tail feathers and eagle's left leg.

228-4 II 2 • C³a (Broken 4ᵗʰ Rt. Star, Normal Third Rev., Die Chip Lower Neck)   (178)   I-2   R-6
Obverse II 2– Die 3– Small die chip at lower rear of neck. *Die marker*– Long thin horizontal polishing line below right cotton boll.
Reverse C³a– Die 3– Two diagonal polishing lines above top arrow feather.

228-5 II 2 • C³a (Broken 4ᵗʰ Right Star, Normal Third Reverse, Line T Top)   (179)   I-2   R-6
Obverse II 2– Die 4– Short diagonal die scratch line at top inside of T in LIBERTY. *Die marker*– Horizontal die scratch just below rear of Phrygian cap.
Reverse C³a– Die 4– *Die marker*– Roughness at top inside of wreath bow with single short horizontal line at lower left inside.

228-6 II 2 • C³a (Broken 4ᵗʰ Rt. Star, Normal Third Rev., Dot Above E)   (193)   I-2   R-6
Obverse II 2– Die 5– Tiny raised dot above E in LIBERTY. *Die marker*– Single vertical polishing line in hair space above lower right hair vee.
Reverse C³e– Die 5– *Die marker*– Single horizontal polishing line between left bow ribbon and left wreath stem.

228-7 II 2 • C³a (Broken 4ᵗʰ Rt. Star, Normal Third Rev., Doubled Phrygian Cap Top)   (?)   I-2   R-6
Obverse II 2– Die 6– *Die marker*– Slightly doubled top of Phrygian cap top, U-US & UNUM towards rim.
Reverse C³a– Die 6– *Die marker*– Long thin vertical die scratch in middle of eagle's left wing.

228A II 2 • C³a (Die Gouge Cotton Bolls & Front Wheat Leaf)   (176)   I-3   R-6
Obverse II 2– Vertical die gouge at base of left cotton boll and long thin die scratch from left side of left boll to right of Y in LIBERTY. Thick die gouge above LI in LIBERTY thru front wheat leaf. Same die as for VAM 222B with point broken on fourth right star.

228B II 2 • C³a (Polishing Line Thru O in OF)   (176)   I-2   R-6
Obverse II 2– *Die marker*– Three vertical polishing lines at middle outside of ear.
Reverse C³a– Long diagonal die polishing line thru O in OF. (Same die as VAM 227.) *Die marker*– Long diagonal polishing line thru lower two berries in first left cluster of left wreath.

229.1 II 8 • C³a (Doubled Top Obverse)   (193)   I-2   R-5
Obverse II 8– Slightly doubled top of Phrygian cap, right wheat leaf, top of left two cotton leaves, LIBERTY on left side and band front, hair front and US UNUM towards rim.

Type II Obverse with C³d Doubled Right Reverse

229   II 2 • C³d (Doubled Right Wreath & AMERICA)   (176)   I-3   R-6

    Obverse II 2– Die chip at top of forehead and fourth right star point is broken.

    Reverse C³d– Some doubled leaves in each cluster of right wreath and bottom inside of AMERICA letters towards rim.

Type III² Obverse with C³ Reverse

230   III²1 • C³a (Normal)   (194)   I-2   R-4

    Obverse III²1– Long wheat leaf below R, close to R, with weak lines. Short wheat leaf between wheat stalks. Thicker bottoms serifs and motto letters. LIBERTY letters are thinner, with shorter serifs on B and R. This is the normal obverse design for most of the Morgan silver dollar series.

230-1   III²1 • C³a (Normal)   (?)   I-2   R-5

    Obverse III²1– *Die marker–* Vertical polishing line thru eye lid front.

    Reverse C³a– *Die marker–* Polishing lines left of eagle's left leg.

230-2   III²1 • C³a (Normal)   (?)   I-2   R-5

    Obverse III²1– *Die marker–* Lines above eyelid front, horizontal line thru bottom of nostril.

    Reverse C³a-- *Die marker–* Short curved line left inside of wreath bow.

230-3   III²1 • C³a (Normal)   (194)   I-2   R-5

    Obverse III²1-- *Die marker–* Polishing line between cotton bolls.

    Reverse C³a-- *Die marker–* Three horizontal polishing lines right of wreath ribbon.

231(revised) III²2 • C³c (Tripled Stars, Doubled Lower Reverse)   (193)   I-2   R-5

    Obverse III²2– Slightly tripled left and right stars, date and all letters towards rim. *Die marker–* Vertical thin polishing lines below eyelid front and tiny die chip on nose above nostril.

    Reverse C³c– Same hub doubling but different die. *Die marker–* Three fine polishing lines above lower right ribbon.

232(revised) III²3 • C³b (Doubled Left Stars, Doubled Left Reverse)   (193)   I-2   R-5

    Obverse III²3– Left stars slightly doubled towards rim, right stars sextupled towards rim, tops of E PLURIBUS UNUM slightly doubled towards rim with both U's of PLURIBUS doubled at bottom inside. Top of cap and right edge of top wheat leaf slightly doubled. Tiny raised dot at back of cheek below ear on some specimens.

    Reverse C³b– Same hub doubling but different die. *Die marker–* Diagonal die scratch from top of right end of olive branch.

PHOTOGRAPHS OF 1878 P 7TF B¹ LONG NOCK VARIETIES

VAM 70 I²12 Doubled Motto Letters

VAM 70 Disconnected Leaves

VAM 70 Die marker– Curved Polishing Line Bow

VAM 79 II/I 35 Doubled Cotton Leaves

VAM 79 II/I 35 Weak Nostril

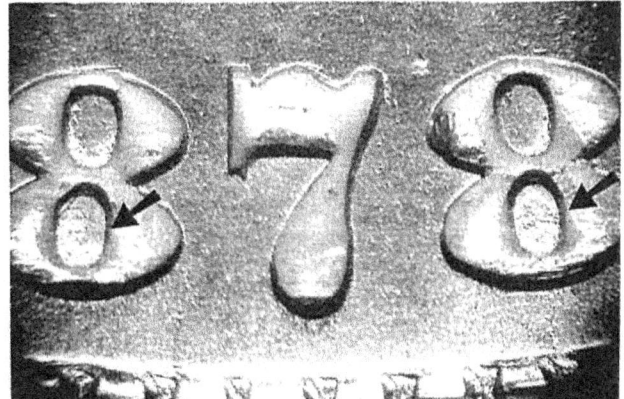

VAM 79 II/I 35 Metal in 8's

VAM 79 Disconnected Olive Branch Leaves

VAM 79 Die Chip Rt. Wreath Top

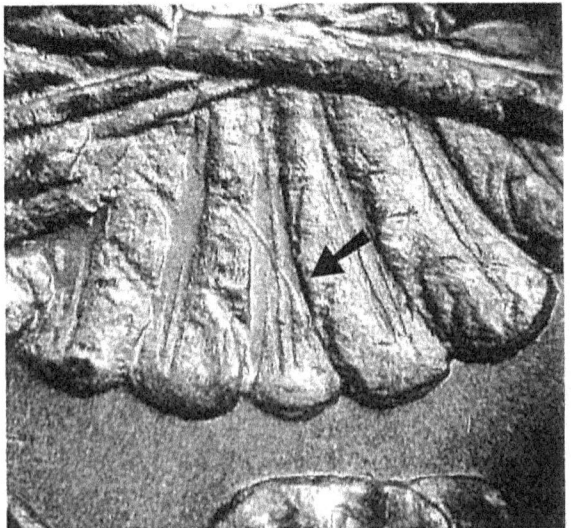

VAM 79 Die marker– Vertical Polishing Line TF

VAM 80 II/I 6 Lines in LIB

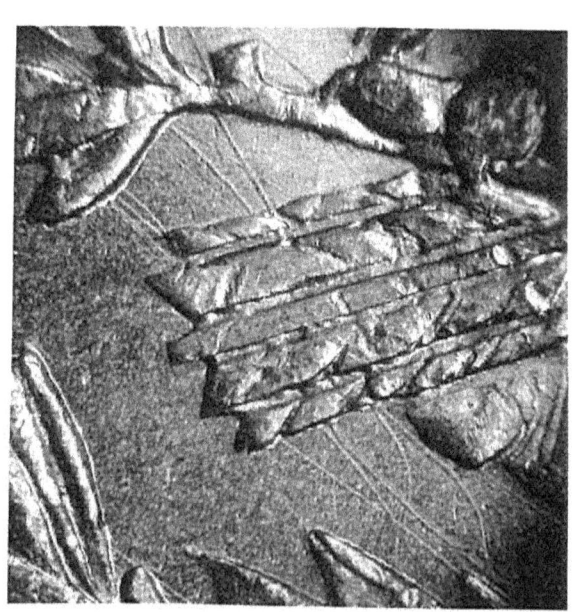

VAM 80 Polishing Lines Tail & Arrow Feathers

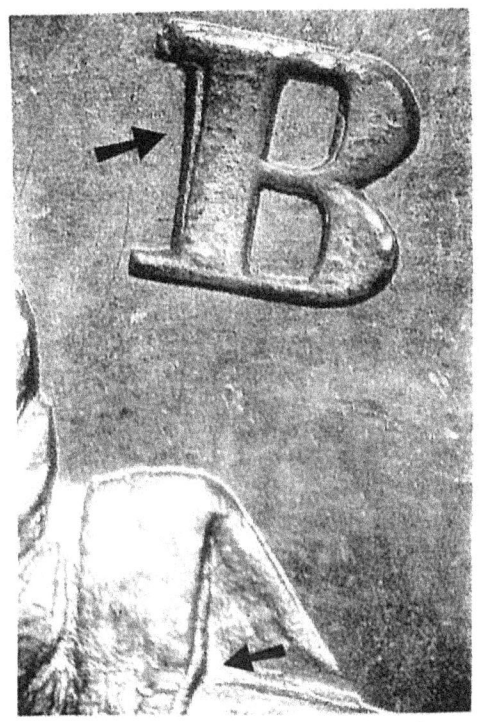

VAM 80 II/I 6 Doubled B & Leaf

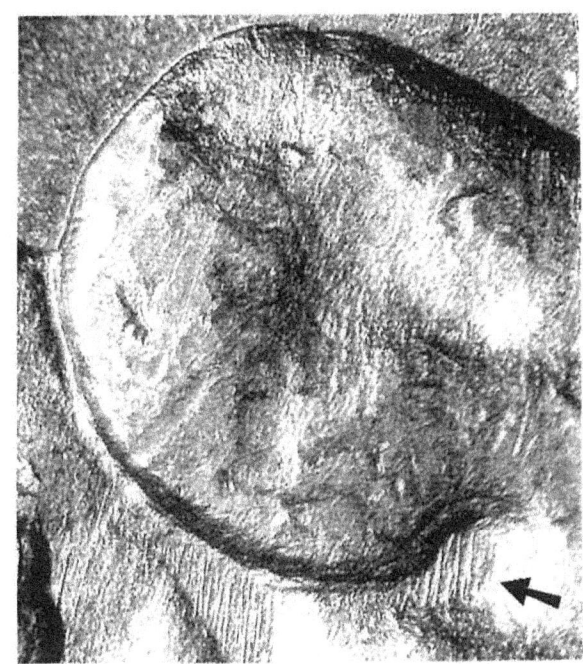

VAM 80 II/I 6 Doubled Cap Fold

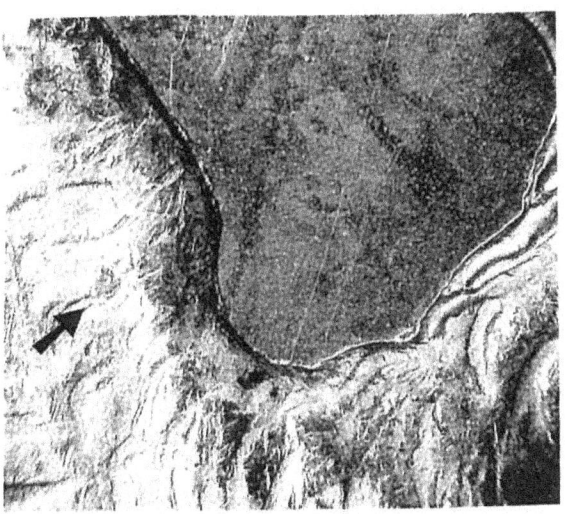

VAM 80 Die Chip Wing Top

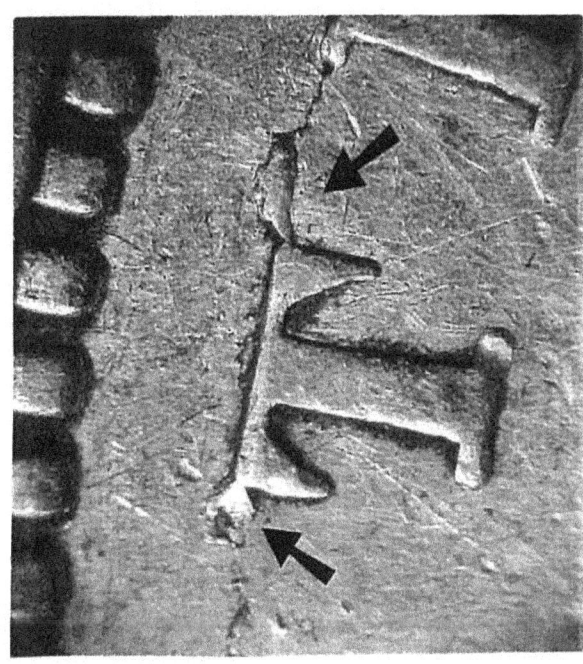

VAM 80A Die Breaks T

VAM 80 Disconnected Leaves

VAM 81 II/I 7 Doubled 1-2 Left Stars

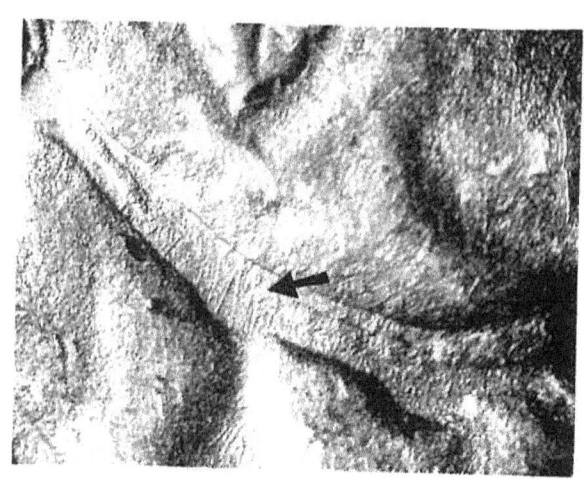

VAM 81 II/I 7
Lines in Ribbon

VAM 81 II/I 7 Spiked P

VAM 81 II/I 7 Doubled Date

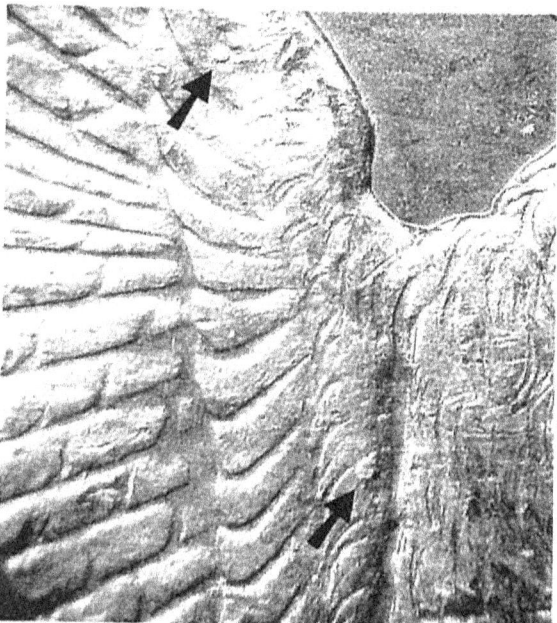

VAM 81 Die Chips on Wing

VAM 82 II/I 10 Die Chip Cap

VAM 82 II/I 10 Doubled 8-8

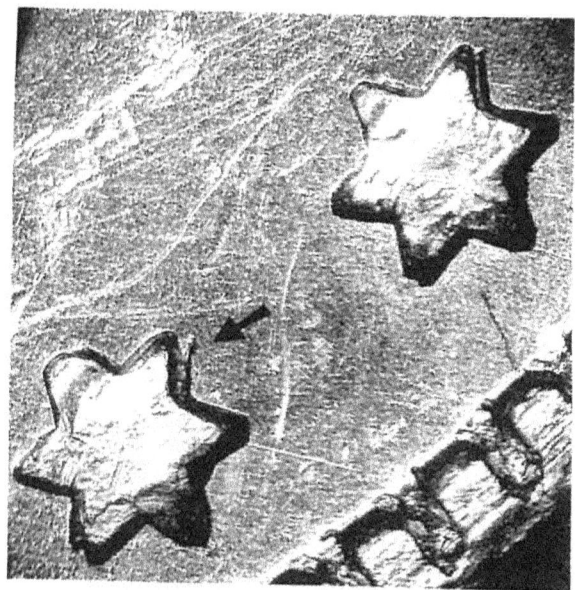

VAM 82 II/I 10 Doubled 1-2 Rt. Stars

VAM 83 II/I 11 Doubled URI

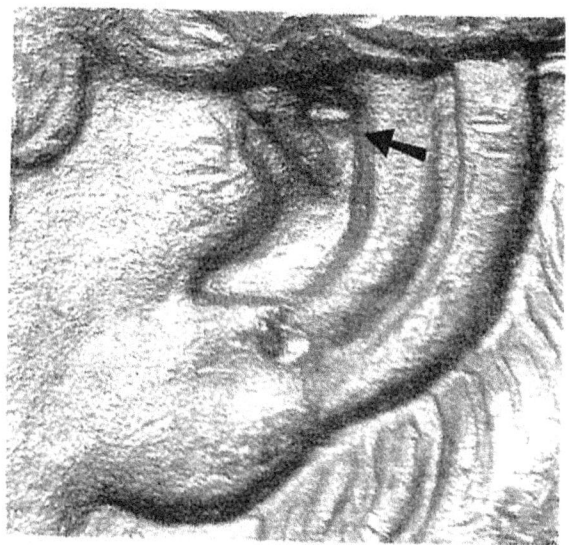

VAM 83 II/I 11 Spike in Ear

VAM 83 II/I 11 Doubled 18

VAM 83 Die marker– Die Scratch Wing Bottom

VAM 83 Over Polished Wing Middle

VAM 84 II/I 12 Dash Below 8

VAM 84 II/I 12 Over Polished L & Leaf

VAM 84A II/I 12 Clashed n

VAM 84 Partially Broken D

VAM 84A Partial Clashed E

VAM 84A Clashed M

VAM 84A Die Chip Wreath

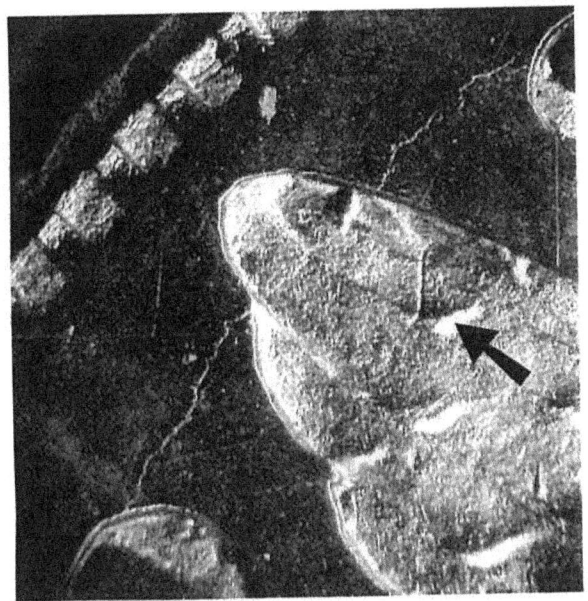

VAM 85 Vertical Thread-Like Die Impression

VAM 85 "7" on A of STATES

VAM 85 Disconnected Olive Leaves

VAM 85 Die Chips & Thread-Like Die Impression

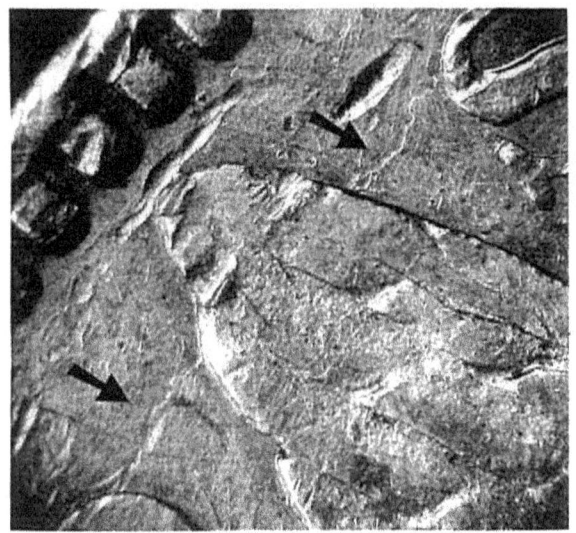

VAM 86 Die Cracks Wing Tip

VAM 86 Short Die Scratches Wing

VAM 86 Disconnected Olive Branch Leaves

VAM 86 Short Die Scratches Eagle's Leg

PHOTOGRAPHS OF 1878 P 7TF B² SHORT NOCK VARIETIES

VAM 100 I¹10 Doubled Motto Letters

VAM 100 I¹10 Doubled 18

VAM 100-1 Die Impression Line

VAM 100-1 Die Scratch A

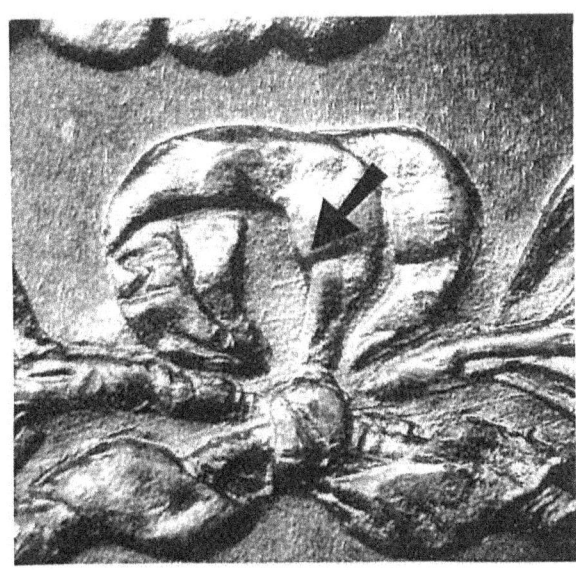

VAM 100-1 Lines in Wreath Bow

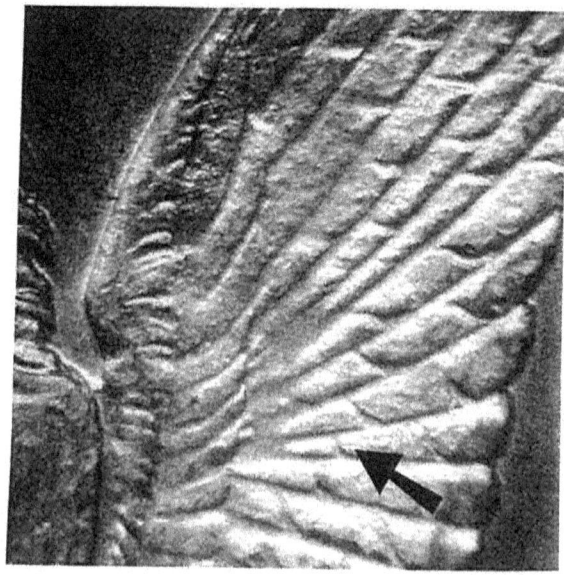

VAM 100-2 Over Polished Wing Middle

VAM 100-2 Lines in Eagle's Rt. Wing

VAM 100-2 Line in Eagle's Left Wing

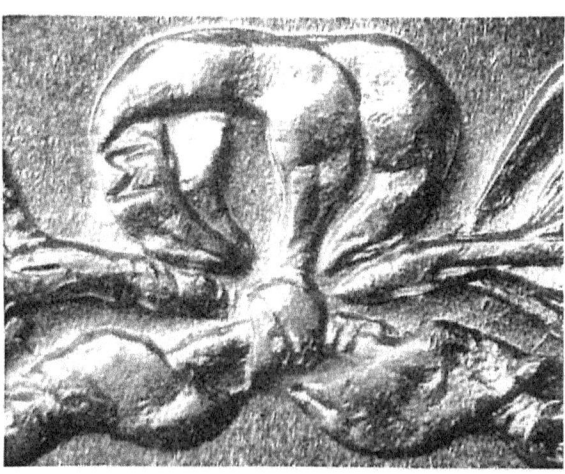

VAM 100-2 Clear Wreath Bow

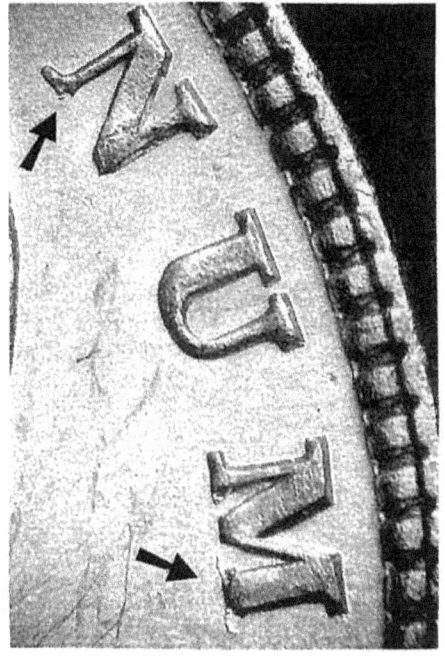

VAM 110 II/I 8 Broken N & M

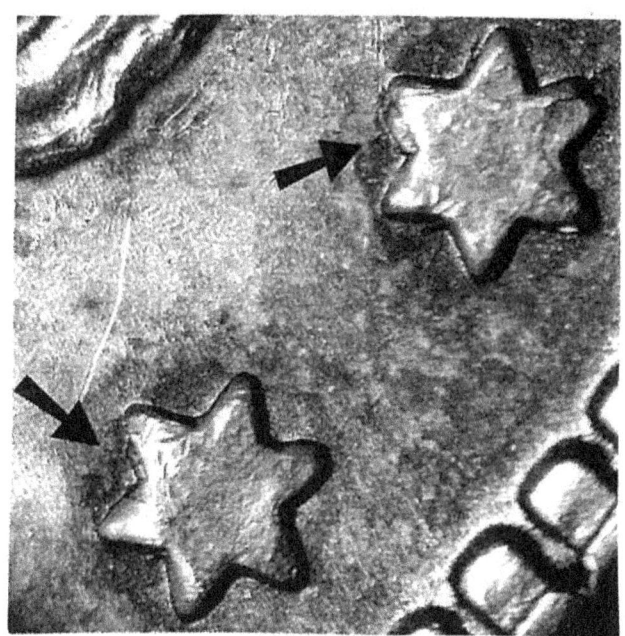

VAM 110 II/I 8 Doubled Rt. Stars

VAM 110 II/I 8 Doubled 18

VAM 110 II/I 8 Doubled 78

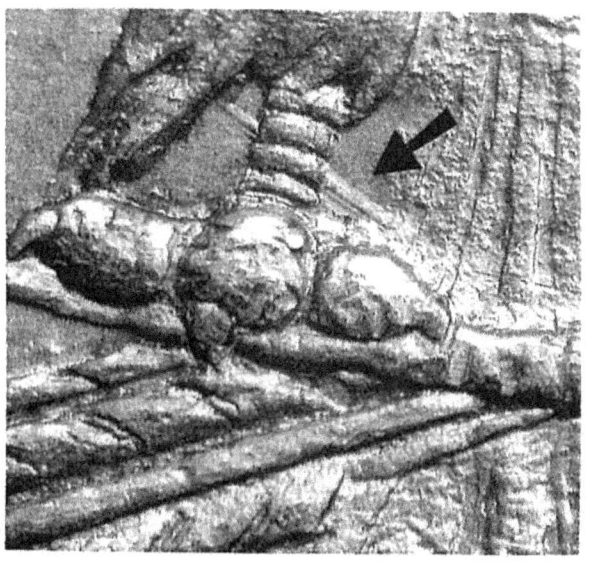

VAM 110 Die Gouge Leg

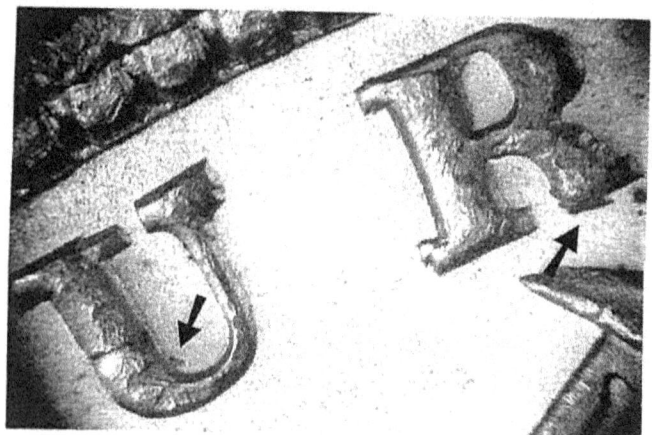

VAM 111 II/I 13 Dropped R

VAM 111 II/I 13 Die Scratch Leaf

VAM 112 II/I 14 Die Scratches Leaves

VAM 112 II/I 14 Bar in B

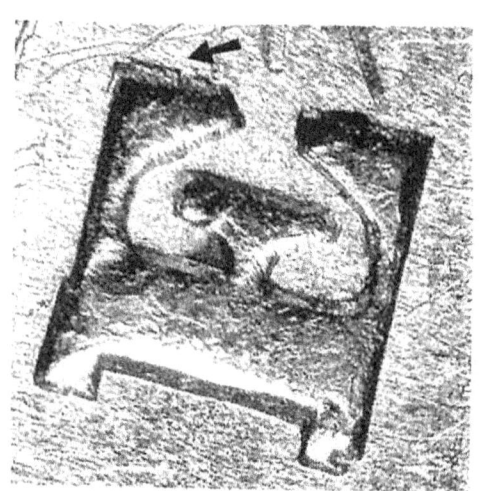

VAM 112 II/I 14 Doubled E

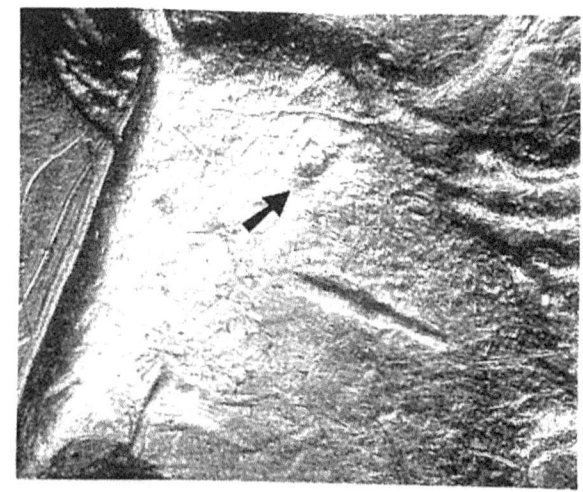

VAM 112 II/I 14 Die Chip Forehead

VAM 112 II/I 14 Doubled 1

VAM 112A Clashed G

VAM 113 II/I 15 Die Flake on Cheek

VAM 113 II/I 15 Doubled 8-8

VAM 114 II/I 16 Over Polished Lower Hair

VAM 114 II/I 16 Doubled R

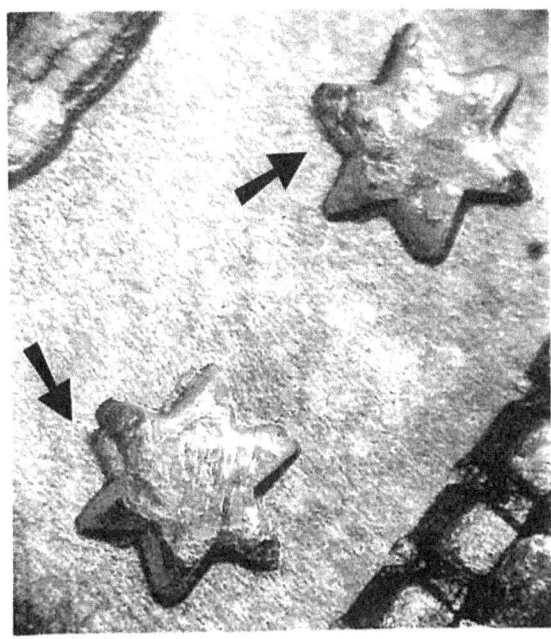

VAM 114 II/I 16 Doubled Stars

VAM 114A II/I 16 Clashed t

VAM 114A Die Chip

VAM 115 II/I 17 Doubled Date & Stars

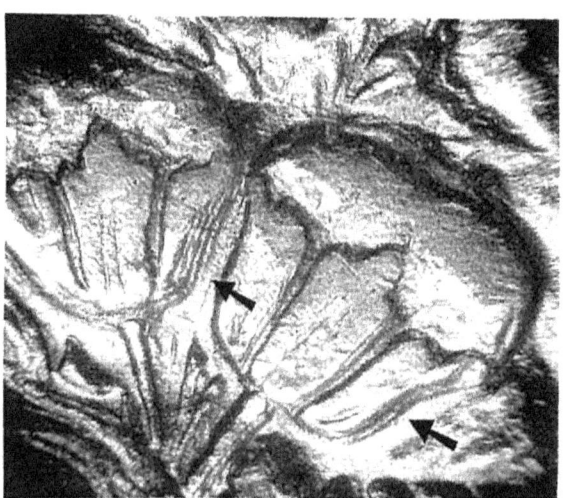

VAM 115 II/I 17 Tripled Cotton Bolls

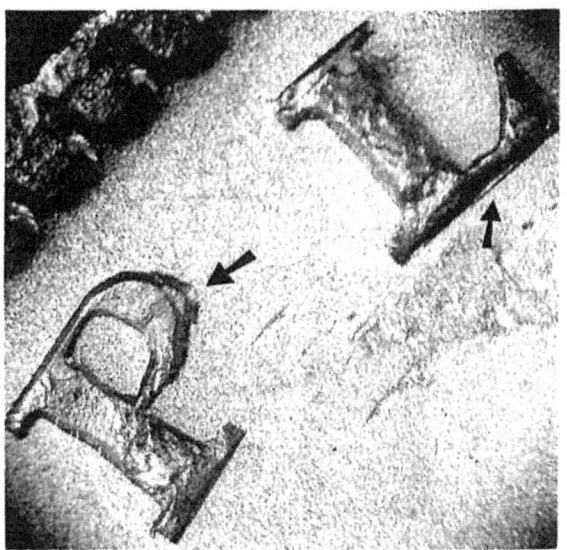

VAM 116 II/I 18 Doubled PL

VAM 116 II/I 18 Doubled R

VAM 116 Die Gouge Third Left Star

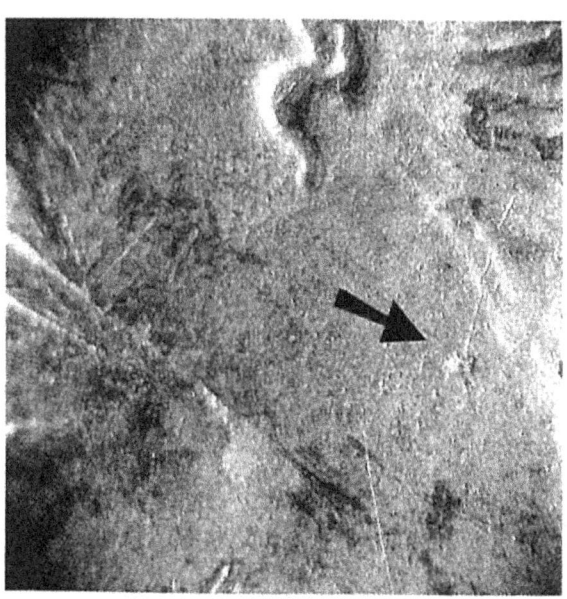

VAM 116 II/I 18 Die Chip & Line

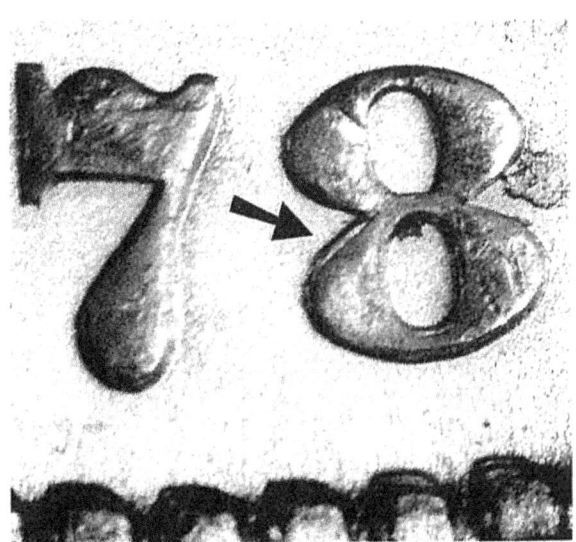

VAM 116 II/I 18 Doubled 8

VAM 116 II/I 18 Two Die Chips

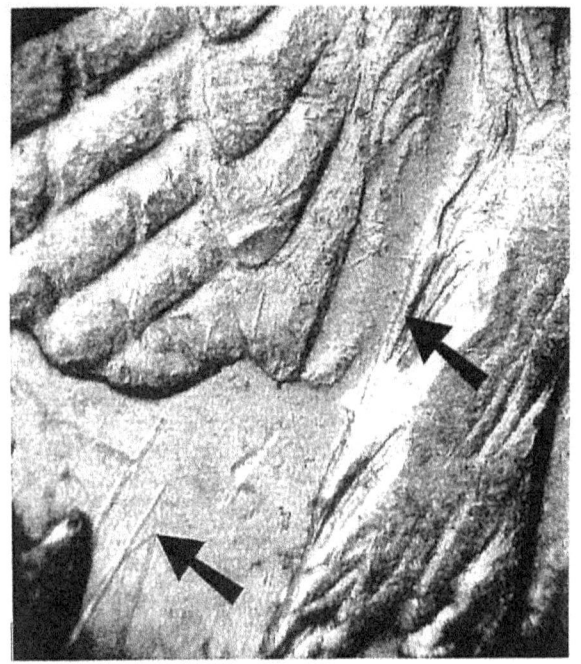

VAM 116A Weakened Feather

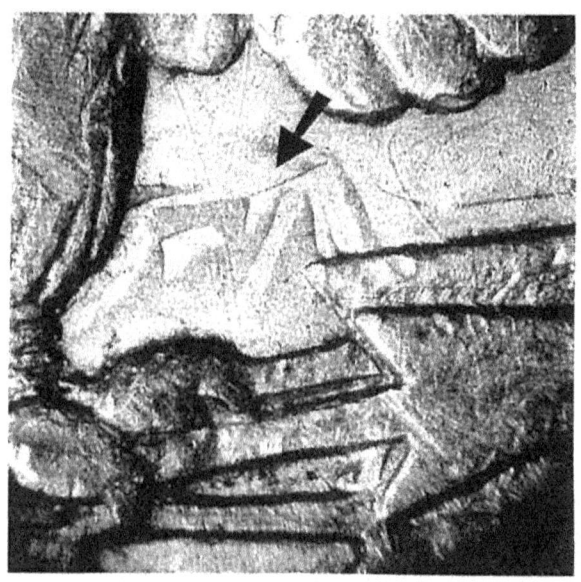

VAM 116A Die Clash Mark

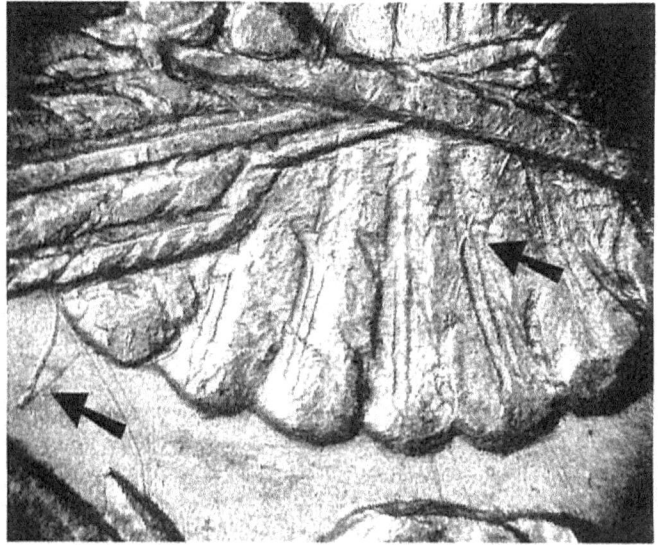

VAM 116A Polishing Lines in Tail Feathers

VAM 116A Gouges Arrow Head

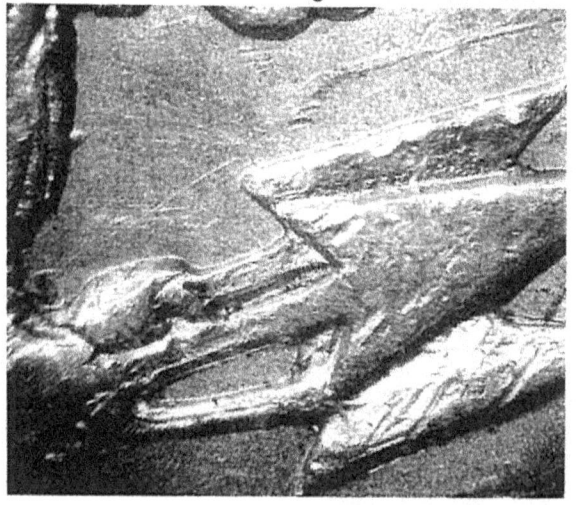

VAM 116B Clash Mark Removed

VAM 116A Gouges in DO

VAM 116B Polished Feather

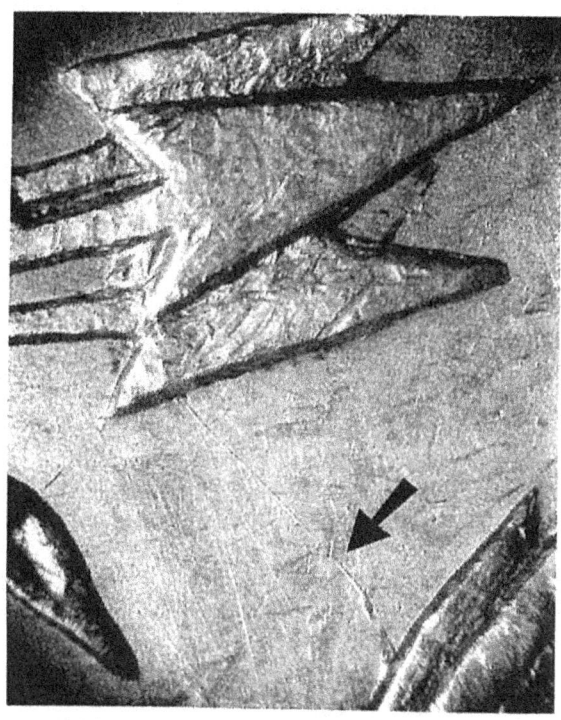

VAM 116B Die Scratch Below Arrow Head

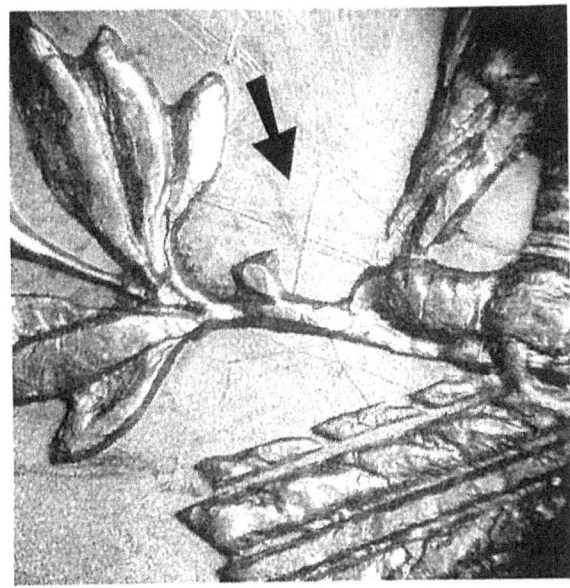

VAM 116B Polishing Lines Above Olive

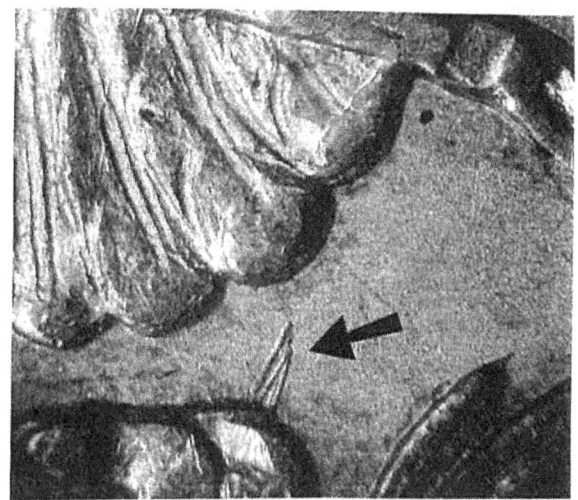

VAM 116C Die Gouge Wreath Bow Top

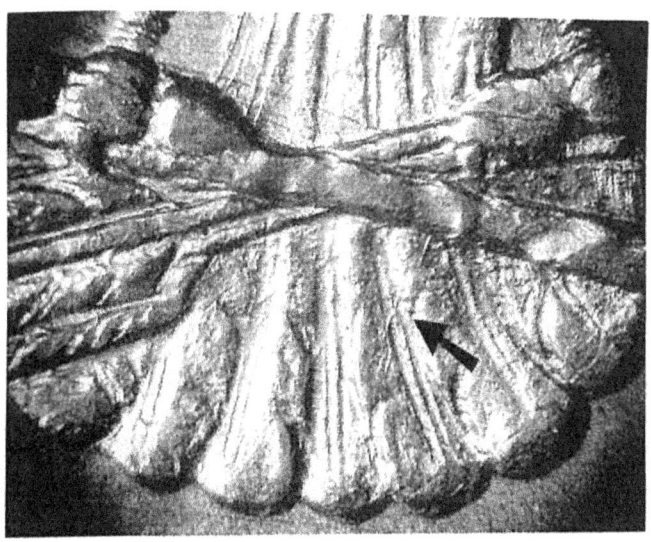

VAM 116B Polishing Lines

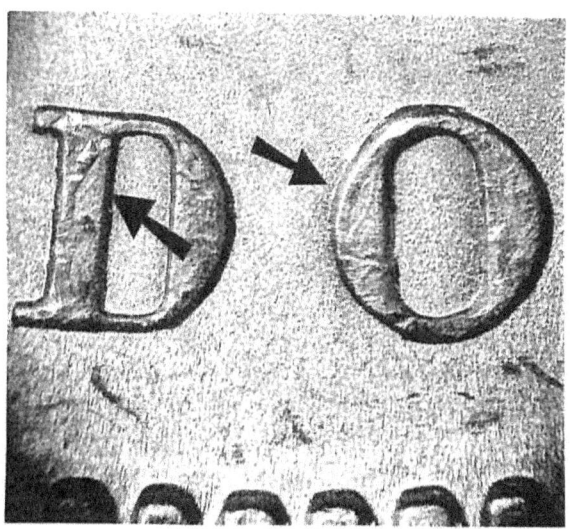

VAM 116C Die Gouges DO

VAM 116C Polished Feather

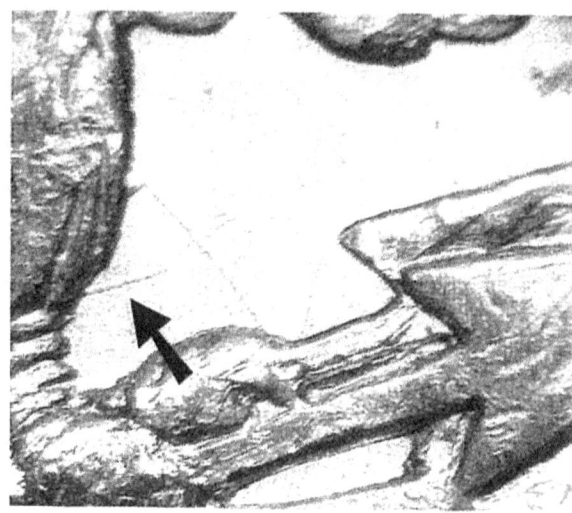

VAM 116C Polishing Line at Leg

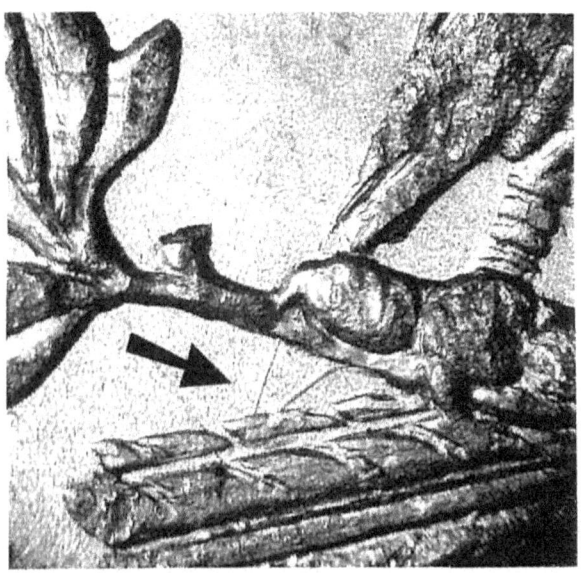

VAM 116C Polishing Lines Above Arrow Feathers

VAM 116C Gouges Top Arrow Head

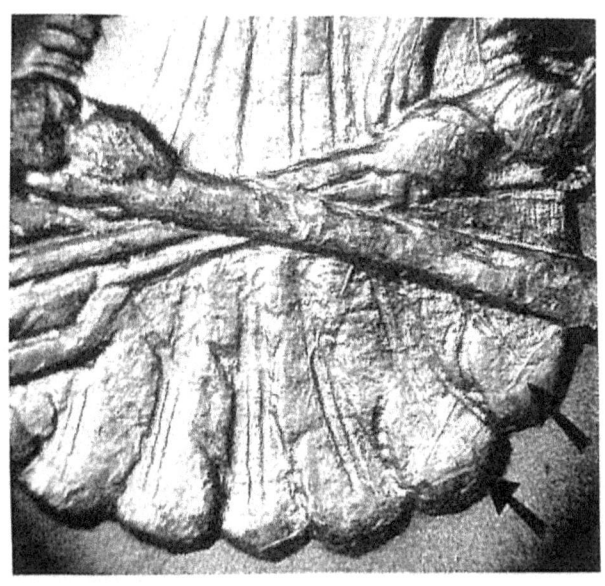

VAM 116C Added Polishing Lines

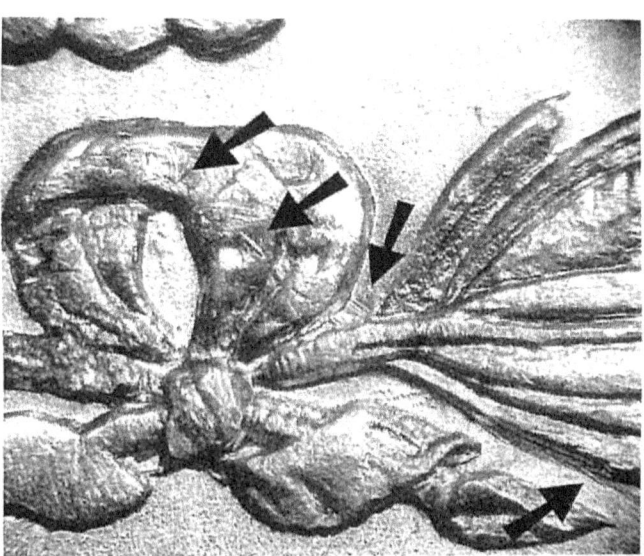

VAM 116C Gouge Wreath Bow

VAM 117 II/I 19 Doubled P

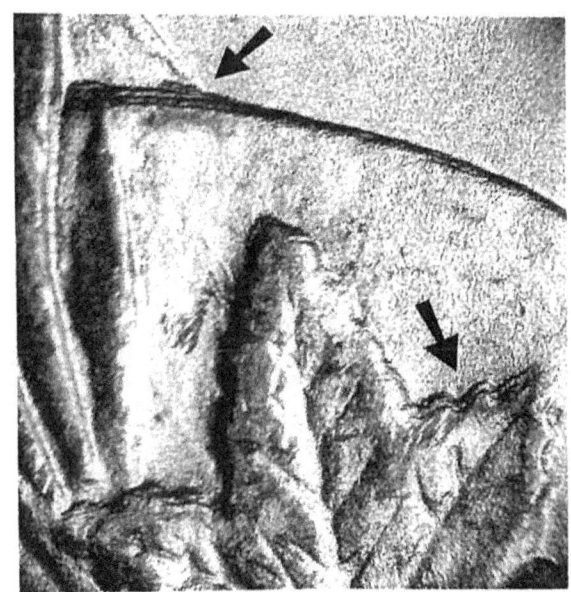

VAM 117 II/I 19 Doubled Cotton Leaves

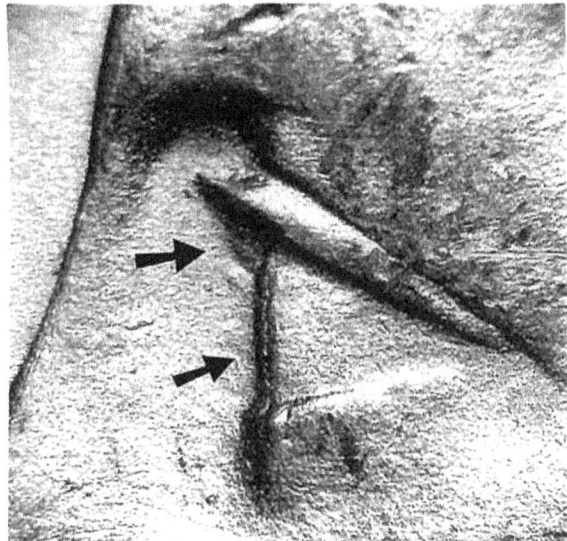

VAM 117 II/I 19 Doubled eye, Tripled Eyelid

VAM 117 II/I 19 Tripled Second Rt. Star

VAM 117 Engraved Vertical Bars

VAM 117 Engraved Vertical Bar

VAM 118 II/I 20
Shifted P

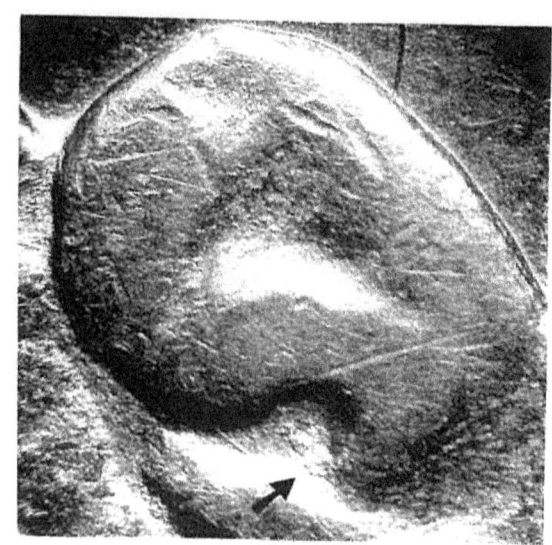

VAM 118 II/I 20 Die Chip Cap Fold

VAM 119 II/I 21
Shifted E

VAM 119 II/I 21 Tripled Ear

VAM 120 II/I 31 Doubled R

VAM 120 II/I 31 Doubled P

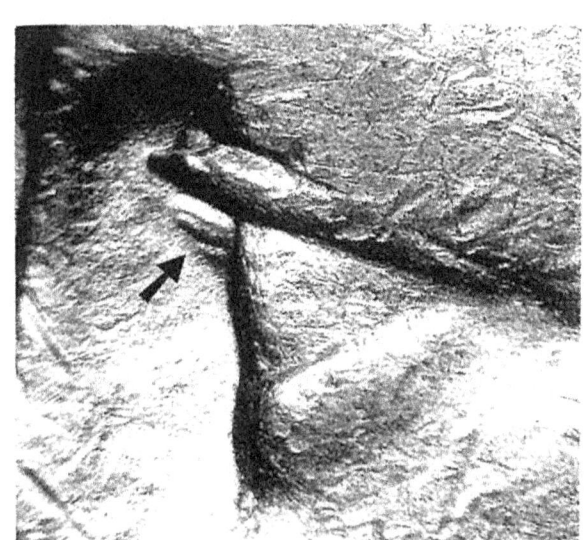

VAM 120 II/I 31 Spikes Below Eyelid

VAM 121 II/I 38 Doubled P

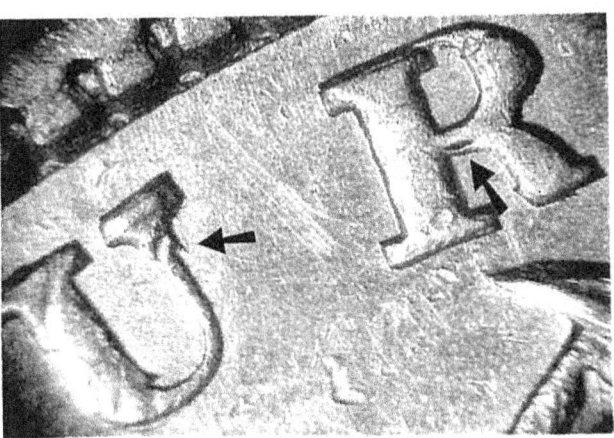

VAM 121 II/I 38 Doubled UR

VAM 121 II/I 38 Die Chip Eye Front

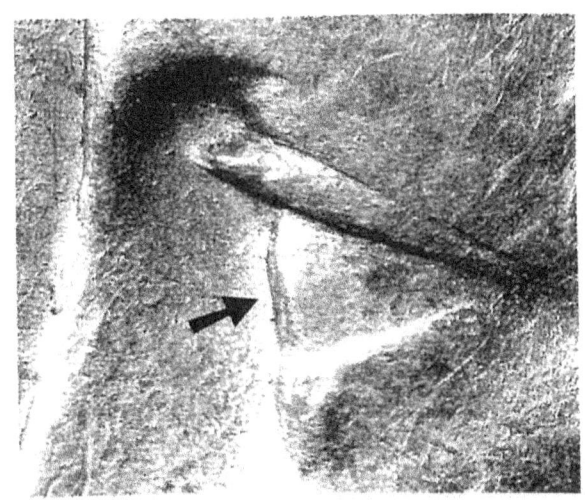

VAM 122 II/I 36 Doubled Eye Front

VAM 122 II/I 36 Doubled Motto

VAM 122 II/I 36 Doubled Rt. Star

VAM 123 II/I 40 Doubled Seventh Left Star

VAM 123 II/I 40 Doubled R

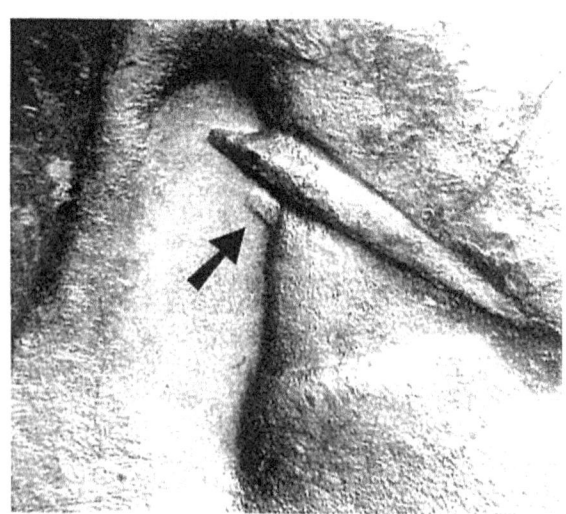

VAM 123 II/I 40 Spiked Eye

VAM 123 II/I 40 Line in Cap

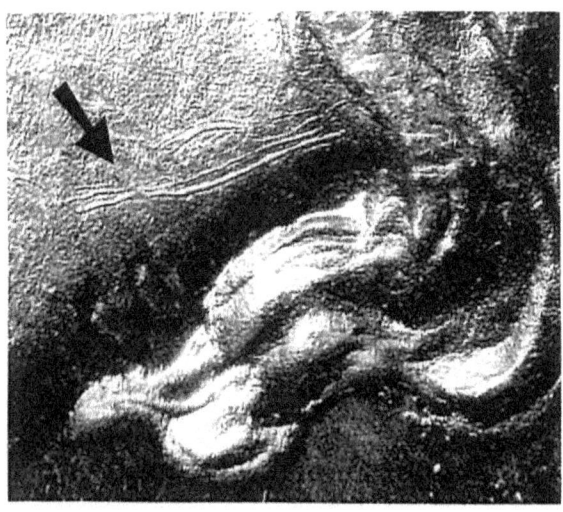

VAM 123 II/I 40 Lines Rt. of M

VAM 123 II/I 40 Lines in Hair

VAM 123 II/I 40 Doubled U

VAM 123 II/I 40 Doubled M

VAM 123 II/I 40 Doubled 8-8

VAM 123 II/I 40 Doubled 1-3 Rt. Stars

VAM 123 Engraved Wing Feather

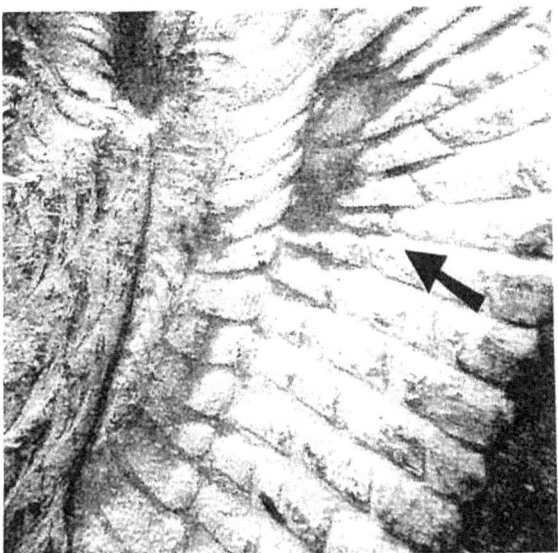

VAM 123 Over Polished Wing

VAM 130A Die Gouge IB

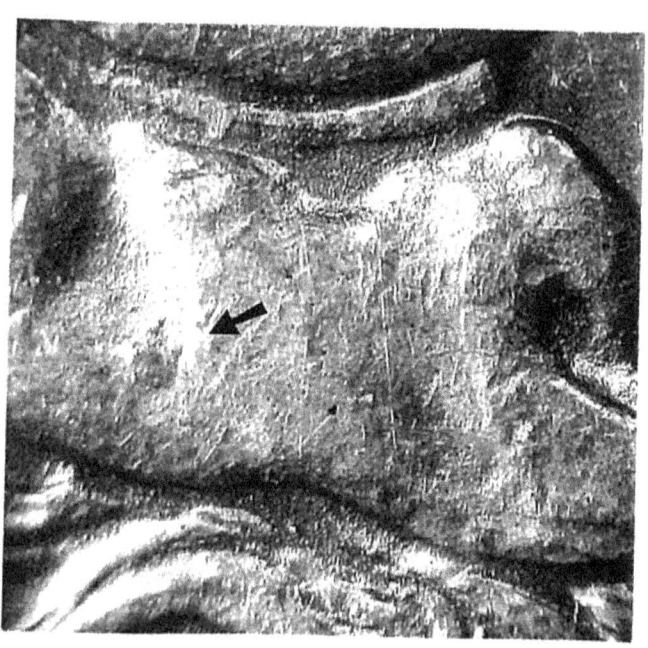

VAM 130A Die Chip Lower Cap

VAM 130B Spike Eyelid

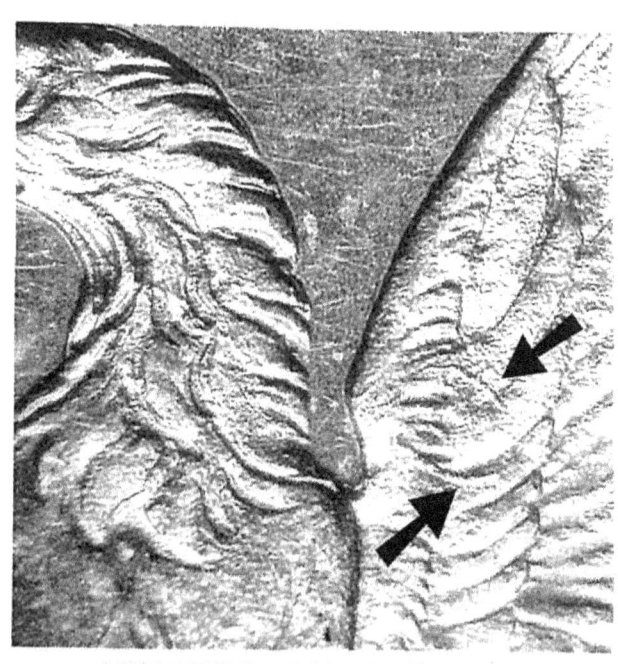

VAM 130B Semi-Circular Gouges

VAM 130C1 Polishing Line in Y

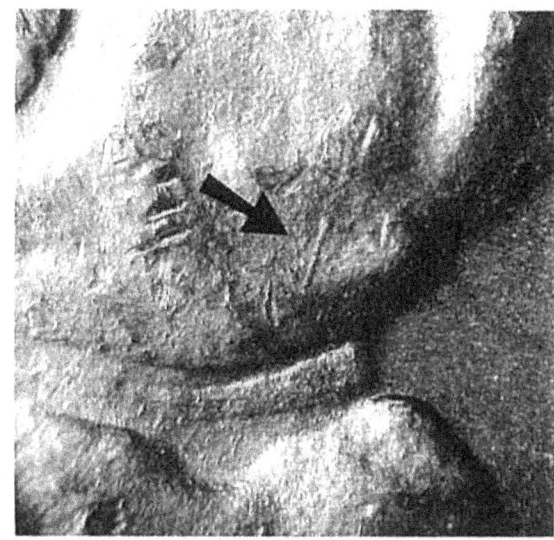

VAM 130C1 Die Scratch Above Cap Ribbon

VAM 130C1 Lines at Wreath Bow

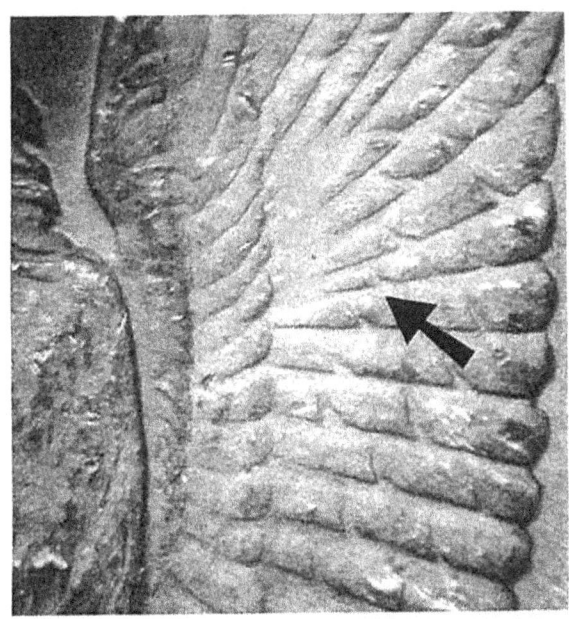

VAM 130C1 Over Polished Wing Middle

VAM 130C2 Die Break Above Cap

VAM 130C1 Die 2 Polishing Line R

VAM 130C3 Die Break R

VAM 131 Die 1– Dot Below Earlobe

VAM 131 Die 1– X Polishing Lines

VAM 131 Die 1– Polishing Outlines LLAR

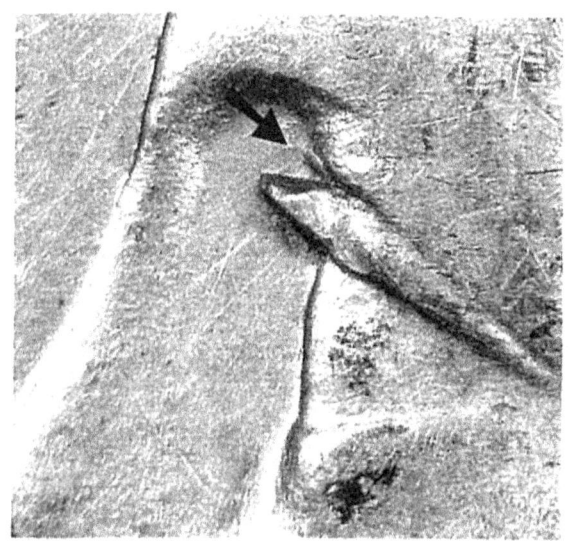

VAM 131 Spike Above Eyelid

VAM 131B Line RT

VAM 131A Die Chip & Line Hair

VAM 131C1 Scratch Thru IB

VAM 131A Die Scratches Eye Front

VAM 131C1 Doubled PL

VAM 131C1 Doubled R

VAM 131C3 Die Breaks O & S

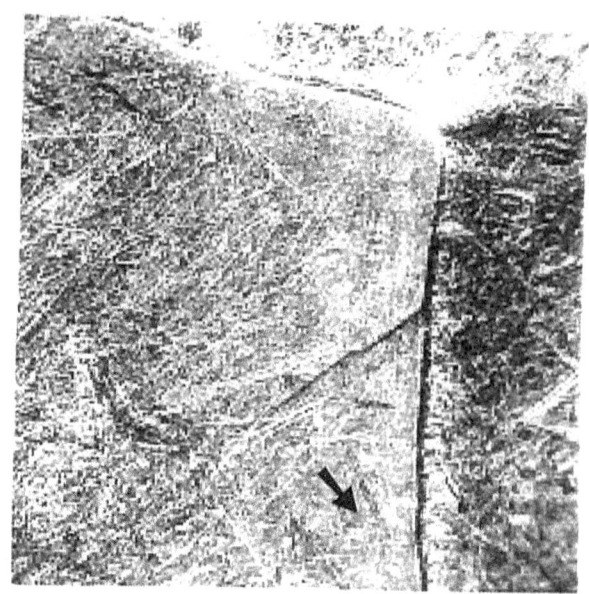

VAM 131C2 Clashed n

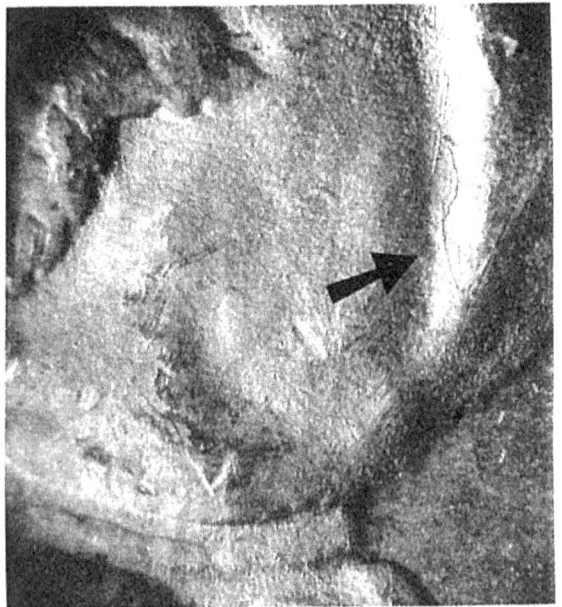

VAM 132 Die 1 Curvy Die Scratch

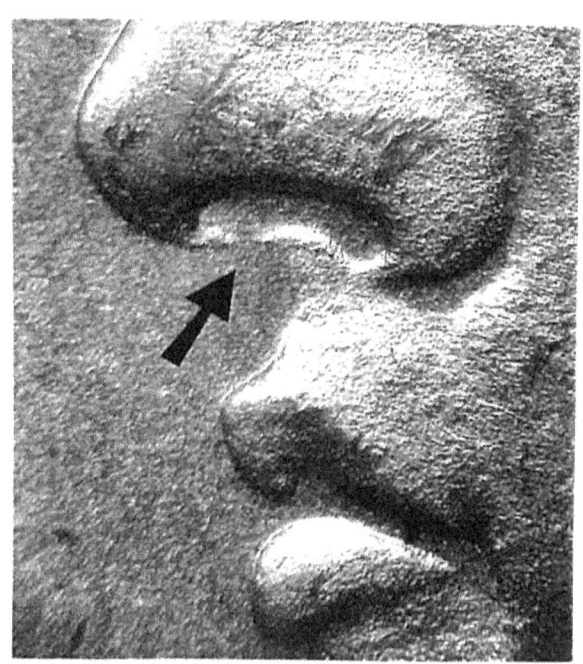

VAM 132 Partial Missing Nostril

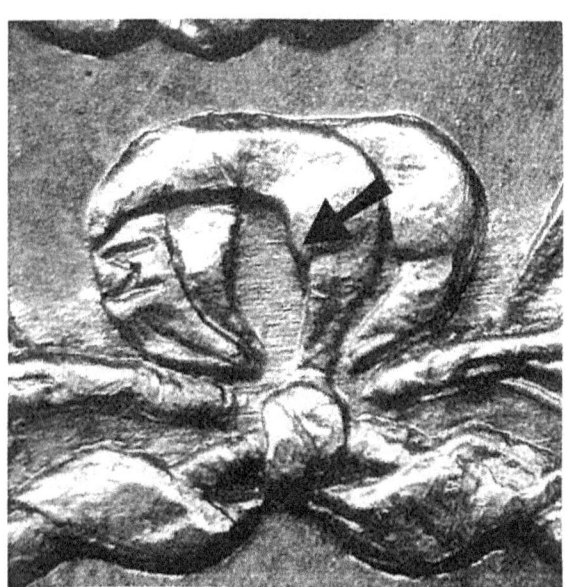

VAM 132 Die 1 Polishing Lines Bow

VAM 133 Doubled Motto

VAM 133 Polished Wing Splotches

VAM 133 Doubled PL

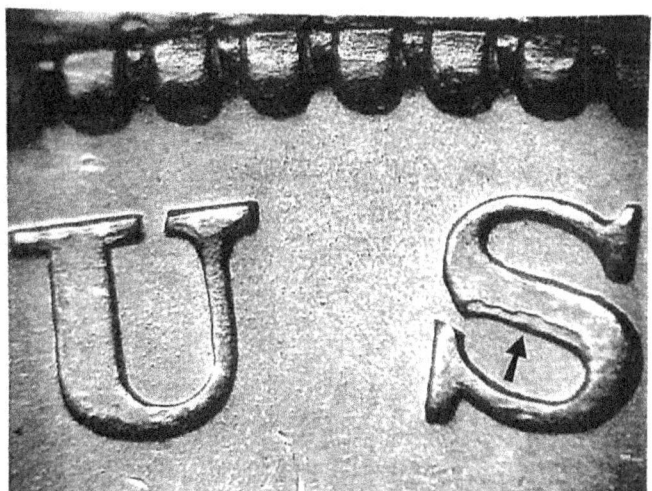

VAM 134 II 7 Doubled UR-BUS UNU

VAM 134 II 7 Line Rt. Wheat Leaf

VAM 134 B²h Polishing Lines

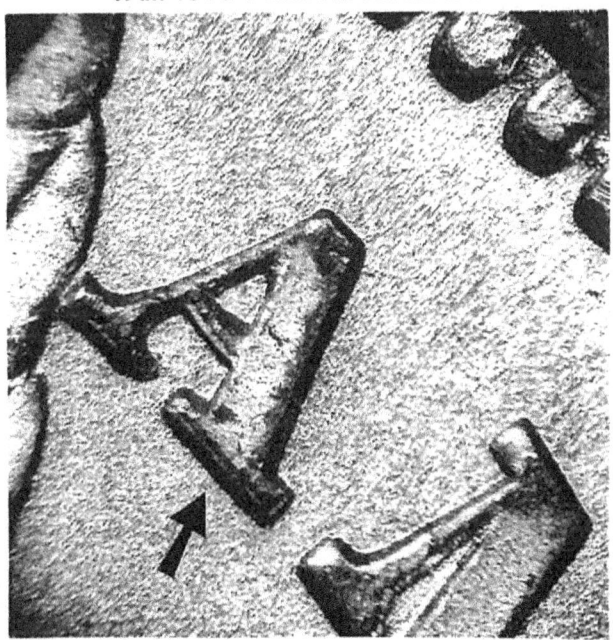

VAM 134 B²h Doubled Legend

VAM 134 Polishing Line Around Olive Branch

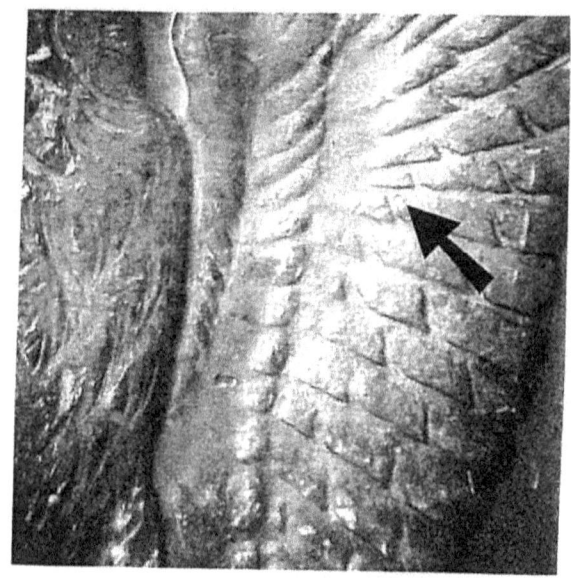

VAM 140 Over Polished Wing Center

VAM 140 Over Polished Wing

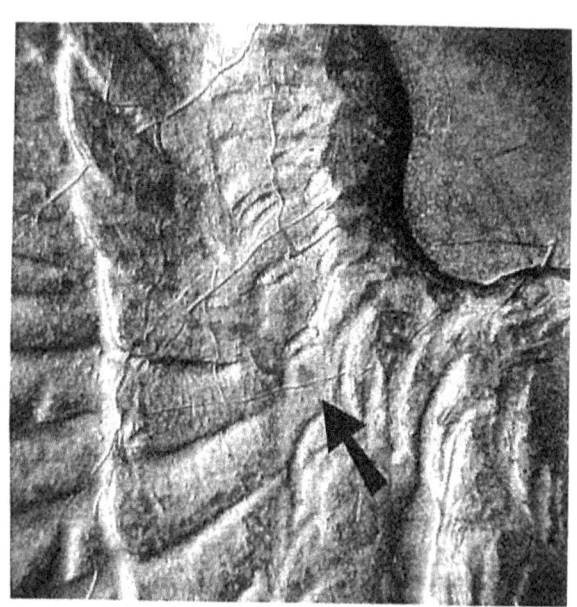

VAM 140A Die Scratches Wing

VAM 140A Die Scratches Legs

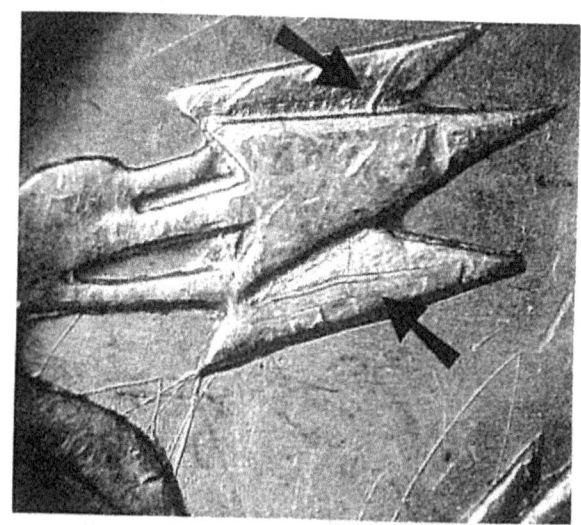

VAM 140A Die Scratches Arrow Heads

VAM 141 B²i Engraved Wing Feather

P VAM 141A Thread-Like Impression

VAM 141A Die Gouge Wing

VAM 142 II/I 22 Doubled 8-8, Tripled 7

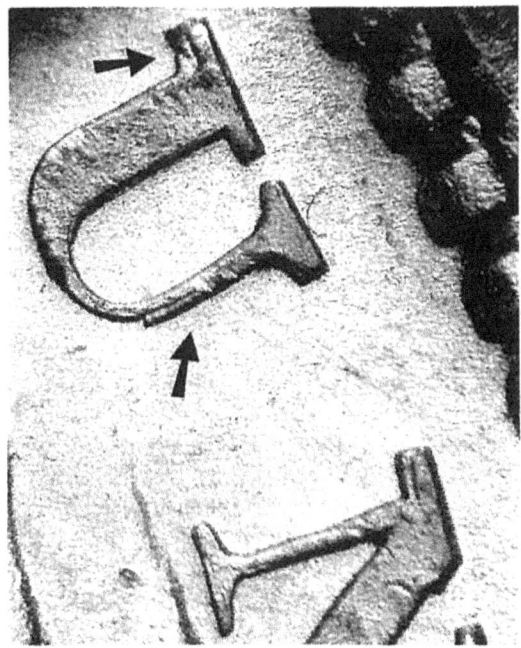

VAM 142 II/I 22 Doubled U

VAM 142A Die Chips

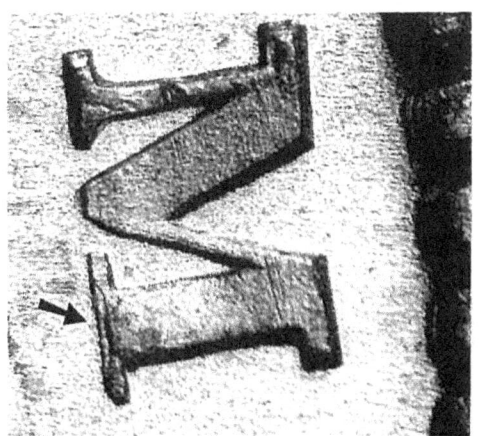

VAM 142 II/I 22 M Split Serif

VAM 143 II/I 23 Doubled Left 8

VAM 143 II/I 23 Spiked Eye

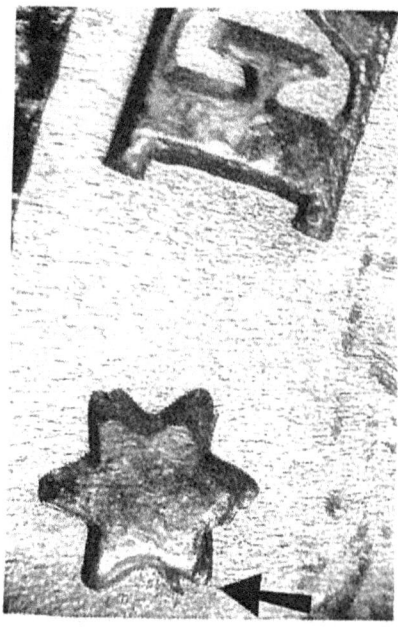

VAM 143 II/I 23 Doubled Seventh Left Star

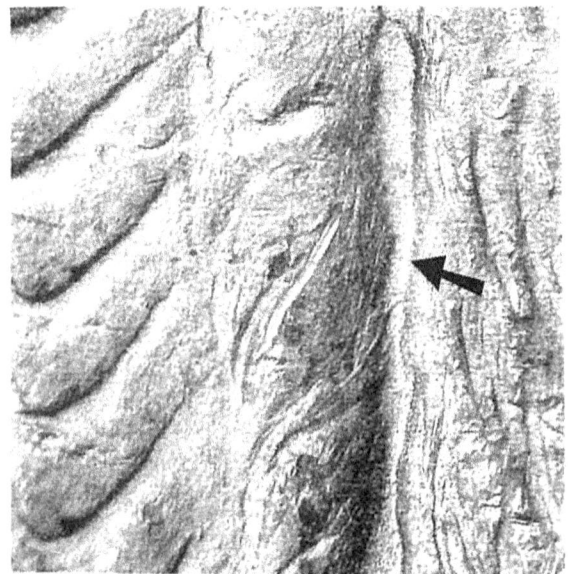

VAM 143 Engraving Lines

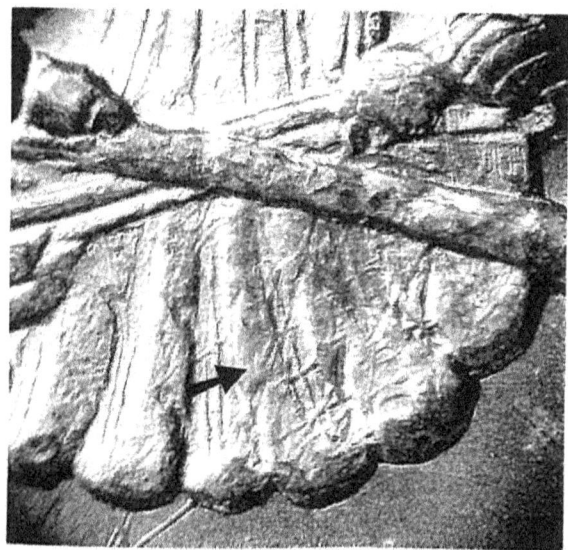

VAM 143 Die Scratches in Tail Feathers

VAM 143 Engraved Wing Feathers

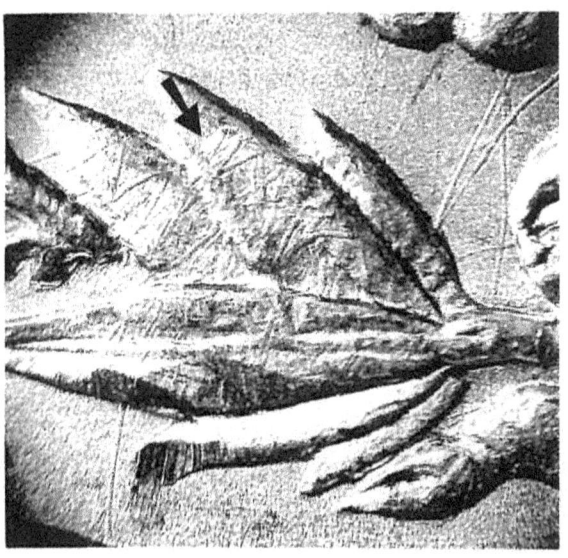

VAM 143 Die Scratches Wreath Leaves

VAM 144 II/I 24 Doubled Left Stars & E

VAM 144 II/I 24 Doubled Ear

VAM 144 Over Polished Wing

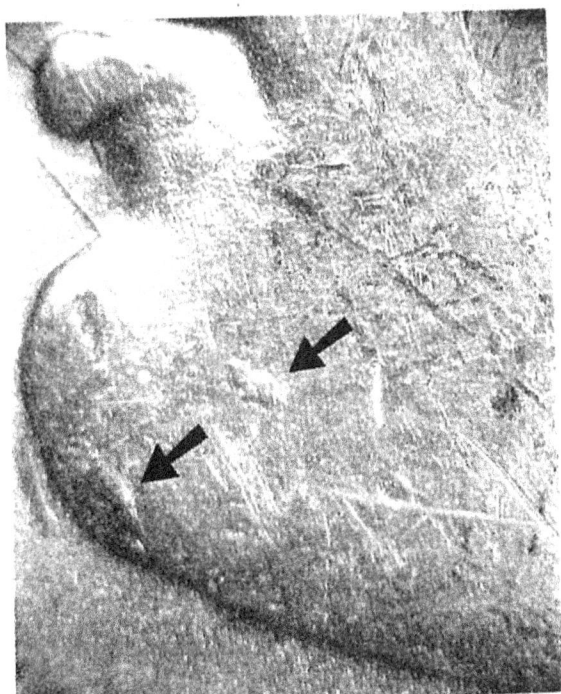

VAM 144 II/I 24 Die Chips on Chin

VAM 144 II/I 24 Doubled Date

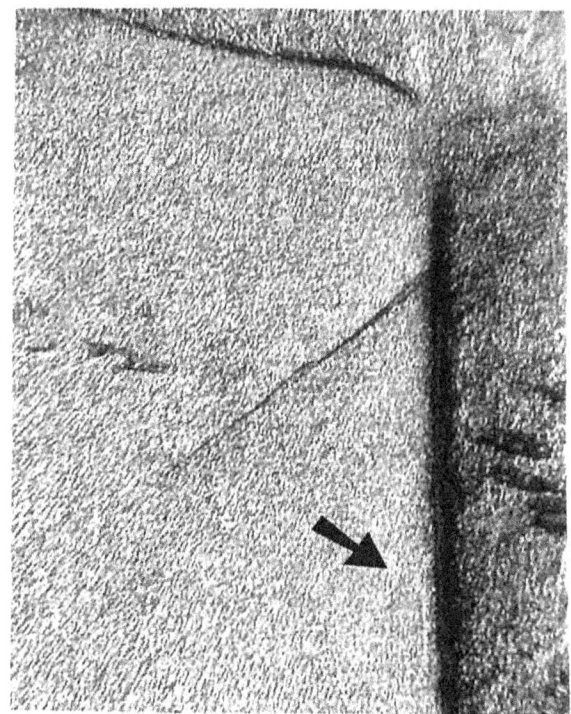

VAM 144A II/I 24 Clashed n

VAM 144B II/I 24 Dot Next to 8

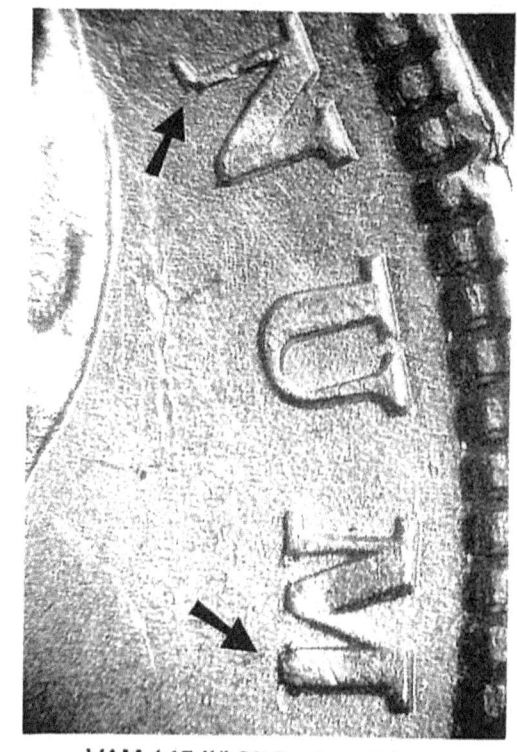

VAM 145 II/I 25 Broken N & M

VAM 146 Lines in E, R, Y

VAM 145 II/I 25 Doubled 1-7

VAM 146 B²j Engraved Wing Feather

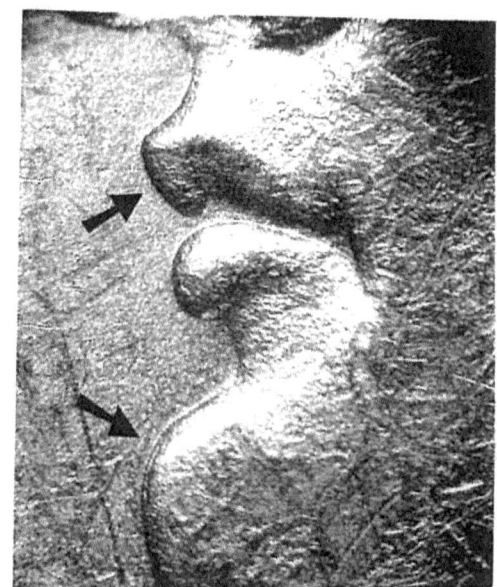

VAM 146 Slightly Doubled Profile

VAM 163 II/I 26 Shifted U

VAM 163 II/I 26
Doubled M

VAM 164 II/I 27 Broken R

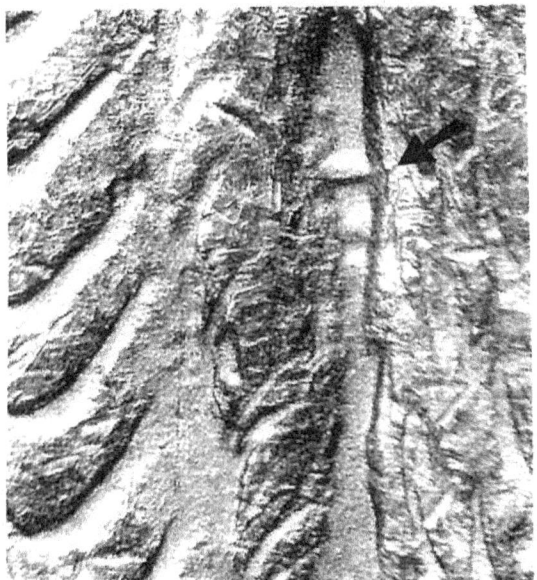

VAM 164 Three Die Gouges

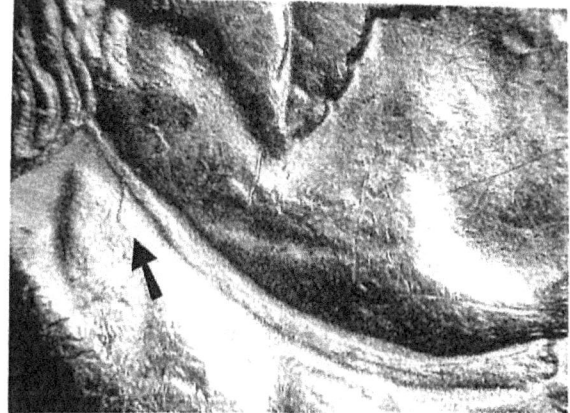

VAM 164 II/I 27 Line Cap Ribbon

VAM 164 II/I 27 Doubled PL

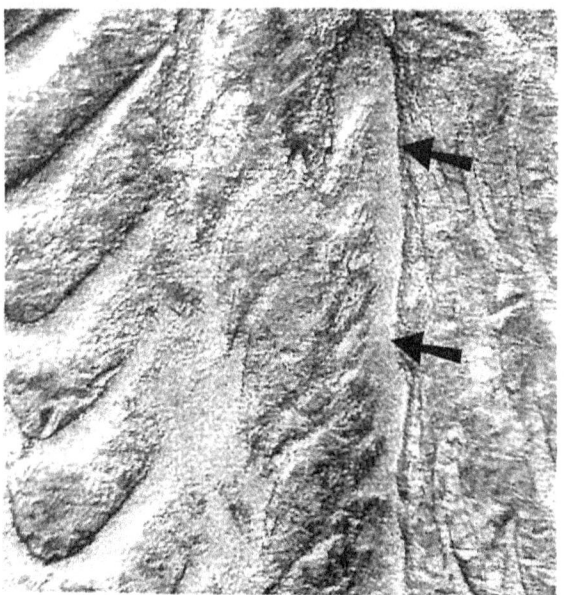

VAM 165 Diagonal Engraved Bars

VAM 165 II/I 28 Doubled PL

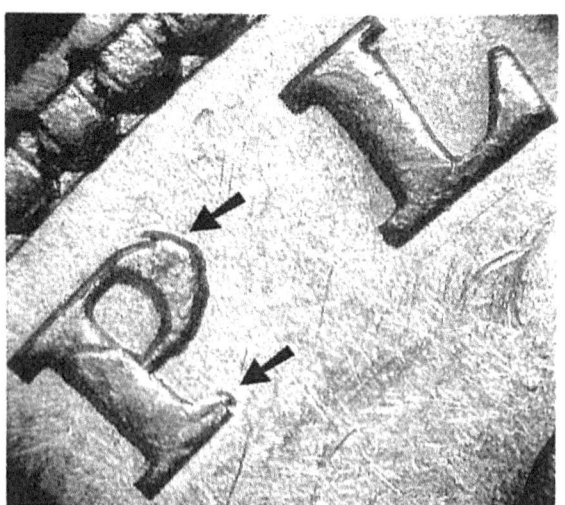

VAM 166 II/I 29 Spiked P

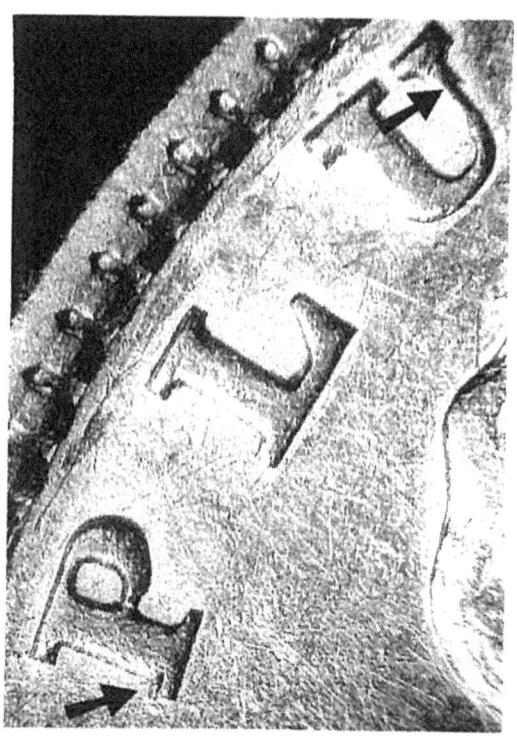

VAM 167 II/I 30 Spiked P

VAM 165 II/I 28 Doubled UR

VAM 166 II/I 29 Bars Under Eyelid

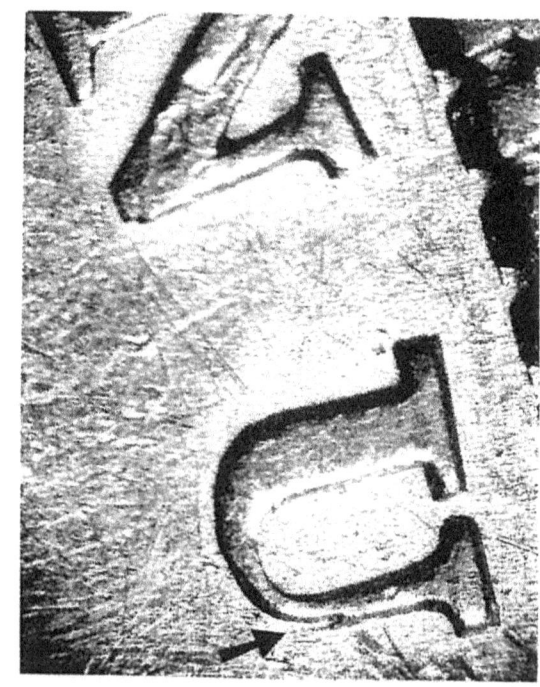

VAM 167 II/I 30 Doubled U

VAM 167 II/I 30
Beveled Inside 8

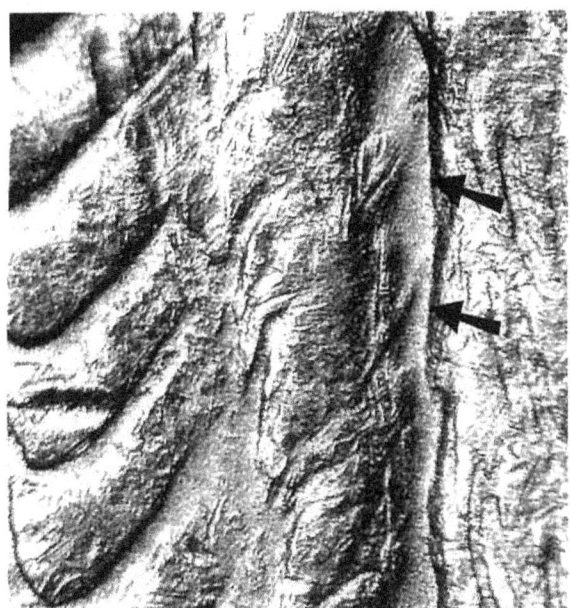

VAM 168 Engraved Bars

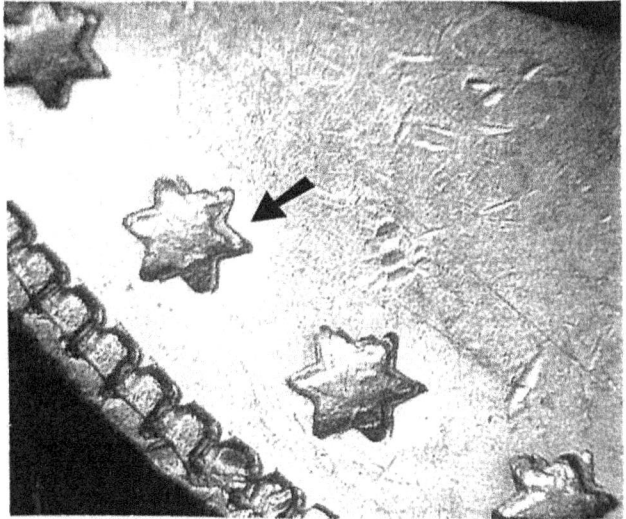

VAM 169 II/I 32 Quadrupled Left Stars

VAM 168 Engraved Vertical Bar

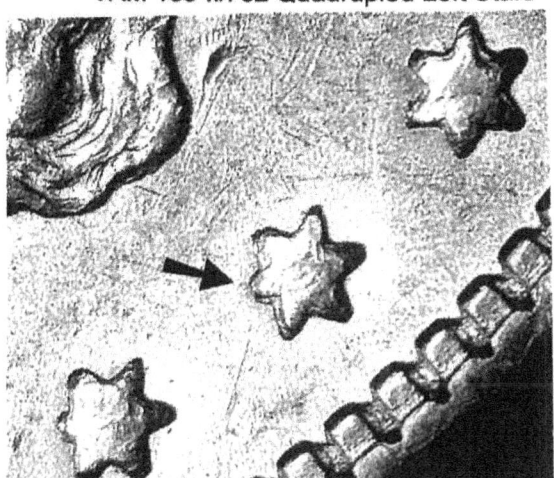

VAM 169 II/I 32 Doubled 3-5 Rt. Stars

VAM 169 II/I 32 Die Chip Cotton Leaf

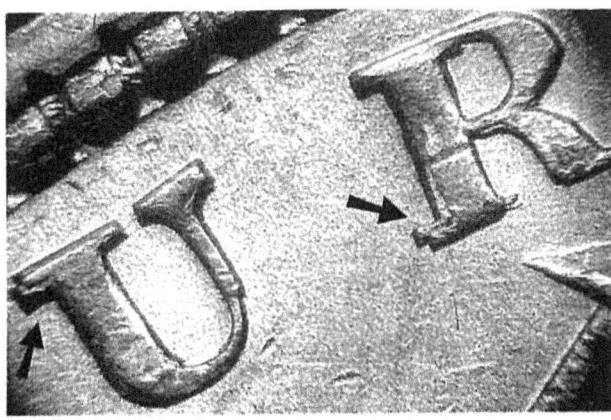

VAM 170 II/I 33 Doubled UR

VAM 170 II/I 33 Doubled Date

VAM 170A Die Chips Cap

VAM 171 II/I 34 Doubled Cotton Bolls, Cap

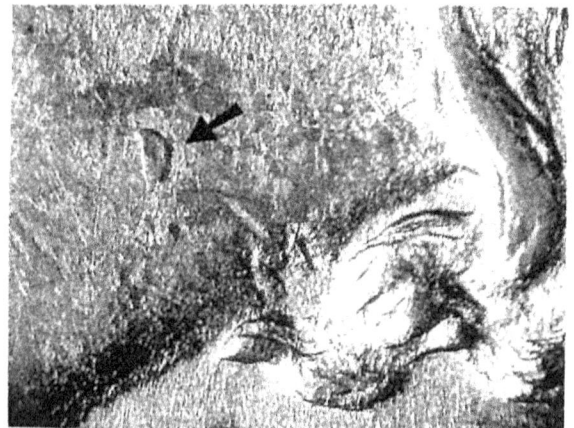

VAM 170 II/I 33 Die Chip Neck

VAM 171 II/I 34 Doubled P

VAM 171 II/I 34 Tripled R

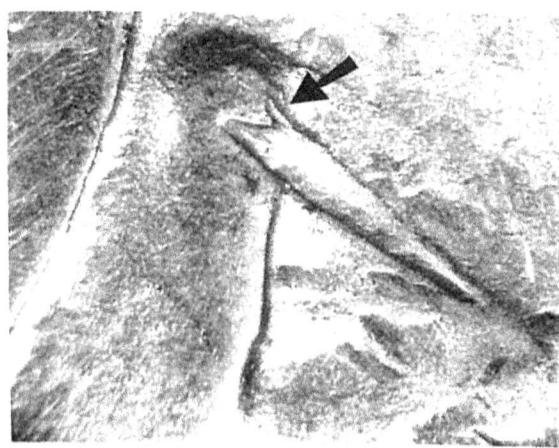

VAM 185A Spike Above Eyelid

VAM 185B Die Scratch Thru I-R

VAM 186A Spike Above Eyelid

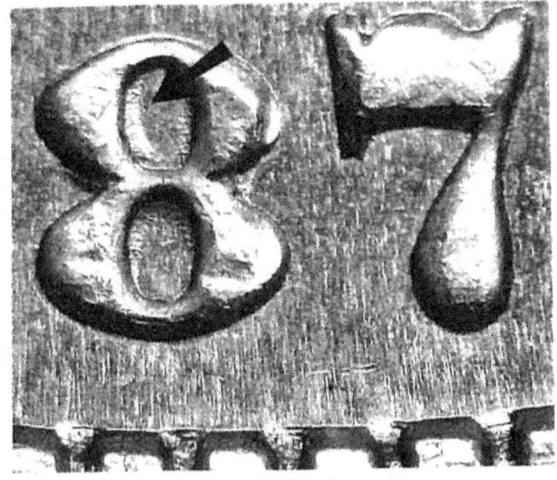

VAM 186A Metal in 8

VAM 186B Die Chips in 8

VAM 187 Doubled R

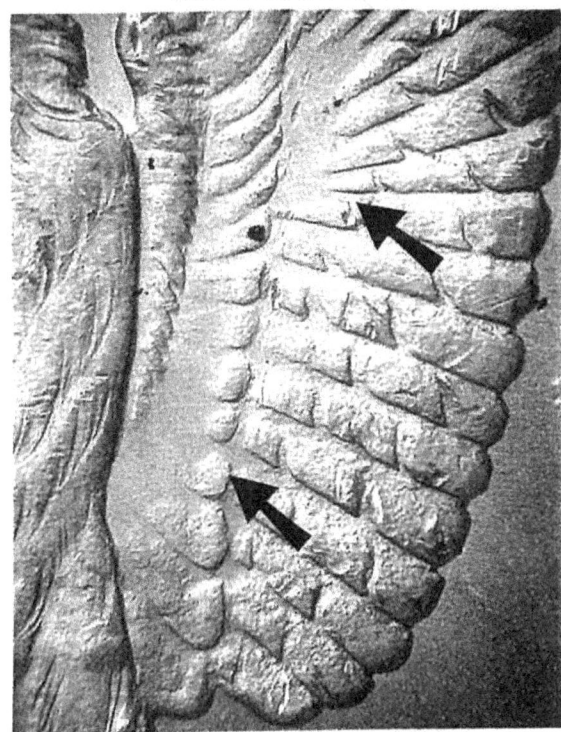

VAM 186B Over Polished Wing

VAM 187
Spike Below
Eyelid

VAM 187 Doubled UN

VAM 189 Engraved Wing Feathers

VAM 189 B²g Engraved Wing Feather

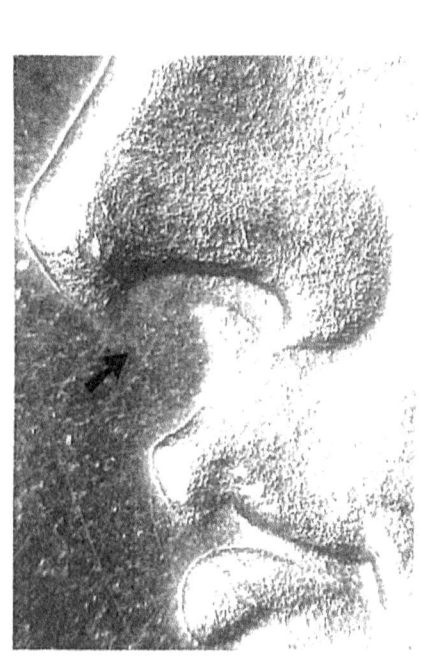

VAM 190 Missing Nostril

VAM 190A Clashed n

VAM 188 Washed Out L

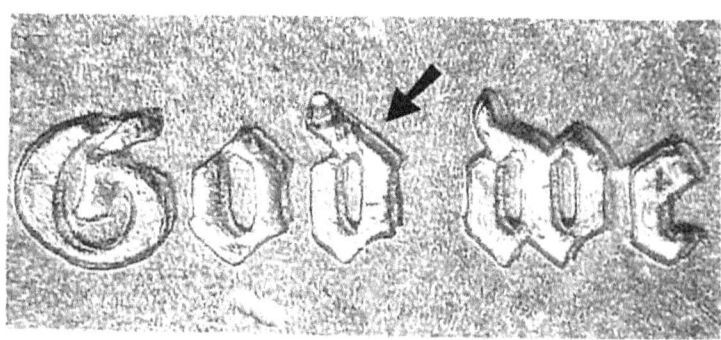

VAM 190 B²d Doubled Motto

VAM 190 B²d Doubled Wing Feathers

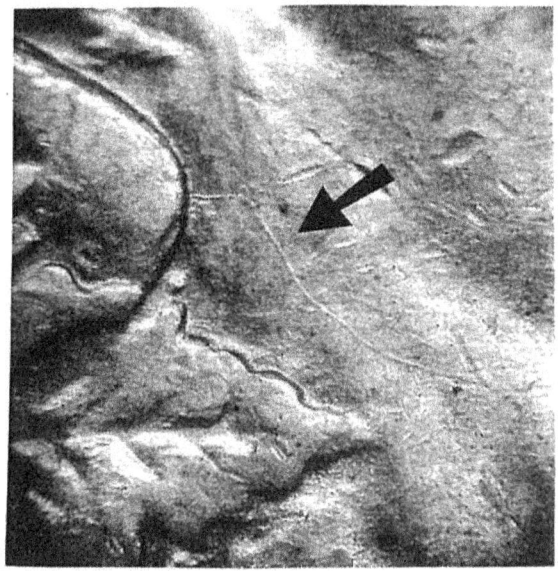

VAM 195 Polishing Line Cotton Boll

VAM 195 B²e Broken D Bottom

VAM 195A B²e Broken D

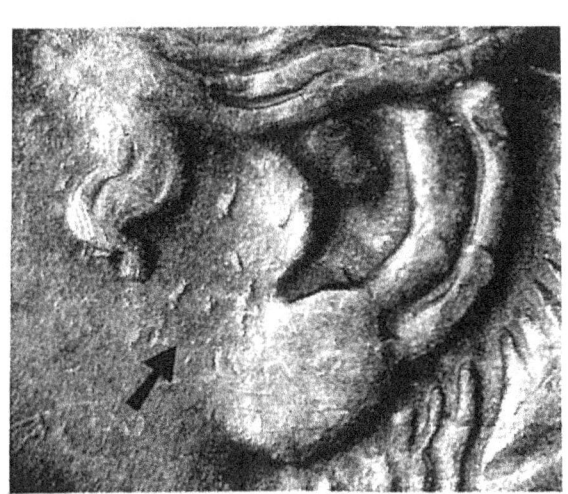

VAM 195A Die Chips Ear Front

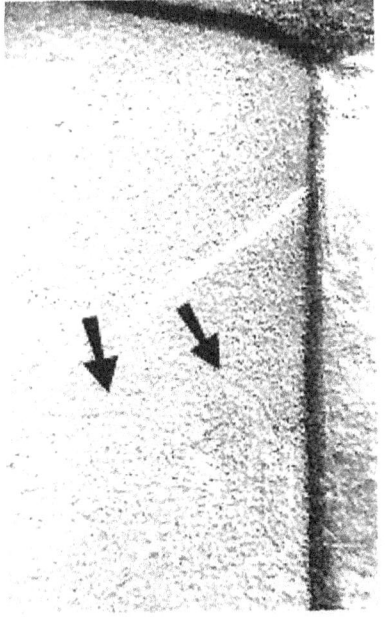

VAM 196A Clashed In

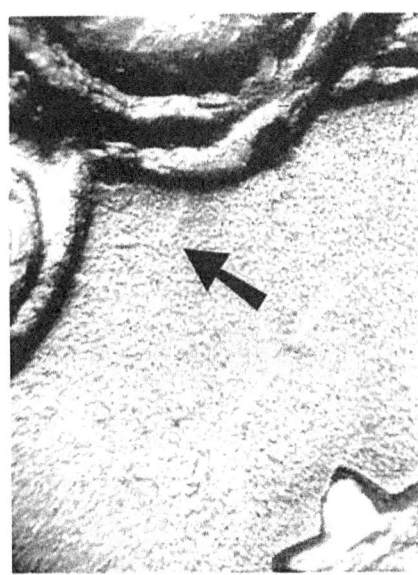

VAM 196A Clashed st

VAM 197 B²f Missing Wing Feathers

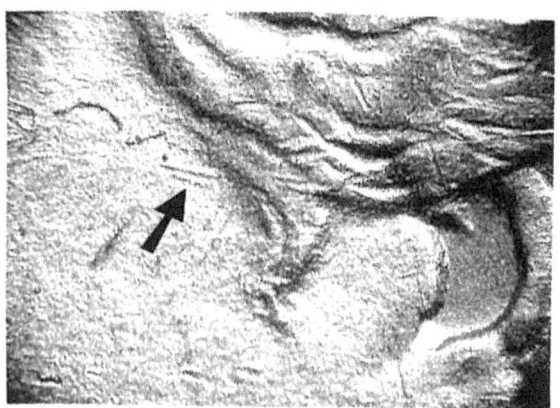

VAM 200 II/I 39 Double Lines Ear Front

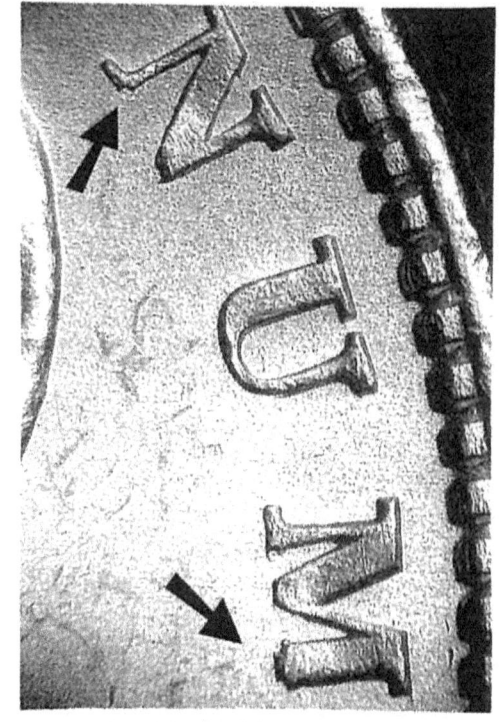

VAM 200 II/I 39 Broken N & M

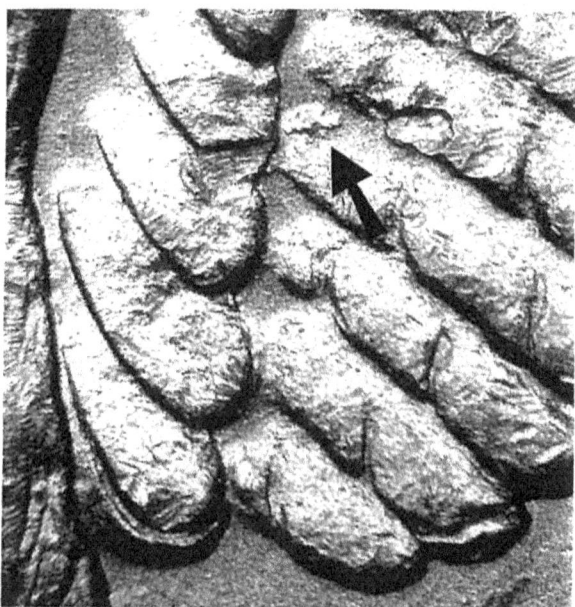

VAM 200 Die Chip Feather

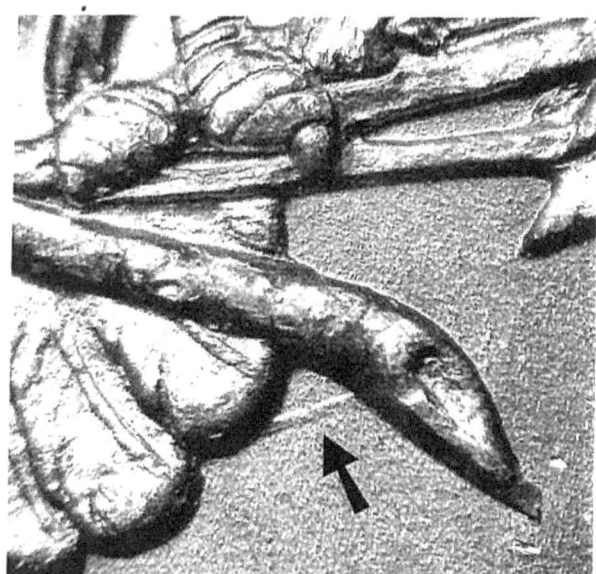

VAM 201 Die Scratch

VAM 200, 201, 202 Die Chip D

VAM 202 Doubled Date

VAM 202 Diverging Polishing Lines

VAM 202A Clashed M

VAM 202A Clashed n

VAM 203 Short Wheat Leaf

VAM 203 Lines in Wing

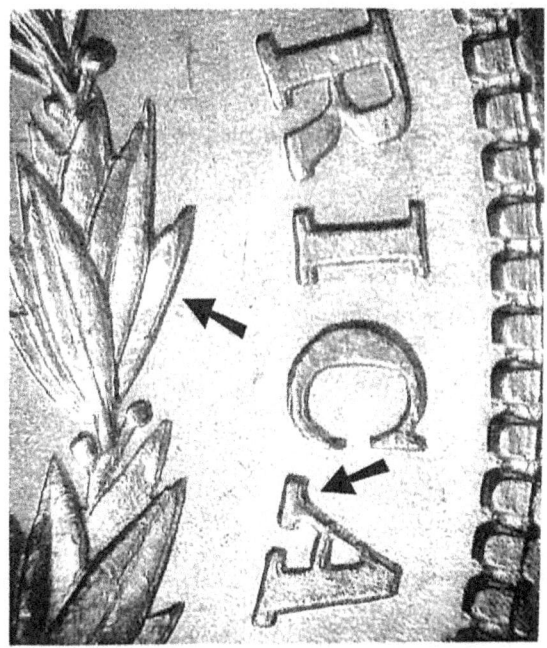

VAM 203 Doubled Peripheral Letters

VAM 203A Clashed n

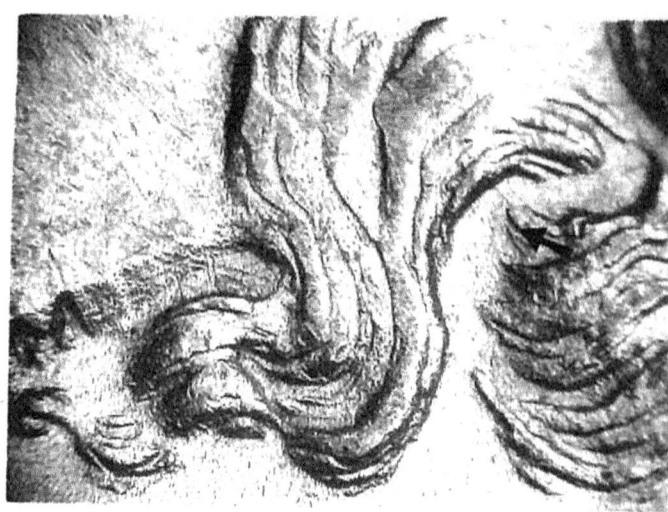

VAM 203A Clashed W

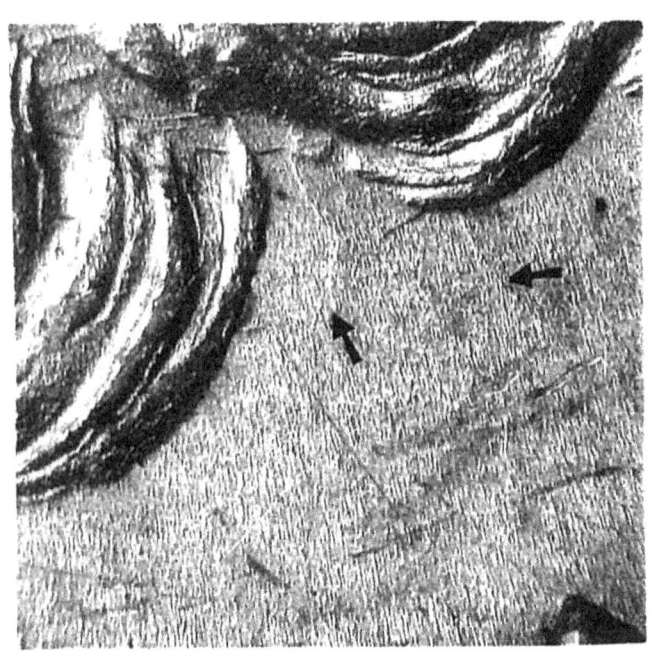

VAM 203A Clashed st

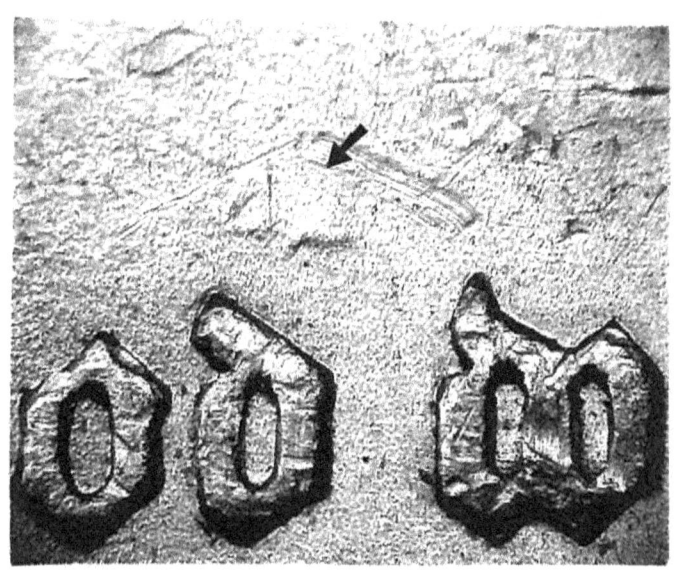

VAM 203A Clashed M

VAM 210 Line Thru Y

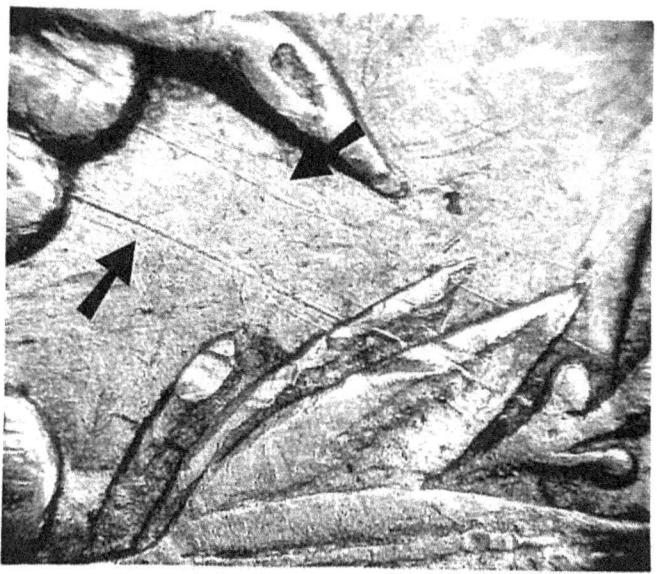

VAM 210 Die Scratches

VAM 210A Line Thru RT

VAM 210A Die Chip Tail Feathers

VAM 210B1 Line Thru IB

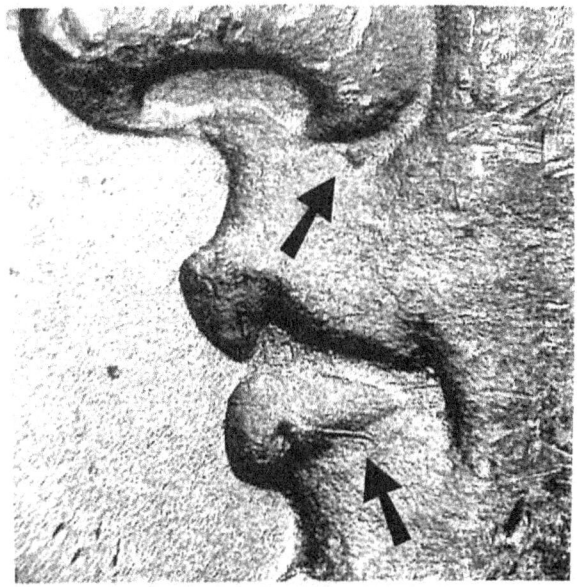

VAM 210B1 Die Scratch & Chip

VAM 210B2 Pitted Forehead

VAM 210B2 Clashed n

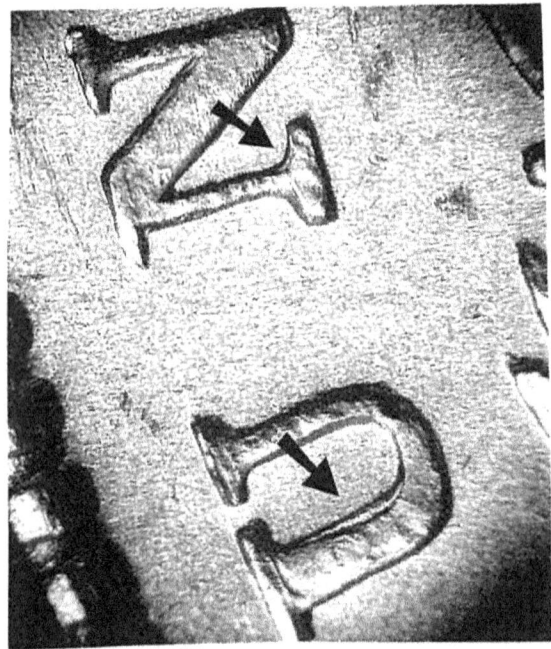

VAM 220 C³b Doubled U

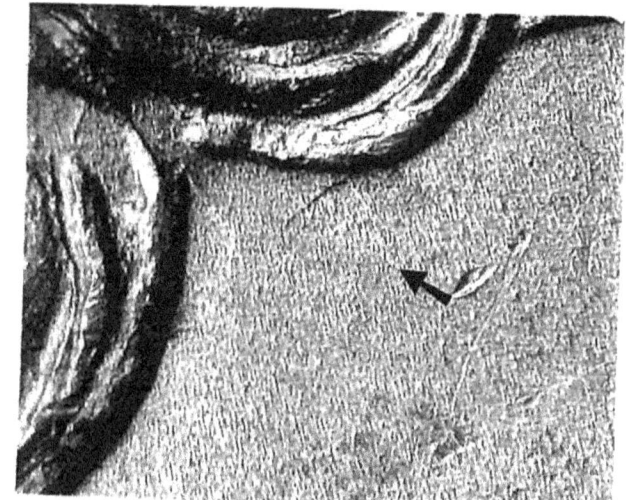

VAM 210B2 Clashed st

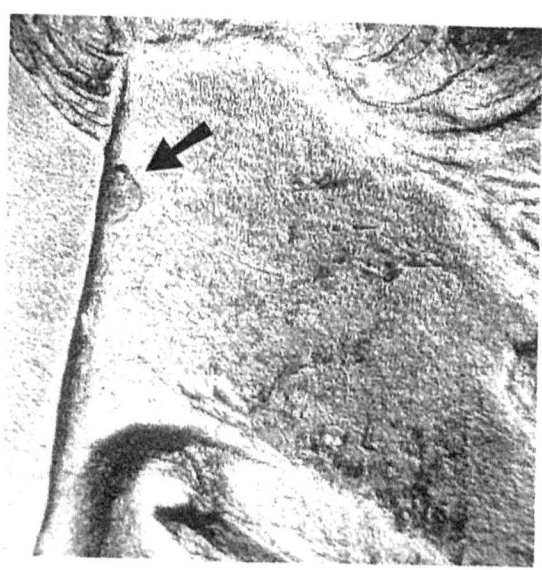

VAM 221-1 Die Chip on Forehead

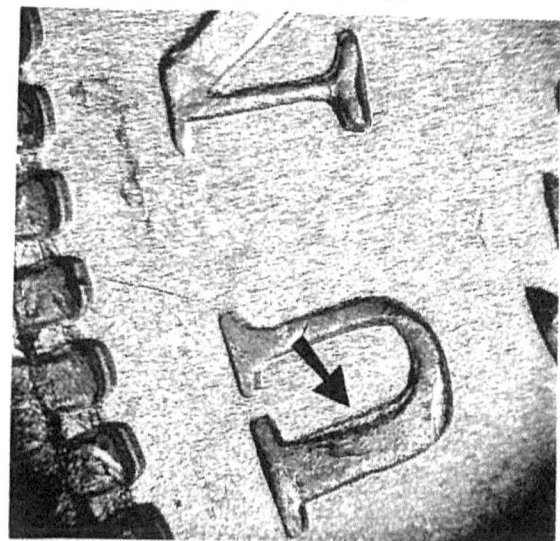

VAM 221-1 C³b Doubled Left Reverse, U

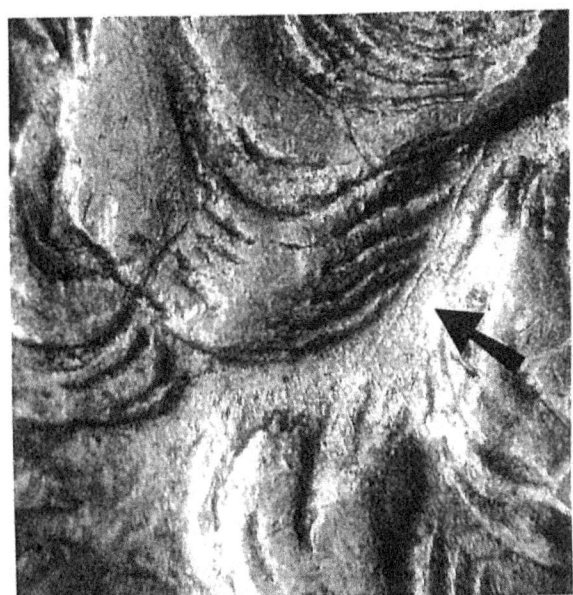

VAM 221-2 Polishing Line in Hair

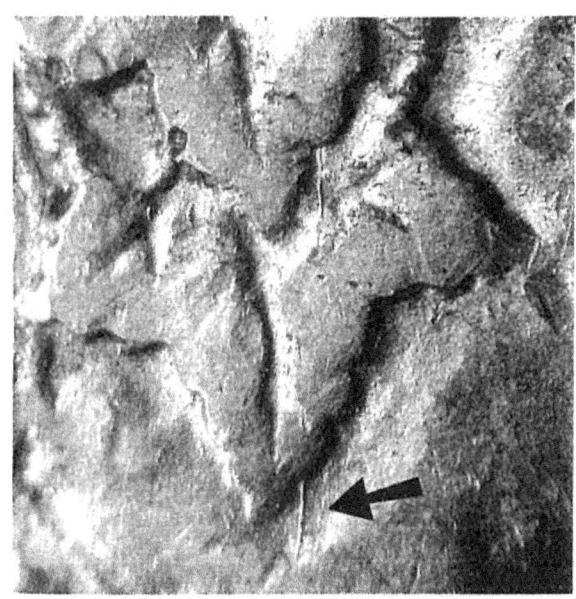

VAM 221–2 Polishing Line Cotton Leaf

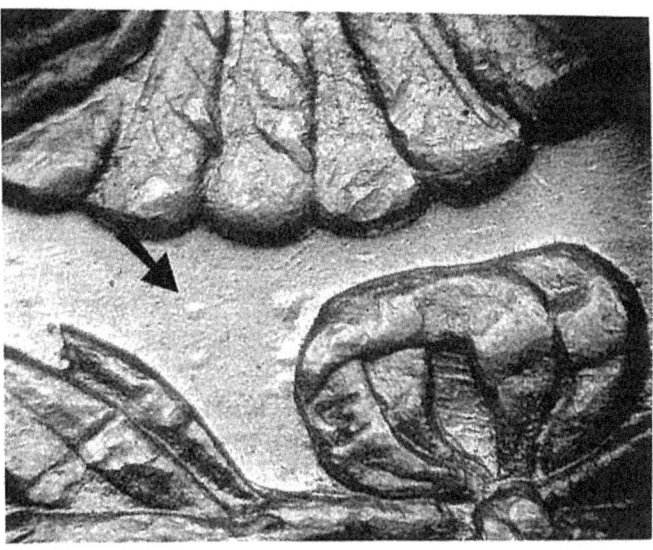

VAM 221A Denticle Impressions

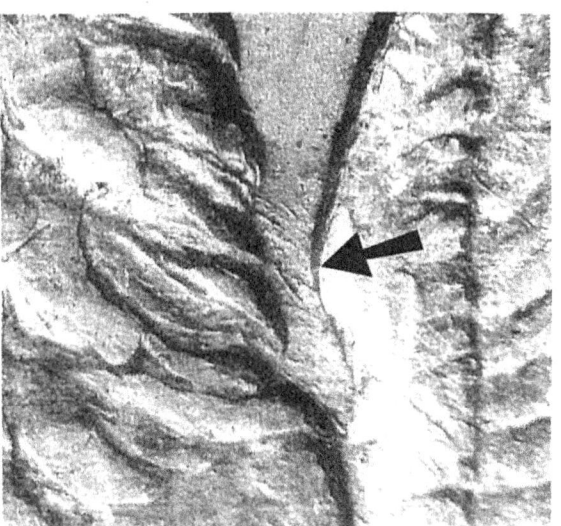

VAM 221-2 Polishing Lines Wing-Neck Gap

VAM 222A Die Chips on Mouth

VAM 222B Die Gouge Above L

VAM 222B Die Gouges Cotton Boll

VAM 222C Spiked Eye

VAM 222D Lines in Cap Fold

VAM 222D Over Polished Lower Hair

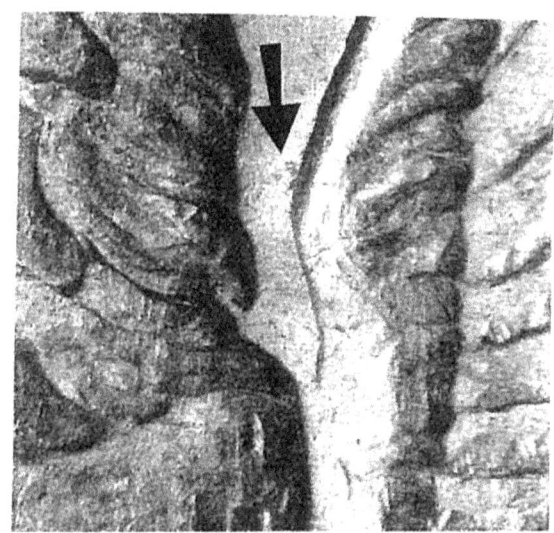

VAM 222D Die Chips Wing-Neck Gap

VAM 223 Doubled Left Wreath

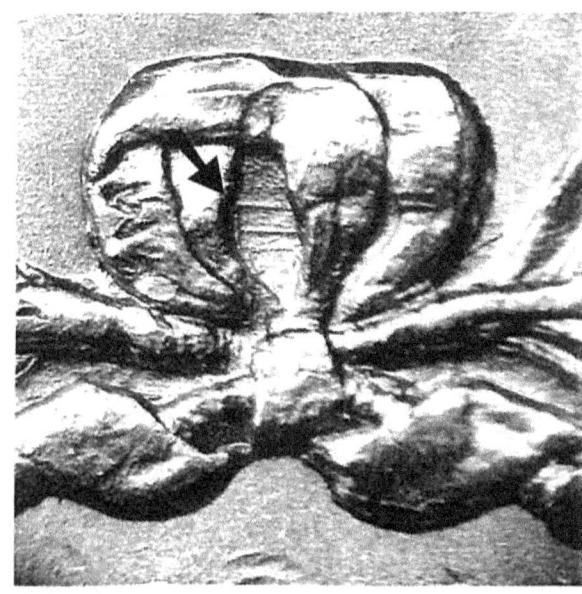

VAM 223 Double Lines in Wreath Bow

VAM 224 Double Horizontal Lines

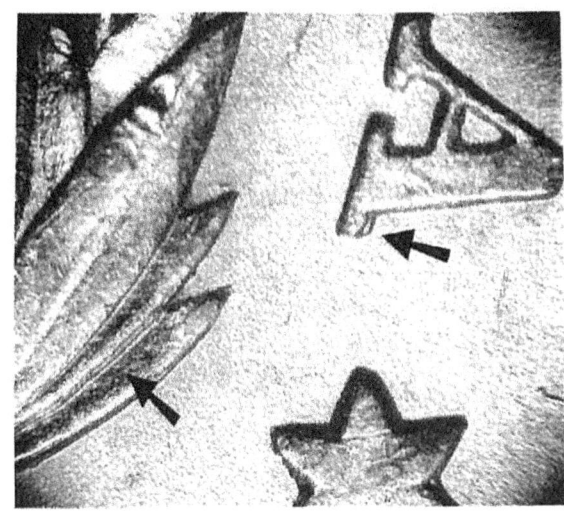

VAM 224 C³c Doubled Lower Reverse, A

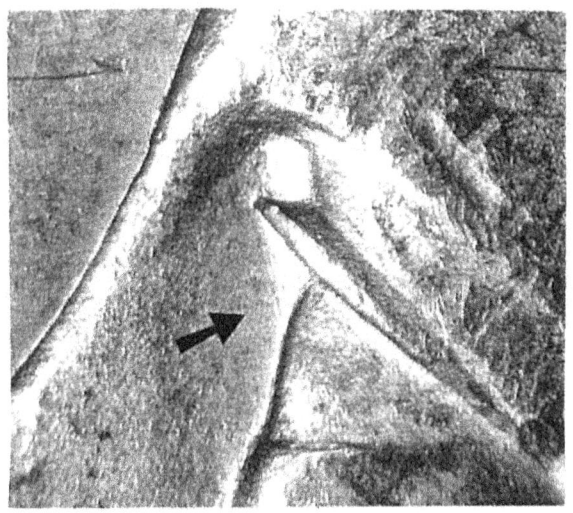

VAM 225 Polishing Lines Eye

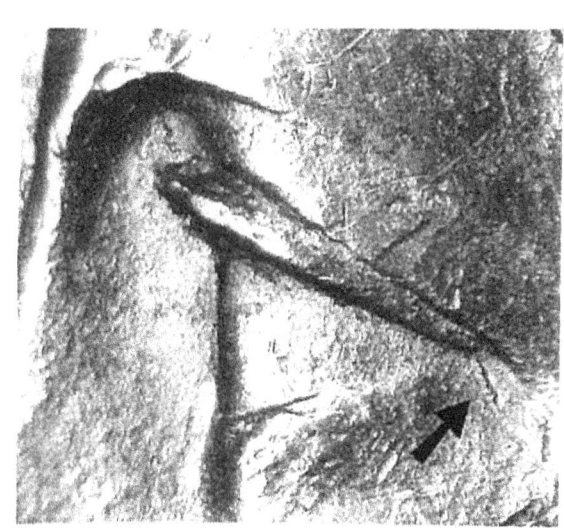

VAM 225 Line Behind Eye

VAM 225A Spiked Eye

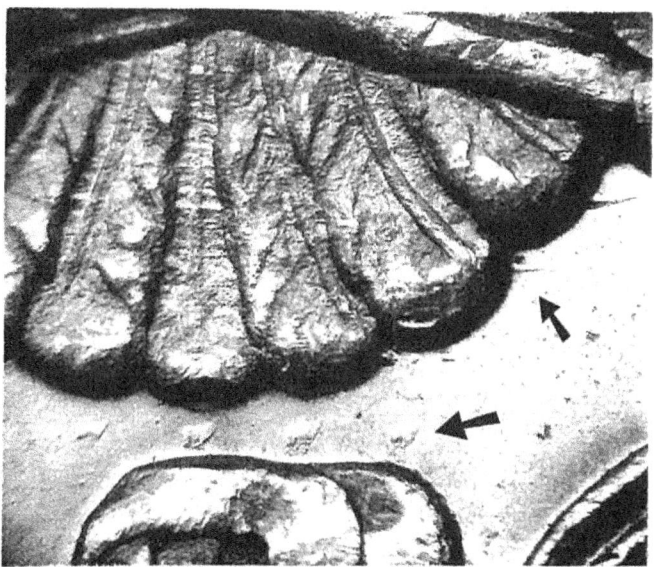

VAM 225A Denticle Impressions

VAM 226 Lines ERT

VAM 226 Line Cap Ribbon End

VAM 226A Clashed n

VAM 226 Three Ticks Leg

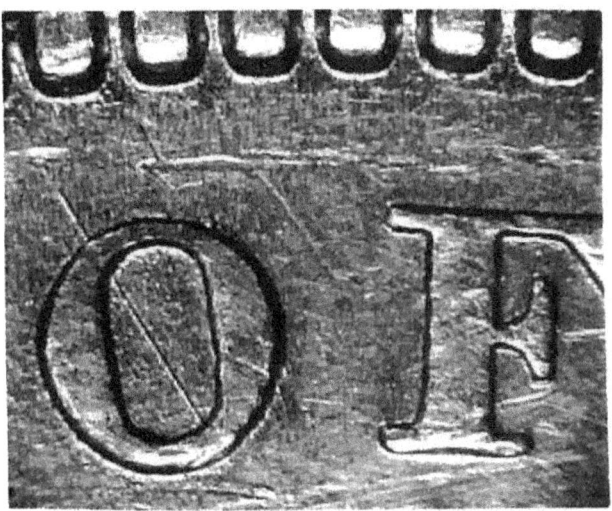

VAM 227 Polishing Line Thru O

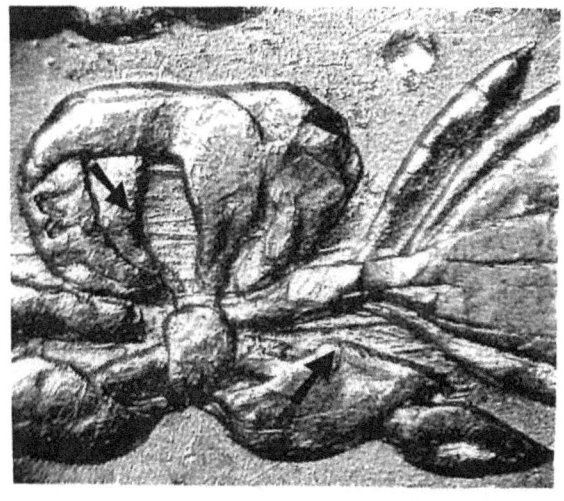

VAM 228 Lines in Wreath Bow

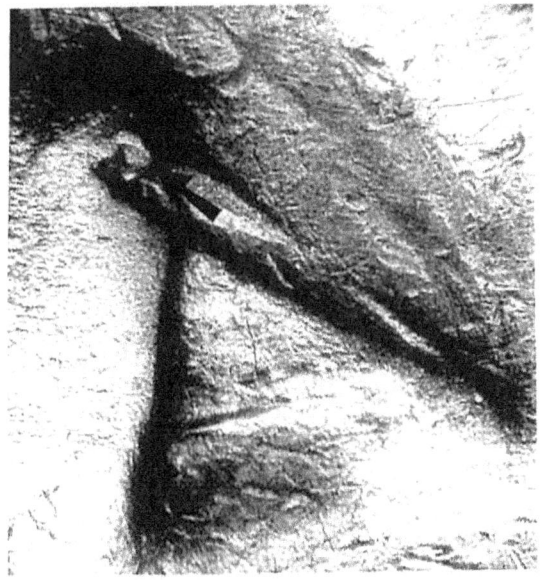

VAM 228-1 Die Chip Eyelid

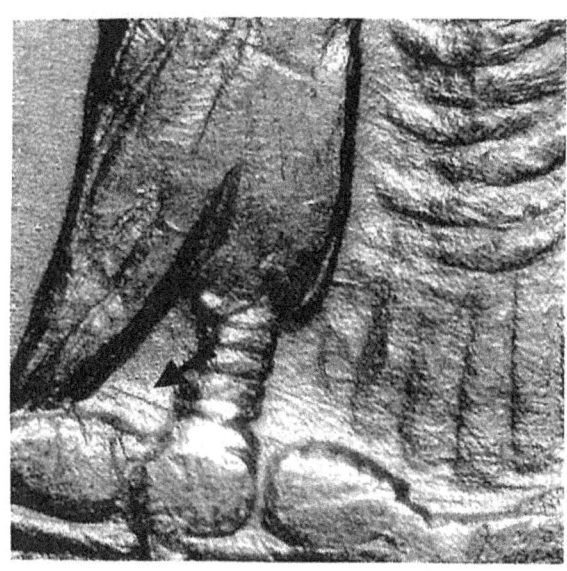

VAM 228-1 Die Scratch Left of Leg

VAM 228-2 X Polishing Lines

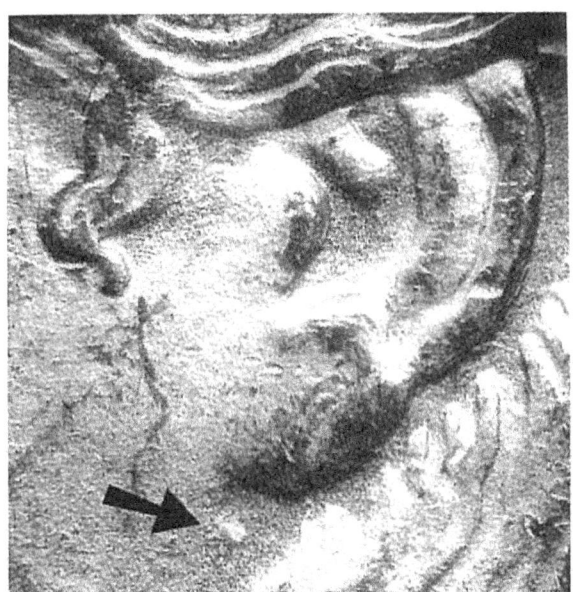

VAM 228-2 Dot Below Earlobe

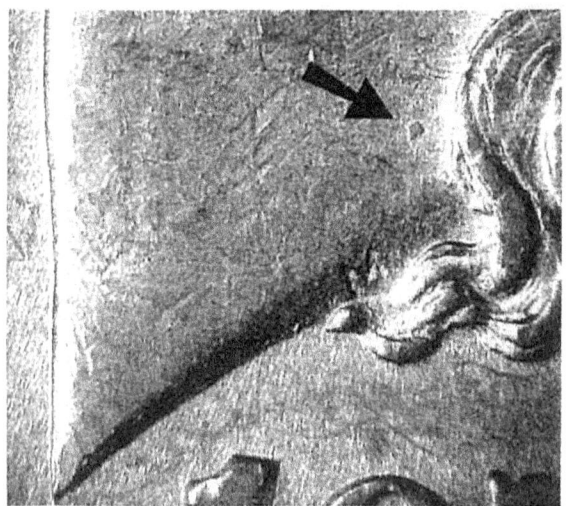

VAM 228-4 Die Chip Lower Neck

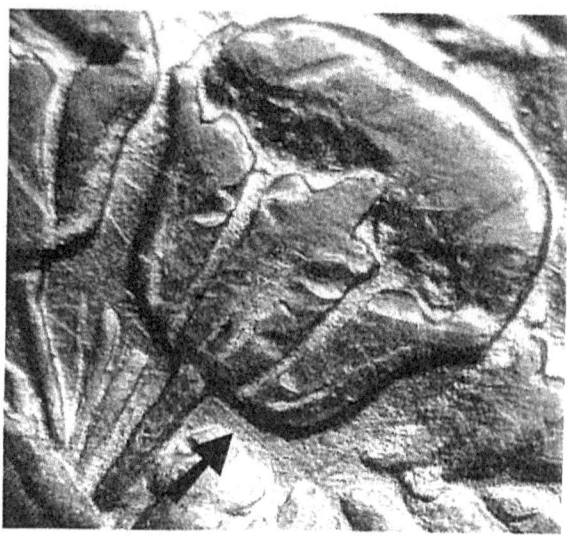

VAM 228-4 Polishing Line Below Cotton Boll

VAM 228-4 Double Polishing Line Feathers

VAM 228-5 Die Scratch Line Y

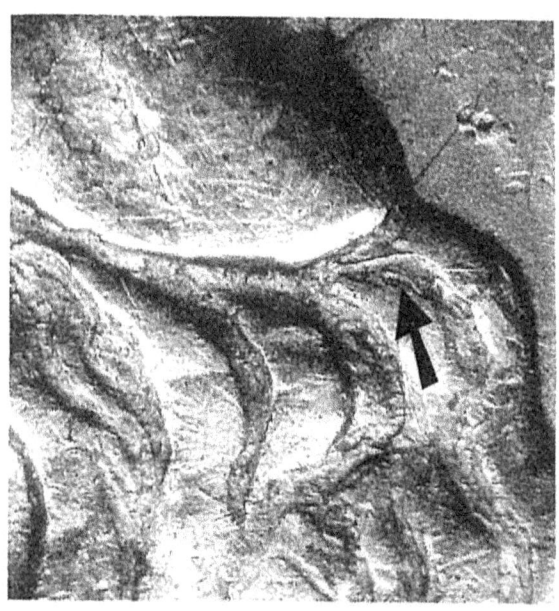

VAM 228-5 Polishing Line Below Cap

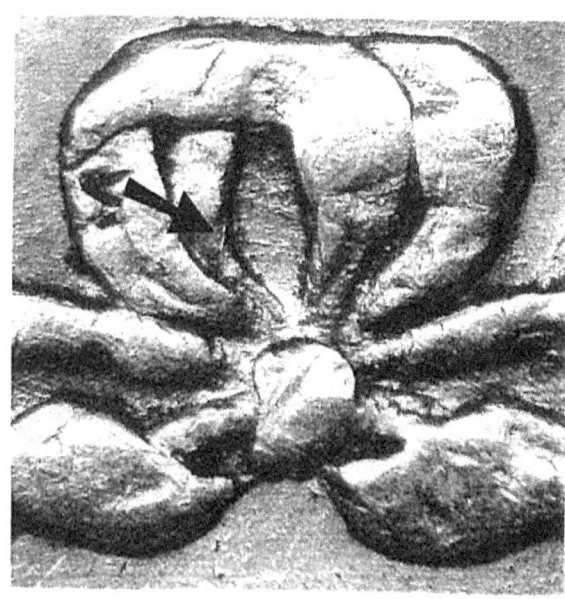

VAM 228-5 Horizontal Line Wreath Bow

VAM 228 Dot Above E

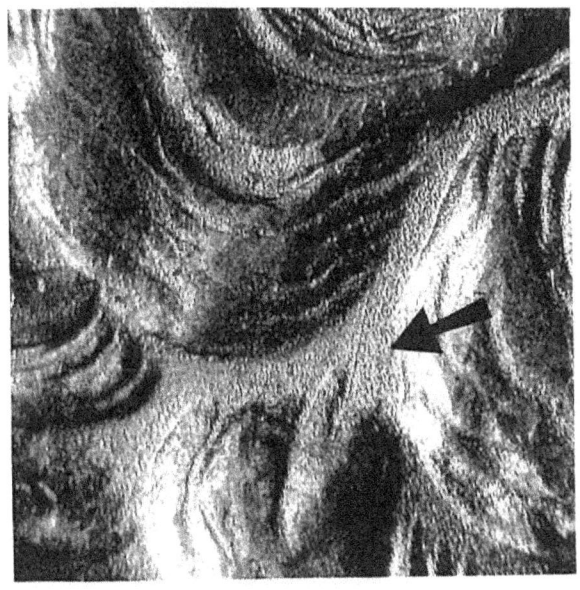

VAM 228-6 Polishing Line in Hair

VAM 228-6 Polishing Line Ribbon

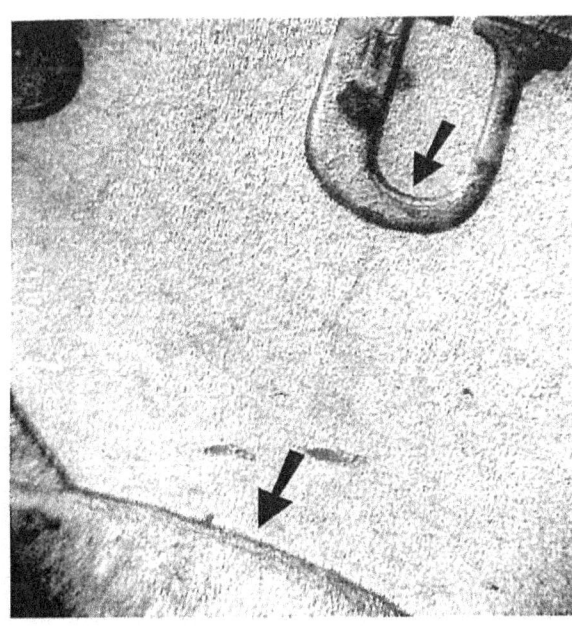

VAM 228-7 Doubled Cap & U

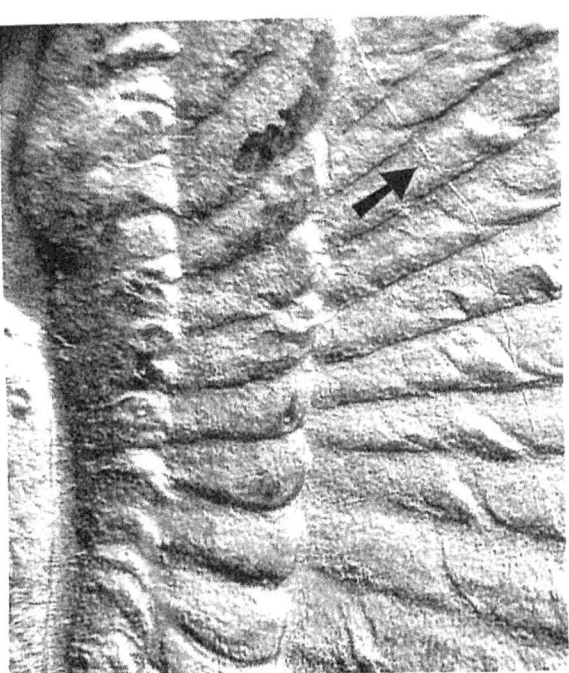

VAM 228-7 Die Scratch Wing

VAM 228B Three Polishing Line Outside Ear

VAM 228B Polishing Line Thru Berries

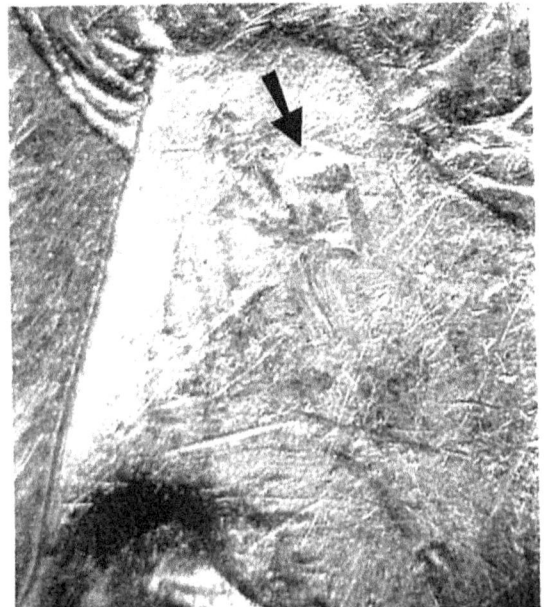

VAM 229 Die Chip on Forehead

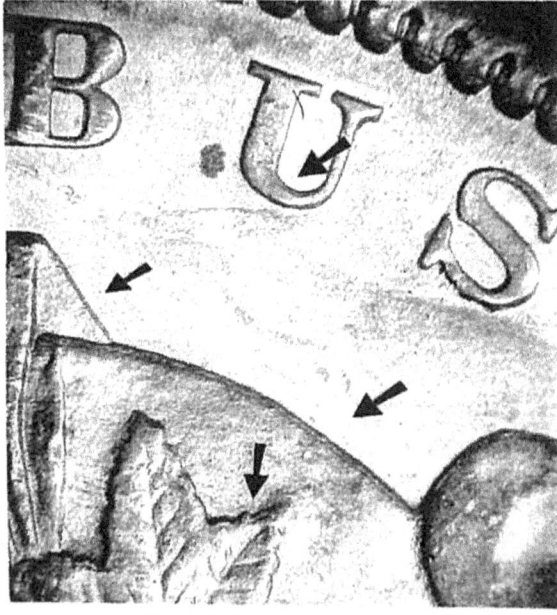

VAM 229.1 Doubled Cap Top

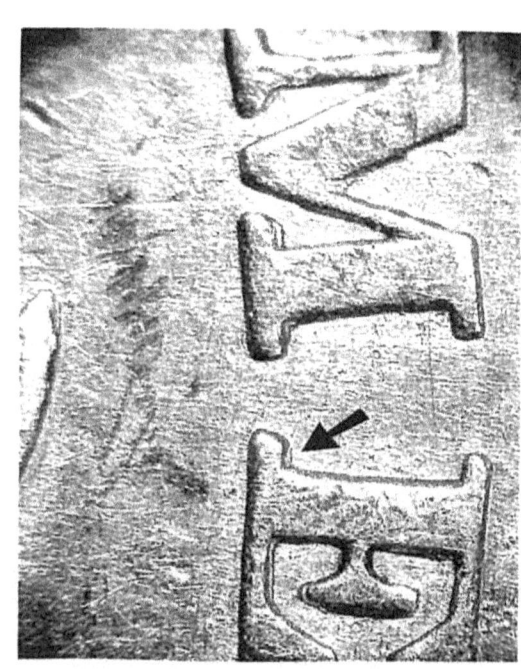

VAM 229 C^{3}d Doubled AMERICA

VAM 230-1 Die Scratch Eye

VAM 230-1 Polishing Lines Leg

VAM 230-2 Lines Above Eyelid

VAM 230-2 Line in Nostril

VAM 230-2 Curved Line in Bow

VAM 230-3 Polishing Lines Bolls

1878 P 7TF VAM 85 "7" on A of STATES

FURTHER REFERENCES

Please check Amazon Kindle for Michael S. Fey, Ph.D., and Leroy Van Allen & A. George Mallis publications. For hard copy print of books, please contact Dr. Fey at RCI, P.O. Box C, Ironia, NJ 07845 or eMail : Feyms@aol.com.

Hard copy books are also available at *The Institute for Silver Dollar Education and Research*, at website: *Ilovesilverdollars.org* or by contacting Executive Director John Baumgart at John.Baumgart@comcast.net

Amazon Kindle

Fey, Michael S. 2019. *The Complete Virtual Guide to Pricing Your Morgan Silver Dollars*. 286 pp. RCI

Van Allen, Leroy, & A. George Mallis. 2023. *Part I or II or III of Three. Comprehensive Catalog and Encyclopedia or Morgan & Peace Dollars*. RCI Total 520 pp.

Leroy Van Allen. 2011. *Wonders of Morgan Dollars*. 139 pp. RCI

Leroy Van Allen. 2013. *Wonders of Peace Dollars*. 273 pp. RCI

Leroy Van Allen. 2006. *Morgan Dollars 8 & 7 Over 8 Tail Feather Story*. 52 pp. RCI

Leroy Van Allen. 2010. *1878 P 7 Tail Feather Morgan Dollar Attribution Guide*. 130 pp. RCI

Leroy Van Allen. 2006. *1878 S Morgan Dollar Attribution Guide*. 139 pp. RCI

Fey, Michael S. 2009 The Top 100 Morgan Dollar Varieties: The VAM Keys

FURTHER REFERENCES

Hard Copy Books

Fey, Michael S. 2019. The Top 100 Morgan Dollar Varieties: The VAM Keys. 286 pp. RCI

Fey, Michael S. 2008. *A Decade of Top 100 Insights*. RCI 174 pp.

Van Allen, Leroy. 1991. *RotaFlip Die Rotation Booklet and Guide*. 1991. RCI

Kimpton, M.D., Mark. 2005. *Elite Clashed Morgan Dollars*. RCI 160 pp

Van Allen, Leroy, & A. George Mallis. 2023. *Comprehensive Catalog and Encyclopedia or Morgan & Peace Dollars*. RCI Total 520 pp.

Van Allen, Leroy 2011. *Wonders of Morgan Dollars*. 139 pp. RCI

Van Allen, Leroy 2013. *Wonders of Peace Dollars*. 273 pp. RCI

Van Allen, Leroy 2006. *Morgan Dollars 8 & 7 Over 8 Tail Feather Story*. 52 pp. RCI

Van Allen, Leroy 2010. *1878 P 7 Tail Feather Morgan Dollar Attribution Guide*. 130 pp. RCI

Van Allen, Leroy 2006. *1878 S Morgan Dollar Attribution Guide*. 139 pp. RCI

Van Allen, Leroy 2013. *Die Gouges and Scratches Peace Dollar Attribution Guide. 109 pp* RCI

Van Allen, Leroy 2008. *1921 Scribbles Morgan Dollar Attribution Guide*. 234 pp. RCI

Van Allen, Leroy. 2013. *Misplaced Date Digits Morgan Dollar Attribution Guide*. 57 pp RCI

Van Allen, Leroy. 2017. *Dashed Under 8 Morgan Dollar Attribution Guide*. 53 pp. RCI

Van Allen, Leroy. 2009. *Overdates and Over Mint Marks of Morgan Dollar Attribution Guide*. 53 pp. RCI

Van Allen, Leroy. 2015. *Denticle & Die Impressions Morgan Dollar Attribution Guide*. 109 pp. RCI

Van Allen, Leroy. 2009. *1921 P Infrequently Reeded or Wide Reeding Morgan Dollar Attribution Guide*. 31 pp. RCI

Van Allen, Leroy. 2011 *Amazing Changing 1921 S VAM 1B Thorn Head Morgan Dollar*. 2011. 22 pp. RCI

Van Allen, Leroy. 2009. *1889 P Doubled Ear Morgan Dollar Attribution Guide*. 32 pp. RCI

Van Allen, Leroy. 2016. *Micro o and Other Counterfeit Morgan and Peace Dollars*. 191 pp RCI

Van Allen, Leroy. 2005. *Micro o Mint Mark on Morgan Dollars*. 32 pp. RCI

Van Allen, Leroy. 2005. *Die Markers for 1921 Morgan and Peace Proof Dollars*. 9 pp. RCI

Van Allen, Leroy and Baumgart, John. 1992-Date Various VAM Book Yearly Supplements. RCI

Leroy C. Van Allen

Leroy Van Allen was born in Seattle and grew up in central California. After completing his master's in electrical engineering at the University of California at Berkeley, he moved to Baltimore, Md, and worked as an electrical and systems engineer. In 1980 he became a full-time coin dealer specializing in silver dollars.

Leroy Van Allen began collecting coins when in grade school, but sold most of them to pay for college. After college he resumed his hobby. He developed an active interest in silver dollars when the mint began releasing previously scarce date New Orleans dollars through banks in the 1962 Christmas season. In 1963 and 1964 he purchased many bags of silver dollars from the Treasury Department in Washington and the Federal Reserve Branch in Baltimore, spurred on by Francis Klaes' booklet on Morgan die varieties. Finding many varieties were not listed in Klaes, he began his own work, examining original mint records and correspondence in the National Archives. His first book, "Morgan and Peace Dollar Varieties," was published in December 1965. All 5,000 copies were sold the first year. In 1966, at the suggestion of Jim Johnson of Coin World's Collector's Clearinghouse, he began a collaboration with George Mallis, who had been making his own studies of these coins.

Leroy Van Allen is a regular contributor to numismatic journals and periodicals. He has served several terms as president of the Maryland Numismatic Society, has been president of the Numismatic Error Collectors of America and secretary of the National Silver Dollar Roundtable for 10 years.

Michael S. Fey, Ph.D.

Dr. Fey is Chairman and Founder of the not-for-profit Institute for Silver Dollar Education and Research (ISDER). He also serves as President, Rare Coin Investments (RCI) for more than two decades. After purchasing the Leroy Van Allen Numismatic Estate in 2022, Fey decided to form ISDER to share information about his love of collecting Morgan and Peace silver dollars. This organization is currently served by a Who's Who Advisory Board of noted silver dollar experts.

Fey was elected to the Board of Governors of the 26,000 member American Numismatic Association (ANA) from 2005-2007. He currently services on the ANA Advisory Board. He was the Senior Instructor for the ANA Summer Seminar at the Colorado College in Colorado Springs, CO for more than 20 years, served on the ANA Consumer Protection Committee, and loaned rare silver dollars for display in the ANA Museum.

He has authored several reference books on Morgan dollars and published a quarterly newsletter for 10 years (A **Decade of Top 100 Insights**), but is perhaps best known as a co-author with his mentor silver dollar expert, Jeff Oxman, for **The Top 100 Morgan Dollar Varieties: The VAM Keys.**

Fey has received many numismatic awards, has been a speaker at major numismatic national conventions. He has discovered more than 50 new Morgan dollar varieties as well as dozens of new varieties in other U.S. and foreign coin series.

He was a Vietnam Era Chemical Officer in the U.S. Army and has interesting athletic achievements as well. His CV can be seen at his RCI website at *http://www.rcicoins.com/curric ulavitae.asp*

An Idea Whose Time Has Come...

There continues to be great interest in Morgan and Peace Dollars. This may be because silver has long been a store of value, and these beautiful cartwheels have been used as U.S. money, in most cases, for more than a century. And with rare dates, mintmarks, varieties and grades of preservation, they can be worth far more than silver. Now, thanks to the efforts of Leroy Van Allen and A. George Mallis, and editor Michael S. Fey, Ph.D., we have a new digital 5th Edition of the **Comprehensive Catalog and Encyclopedia of Morgan & Peace Silver Dollars.** The Institute of Silver Dollar Education and Research (www.Ilovesilverdollars.org) now provides Annual Supplemental VAM lists of new discoveries to ensure the VAM Encyclopedia remains up-to-date. These reference books have become extremely valuable tools for all silver dollar dealers, collectors and investors.

www.ingramcontent.com/pod-product-compliance
Lightning Source LLC
Chambersburg PA
CBHW041117120626
46547CB00019B/2741

*9 7 9 8 9 9 0 2 9 7 0 4 3 *